BREWING UP
A BUSINESS

adventures in
entrepreneurship

BREWING UP
A BUSINESS

from the founder of
dogfish head craft brewery

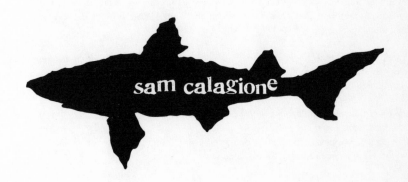

sam calagione

WILEY

John Wiley & Sons, Inc.

Published by John Wiley & Sons, Inc., Hoboken, New Jersey.
Published simultaneously in Canada.

For general information on our other products and services or for technical support, please contact our Customer Care Department within the United States at (800) 762-2974, outside the United States at (317) 572-3993 or fax (317) 572-4002.

Wiley also publishes its books in a variety of electronic formats. Some content that appears in print may not be available in electronic books. For more information about Wiley products, visit our web site at www.wiley.com.

Library of Congress Cataloging-in-Publication Data:
Calagione, Sam, 1969–
Brewing up a business : adventures in entrepreneurship from the founder of Dogfish Head Craft Brewery / Sam Calagione.
p. cm.
Includes index.
ISBN-13 978-0-471-70868-1 (cloth)   ISBN-13 978-0-470-05045-3 (paper)
ISBN-10 0-471-70868-2 (cloth)   ISBN-10 0-470-05045-4 (paper)
1. Dogfish Head Craft Brewery. 2. Microbreweries—Delaware. 3. Entrepreneurship—Delaware. 4. Small business—Delaware. I. Title.
HD9397.D644C35 2005
338.7'66342'09751—dc22
2005001068

Printed in the United States of America

10 9 8 7 6 5 4 3

For my sweet gal, Mariah.
Since I have met you, I have grown to believe
there is nothing we can't do together.

Contents

Foreword

THE PASSION OF THE INDIVIDUAL

By Michael Jackson*

The cheerful chap on the cover of this book has every reason to smile. The military-looking vehicle behind him delivers only the matériel of sociability. People love him for it.

Sam Calagione does not aspire to sit among the suits at a boardroom table and be a slave to the miltary metaphors of marketing. He fights his own battles, on behalf of people with individual tastes and against the tyranny of timidity, conformity, and the lowest common denominator.

When I first took my pen to the same cause, 30 years ago, my colleagues asked if I had given up serious journalism. Did I no longer want to change the world? Almost all of them took beer seriously, but they nonetheless thought that writing about it was a frivolous pursuit.

Like Sam Calagione, I can simultaneously have fun in my job but pursue it with serious intent. Those of us who are truly demanding about our beer are a minority, but we are by no means insignificant in number, and we are willing to pay more for a brew we like.

For us, good beer is essential to the quality of life. People who love wine or bread or cheese, for example, would take the same view. These are

*Michael Jackson is the world's best-selling author on beer and whisky. His most recent books are *The Great Beer Guide* (DK Inc, New York) and *The Complete Guide to Single Malt Scotch* (Running Press, Philadelphia)

all perfect products for the entrepreneur, but so are scores of others. In my view, a passion for the product is the first essential. If you have a passion, look at that first. Whatever excites your passion, there are surely others who feel the same way.

Passionate beer-lovers are seeking character, with its own individualistic interplay of flavors. Big breweries have the technical knowhow to make such products but their kettles are too large for our market. Their cost accountants want to produce beers low in raw materials and high in acceptability. Their marketing men believe they can think small, but they cannot; well, not small enough. To have individualistic beers, we need small breweries. If you are not passionate about beer, you may be unaware of the renaissance of craft brewing in the United States since the late 1970s.

When I began writing about beer, there were fewer than 50 brewing companies in the US, almost all of them making very similar beers. Today, there are more than 1,500, brewing beers in more than 100 styles. Many of those beers are highly individualistic, but none more than Sam's.

Their individuality is suggested by their names. I especially like Raison D'Etre (both the name and the beer), then he exceeded it with Raison D'Extra.

As his verbal dexterity suggests, Sam was an English major. He studied fiction and poetry. I'm told he takes Walt Whitman to bed with him, though I learned this from a young woman who has no first-hand knowledge of that. I think she wished she had. "You are spending the whole day with Sam Calagione. Tomorrow!? He's the Robert de Niro of brewers!" He hasn't made a feature film yet, but he has been a Levi's model and made a rap record.

Sadly for female admirers, he seems to have found the perfect wife while still at college. He has the ingenuity to invent new equipment for the brewhouse, and the muscle to row his beer across the Delaware river.

Now it turns out he can write a book, too: brisk, readable, and instructive. A man of such diverse attributes, abilities, and achievements sets an example that makes us all look deficient.

What can we do about this? I can write a foreword, which aggrandizes myself: I become someone whose blessing he needed. And you? Read the book and brew up your own business. You don't have to make beer. Just make a million . . .

Preface

In my college days I was an English major (fatefully, I minored in beer drinking . . . one man's disciplinary probation is another man's vocational research). I have always enjoyed reading more than studying. When I had an epiphany to open a brewery, I figured I could learn everything I needed to succeed in business by reading business books. Boy, was I wrong. However, I did learn a lot from reading great books by and about the business leaders that came before me. I have a shelf full of them. I especially enjoy books about entrepreneurs who started little companies with big visions. Stories about women mixing up hand lotions in their home blenders and packing them in ketchup bottles, or guys cooking up the revolutionary sole (soul) of a running shoe in their waffle makers. But nearly all of these books remain only three-quarters read. I earmarked and underlined hundreds of inspirational philosophies and schemes that motivated me toward my dream of opening my own company. But I always seemed to lose interest in these stories at about the same point—just after the hero slays the dragon and brings the great idea to market, when the MBAs, bankers, and accountants bum-rush the stage and in the flash of a moment the company goes public. When my eyes come across that horrific, inevitable phrase, "maximizing shareholder value," they pretty much glaze over.

Entrepreneurs are fueled by risk and an inherent desire to make their mark in their world. In growing Dogfish Head I've done a lot of things right and a lot of things wrong. What I am most proud of is having done so many things. Everybody has dreams and ideas; our imaginations should be our most treasured assets. But the self-esteem and courage needed to continually face the Sisyphean task of moving your idea from imagination toward reality is what propels an entrepreneur forward. Everyone has great ideas, but successful businesspeople tend to be better at *executing* great ideas. The sense of accomplishment that comes with this execution gives us the buzz we seek. This buzz would not be half as resonant if there were no risk involved. Executing your idea while fully aware of the risk enhances the natural buzz. When it comes to brewing up a business, I haven't always known exactly what I am doing. The results of some of my efforts bear this out. I'm okay with that, and if you are in business for yourself or considering heading in that direction, you need to be okay with that, too. I am confident that even if you fall down in business and have to pick yourself up and start afresh every day, the courage that comes with embracing your struggle will be well worth it.

It's that feeling of handing a cupful of moisturizer to the first customer, or watching the athlete take the first turn around the track in Aunt Jemima shoes, that feeling of *Oh my God! What am I doing?* is the most holy feeling an entrepreneur can experience. In my mind, it speaks to a basic and beautiful human condition—the rush of adrenaline. The fight-or-flight predicament. Not knowing if you are going to survive, if your idea is going to be embraced, is an exciting, daunting, and addictive feeling for an entrepreneur. It is our Raison D'Etre. And you can maintain and amplify that feeling regardless of what stage your business is in—even if you are still in the planning stages. It just seems to me that going public is by definition anti-entrepreneurial. You cannot let the tail of money wag the dog of inspiration.

Of course, there are legitimate reasons why a company goes public. I just can't think of any off the top of my head. (I have promised my coworkers that the day Dogfish Head goes public I will dive into our largest fermenting vessel and tread beer for an entire 8 hour workday.) This book is not really for the folks faced with the challenge of bringing their companies public. This book is for the rest of us—the majority of us. Over 95 percent of the companies in America are privately owned. Over 80 percent of these are considered small companies—companies with revenues of less than $10 million. It is a documented fact that the Number One reason small companies go out of business is lack of capital. Lack of capital is pretty much my middle name. I'm almost sure we were the only commercial brewery to ever accept delivery of a brewing system from the back of a UPS truck.

When we opened our doors, we had the dubious distinction of being the smallest brewery in the country. Today Dogfish Head is the fastest-growing brewery in America. We are still tiny, but we are growing strong. And we are still learning from our mistakes. We've made more than a few. (Note to self: Do not put peppercorns and lavender buds in a beer and expect people to beat down your door for a pint of it.) But the one thing we have successfully done is establish a small brand that stands for quality and innovation. We have built this brand through our own belief and determination in what we are doing and the shared belief of our coworkers and customers. We grew our revenues by over 50 percent last year to $8 million. We built this brand spending less than 1 percent of our revenue on advertising. I will share some of the defining moments in the Dogfish Head corporate evolution that were monumental learning experiences. I will regale you with stories of exploding stainless steel tanks, building and rowing a boat full of beer from Delaware to New Jersey (our first export), selling T-shirts at trucker stops for gas money on the way home from beer festivals, and worse. But mostly I hope to commiserate and celebrate the amazing feeling of what it means to be an entrepreneur. Say it with me as you bring this book to the cash register, *Oh my God! What am I doing?*

Acknowledgments

In addition to my wife and partner, Mariah, there are a number of people I am thankful to have worked and lived with. I raise my pint glass to you for a number of reasons:

For my children, Sammy and Grier. Thank you for waiting up for me in the evenings. I have enjoyed our bedtime stories as much as you.

For my family, especially my sisters, Christa and Myka, and my parents, Sam and Mary, who bought me the book *When Bad Things Happen to Good People* the day I got kicked out of high school. Through your limitless support and direction we have learned that good things can happen to good people as well. As Dogfish Head has mutated from a family vacation place to a business that we built, it has always felt like home.

For all of my amazing friends, who I'm pretty sure would love me even if I didn't own a brewery.

For my agent, Clare Pelino, for having the vision for this book before any of us did.

For my editors at Wiley, Matt and Shannon. For believing in this book and encouraging me every step of the way.

For the artists/entrepreneurs/businesspeople who have inspired me and motivated me to put my thumbprint, however small, on the world. Especially Andy Warhol, Marcel Dzama, Matthew Barney, Bruce Weber, and Dave Eggers.

For all the other small breweries fighting to stake their claim in the competitive American beer scene. Slow and steady wins the race.

Last, but foremost in terms of inspiring the creation of this book, are the people who have worked beside me throughout the creation of our company. Dogfish Head is where we are today because of the hard work, dedication, compassion, and creativity of all the amazing women and men who have built this company alongside me. Keep up the great work, guys. From your father/son/brother to the rest of the Dogfish Head family, I say thank you, and boy do I mean it.

chapter 1
THE UNCONVENTIONAL BEGINNINGS OF AN ENTREPRENEUR

My dad backed our red pickup truck beneath the second-story window of my dormitory bedroom. My friends in the next dorm room initiated a grand send-off by blasting Frank Sinatra's "That's Life" out their windows as we threw green garbage bags filled with clothes, cassettes, and books into the back of the truck below. I received this rousing tribute partly in acknowledgment of my proud Italian-American heritage, but mostly because I had just been kicked out of prep school a mere 2 months before graduation. My father drove me home in silence. When we reached the driveway of our house, he said simply, "Sammy, sometimes you're a tough kid to love."

I was so disappointed in myself at that moment. Yes, I was disappointed because I had let my father, my biggest supporter in the world, down to a cosmic degree. But I was mostly disappointed in myself because I had just lost the connection to the place where I had learned who I was and who I wanted to be. The place where, I would later realize, I decided to be an entrepreneur. For better or worse, I figured out who I was and who I wanted to be while I was attending Northfield Mt. Hermon School—the high school started by the world-renowned evangelist, D.L. Moody. The school I never graduated from.

Not that I didn't deserve to be kicked out. The administrators there finally sealed my fate under the blurry and all-encompassing "Accumulation of Offenses" section of the student handbook. I can recount a number of said offenses accumulated in my 3 years there, and I think I should recount them again now. Looking back, I believe these offenses were indicative of the entrepreneurial fire I had burning within me.

I came right out of the gate with a willingness to embrace risk. I set the record for the earliest point in the school year when a student was placed on disciplinary probation. I had grown up in the town next to the school, and I wanted to show my two best friends the beauty of my new school as well as the beauty of the girls at my new school.

We snuck out my parents' station wagon in the middle of the night and headed to campus. Just three sophisticated 16-year-olds, smoking cigars and listening to Journey. We approached the school in a covert fashion that we thought would surely allow us to elude campus security. Instead of using the road, we drove up the football field, through the quad, and straight into a motion-detecting light. Not into the shaft of light, mind you, but into the pole that was holding the light itself. It detected our motion. We were greeted by a dorm parent who soon invited campus security to the party, and the rest was history.

My next year marked the second phase of my delinquent entrepreneurial development in which I exhibited ambition and an ability to organize coworkers toward a common objective. Our objective at this juncture—not getting kicked out.

In my junior year, I was not permitted to attend the prom. So another junior classmate and I designed a foolproof plan. We would act as chaperones for a bunch of senior friends who would be attending the prom. We decided to do this in style: A Winnebago was rented, beers were procured, bow ties were straightened. We headed off to the prom but never reached our destination as much beer drinking, pool hopping, and roof surfing ensued. While going down the highway at 60 miles per hour sitting Indian style on top of a Winnebago seemed like a good idea at the time, I can see now that it probably was not. The local authorities felt similarly, and we received a two-cruiser escort back to campus.

They had us now. I believe that was the actual phrase used by the teacher who the authorities handed us over to. We were all separated into different rooms so as not to corroborate our stories as we awaited our morning tribunal. The Winnebago was locked safely on campus, nearly overflowing with the various and sundry contraband. But this is where it turns into a story of uncommon valor and the creation of a united front committed to reaching a shared goal: beating *the man*. Walkie-talkies were employed, as were bicycles, and door-opening coat hangers. We even used the sheets-tied-together-to-rappel-out-the-window motif celebrated in nearly every prison-break movie.

The following morning we were called to meet outside the Winnebago. There was a short, self-congratulatory speech by the teacher that mostly revolved around our foolishness for actually thinking we could get away with it. The door swung open and revealed . . . nothing but a very clean and contraband-free recreation vehicle. We were set free for lack of evidence. In the middle of the night we had successfully executed Project-Break-Back-In-and-Throw-It-All-Out. We even made sure there was a vase of fresh-cut flowers on the dining table in the camper.

By senior year my entrepreneurial spirit knew no bounds. After the Winnebago incident, the powers that be decided to keep an eye on me. They said I could come back but only on the grounds that I live on campus in a dormitory. They didn't realize that my friends had formed a juvenile-delinquent all-star team by signing up to live in the same dorm. We each had diverse talents but shared a common love of partying and rule breaking. This would be the setting of my first endeavor into the beer business. I would visit my parents on the weekends, borrow the car, and cruise liquor stores for sympathetic, western Massachusetts, libertarian hippies willing to buy me beer as I waited in the shadows. I would return to school and parcel out the booty. There would always be an extra six-pack in it for me—the business-man. This proceeded throughout the year without a hitch. Yes, our beer-addled behavior sometimes raised suspicion. Like when a faculty member opened the door to the recreation room only to find us playing two-on-two Ping-Pong wearing nothing but tube socks and ski goggles. But my luck couldn't last, and I tempted fate. The businessman got caught and was put out of business.

YOUR CALLING: FINDING YOUR PASSION

There are a number of reasons why my time at Northfield Mt. Hermon was so crucial to my development as a creative person. The most important is that it was the place where I met and began to date my future wife, Mariah. At that time, aside from reading and writing, being with Mariah was one of the only things I was good at. I actually met Mariah's mom, Rachel, first. She was friends with my favorite teacher, Bill Batty, and was at his house visiting his family for the weekend. Some friends and I were there that evening hanging out with Bill and his son John, who was a classmate of ours. Mariah's mom made brownies for us that I was sure were the best I had ever tasted. She told me her daughter had just started her first term at NMH, and I told her that if her daughter could cook anything like her mom I was going to marry her someday. Within a couple of months I was dating Mariah, and we've been together ever since.

We began dating when we were all of 16 years old, so we've pretty much grown up together. Our personalities evolved to complement one another's strengths and weaknesses. We attended different colleges in different parts of the country, spent separate semesters abroad in Australia, and still worked hard to see each other every chance we got. So much time and distance apart is not easy on a relationship, but through it all I got my first taste of how, if you want something bad enough and are willing to do anything necessary to make it happen, you *can* make it happen. This lesson has served me well in love and in life. Mariah was always the first person I went to for support and advice on the challenges we faced in the early years at Dogfish Head. She became my true partner in the company in our third year in business, and we've worked side by side to grow Dogfish Head since then. She is much more focused and practical than I am and has been as equally committed to guiding Dogfish Head toward where we are today as I have. There are a million reasons why I love Mariah, one of which is that she is undoubtedly the only person in the world who has higher expectations of me than I have of myself. She is never surprised when we achieve great things; she would expect nothing less. I sensed that the first time I met her at NMH, and even more so after I was kindly asked to leave the school. In those first few weeks apart, our relationship became more difficult but also more rewarding as I saw she was willing to stand by me.

What sounds like a sad ending to a high school career was actually a pretty revelatory beginning. As I mentioned, getting kicked out of high school was one of the worst things to happen to me because it was where I learned who I was. On the day I got kicked out I also came to recognize the person I wanted to be. I wanted to create. I wanted to make something that was a reflection of myself. At first I wanted to be a writer, and I went off to college as an English major with the hopes of doing just that. Yes, I'm one of the elite fraternity of people in the country who graduated from college without ever actually receiving a high school degree. . . . We aren't exactly Mensa.

RECOGNIZING YOUR STRENGTHS

Because beer has always played an important role in my life, I continued to hone my creativity with and passion for beer while at college. I designed an all-weather, thrift-store reclining chair that actually contained a covert compartment that held a keg. When security showed up to bust a party, we'd sit on the chair and ask, "Keg, what keg?" I proudly contributed toward the invention of a drinking game called Biff that involved squeegees, milk crates, a Ping-Pong ball, and four contestants dressed only in tube socks and ski goggles (if it ain't broke, don't fix it). I graduated from college and realized I was more passionate about beer than a career in writing. So I started making my own beer and decided I wanted to open a brewery.

As an entrepreneur—as a person—you have to ask yourself what is your defining inmost thought. And then you have to do everything you can to express this belief to the people around you. I learned to love to read and write and express my creativity at Northfield Mt. Hermon. My inmost thought when I was first enrolled at Northfield Mt. Hermon was: "Rebel against authority in order to express yourself." This is pretty much the same defining instinct that drives me today, but I've been fortunate enough to find a constructive outlet for this angst. I've created a company that subverts the definition of beer put forth by the "authorities" at Budweiser and Coors.

If you did not earn a business degree or follow a clear and common path to create your business, you know there is no prescribed method to ensure success. I'm sure that majoring in business or getting an MBA gives you more tools and familiarity with the mechanics of business. But tools are useless unless you are able to use them. You could have the best set of tools in the world but if you are not ready and capable of working with them they are useless to you. If you believe in your idea enough to make it happen, it must be a powerful idea. The way you harness the power of that idea is to believe you are the only person capable of making that idea a reality. Once you have this mind-set, you will see that the tools are not what builds a strong company—it's the builder.

Opening a brewery—opening any business—seems like an impossible feat from a distance. But it starts with a faith in yourself—a belief that just because something hasn't been done before doesn't mean it shouldn't be done at all. If anything, the more impossible your business idea seems to the world at large, the more opportunity there might be for you to succeed. Thomas Edison didn't invent the lightbulb from scratch, but he was the first to imagine an entire country illuminated and powered by electricity. He set to work not just to create a durable lightbulb but to create an entire industry while naysayers around him predicted his failure. If you are going into business, the core of your strength lies in your ability to picture a world in which your idea makes a difference. However big or small that difference may be, however many people's lives your idea ends up affecting, you need to recognize and celebrate your opportunity to make a difference. The lightbulb that went off above Edison's head was not so much an actual physical lightbulb as it was a vision of a world in which he could make a difference.

TAKING RISKS: BEING A BUSINESS PIONEER

One of my earliest and fondest childhood memories is being shot in the back with a real arrow by my father as I rode a horse. He loaded the car with me, a camera, a bow, an arrow, and some ridiculous, kiddie Western clothes he bought on a business trip to Texas. We drove to a farm that didn't belong to anyone we knew but had a very old horse that he felt confident wouldn't run away if he placed me on its back. He stuffed a flat piece of lumber under my shirt and jammed an arrow through the shirt into the wood. He placed me on a horse and "shot" me as I was doing my best wounded-cowboy impression. He was putting together a slide show for a group of fellow oral surgeons. He planned to end his lecture about a new, unorthodox tooth-implant system he had created with that picture of me on a horse with an arrow in my back. The message revolved around the perception of risk that comes with trying something new. The pioneers were the ones who risked their lives in order to create a new community in a new land. All small businesspeople are pioneers, and their companies are the hearts of their communities.

Of course there is risk that comes with being a pioneer, but the risk is minimized if the community is built on an impressive set of values; impressive in that they make an impression on the lives of the people who come in contact with them. These values start at home and shouldn't be separate from your professional values if you are going to succeed. I think I sensed this idea emanating from my father even then, at the moment he was shooting me with an arrow.

The only predictable thing in the world of business is that the future cannot be predicted. Going into business is about embracing the unknown. You recognize very quickly that there is no safety net to catch your fall. While you cannot recover what could be lost by taking those risks, even many failed entrepreneurs agree that those risks are well worth taking. You have to believe in yourself and the integrity of your idea to really make a go of it. Business integrity is a combination of your values and work ethic and the value of your product or service to potential customers. To connect your values with your product takes education. First you have to educate yourself on how to get into business; how to apply your own values to those of your business. Then you have to educate your coworkers and customers on what that business is all about. An unwavering faith and devotion to seeing your idea through is critical. This faith will come through your values and your education. No matter how much the daily unknowns of business push and pull you out of your comfort zone, you can execute your ideas if you are anchored by strong values.

VALUES

There are as many different reasons, motivations, methods, and models for starting a business as there are businesses. The one major characteristic consistent in every successful business that survives long past its inception is an adherence to core values.

The values around which you choose to focus your business will form the backbone of your company more so than your business plan, management team, marketing plan, budget, or product line. Your values determine the quality of your product or service, how you treat your customers, the culture of your business, and how you manage employees. The values essential to being a successful entrepreneur are not learned in a classroom or from a book. Values are acquired daily by interacting with people. In business, values are maintained through relationships with employees, colleagues, and customers. Having good business values starts with a single, all-important idea—you either treat people with love and respect or you don't. It may sound naïve and simplistic, but the execution can be quite complex. The manifestation of this respect is reflected in your business offering—it either represents a good value or it doesn't. Before creating a valuable product or service, one must take inventory of personal values. In business it is easy to be conflicted between making a large profit or consistently satisfying customers and coworkers, thereby gaining their trust and loyalty.

Whether you are an MBA graduate running a publicly traded company or a one-person home-based entrepreneur, too often we measure our individual success by our paychecks. We focus on the monetary value attributed to our labor. For a businessperson, this translates to your business's profit margin. While a large profit margin may feel like success for a short while, a company focused entirely on increasing profits will not experience sustained success. To really know success in business is to have your personal values and those of your company perfectly aligned.

FITTING THE PIECES TOGETHER

After graduating from Muhlenberg College in 1992 I moved to New York City because English was the only subject I had excelled in and I had a vague notion that I either wanted to teach or write. I also had a pretty strong notion that I wanted to move to the biggest city in America, go out all night, and revel in my youth. I moved in with a friend and enrolled in some writing courses at Columbia University. To pay the bills I worked as a waiter at a restaurant called Nacho Mama's Burritos. There, I quickly became friends with Joshua Mandel, one of the owners. While the decor and the fare bespoke a Mexican restaurant, Joshua was so passionate about beer that serving unique and high-quality beers became a specialty of the restaurant.

Joshua was one of the first restaurateurs in New York City to seek out not only the obscure import beers but the beers made at small American microbreweries that were just starting to gain favor in a few corners of the world. The restaurant was serving beers like Sierra Nevada Bigfoot, Anchor Liberty, and Chimay Red. We noticed many of the patrons shared our excitement about these innovative brews. I slowly began to realize that my work in the restaurant in general, and selecting, recommending, and serving beer in particular, was very rewarding. There was definitely a pivotal moment when I saw that a core of regular customers at Nacho Mama's actually cared about and trusted my opinion on the unusual, exotic beers we were selling. These were people I admired simply for taking the risk of trying something new. Like me, they were ready and willing to experiment. They trusted my understanding of what they were looking for. They trusted themselves enough to make up their own minds about the quality of the beers we served. I remember taking great pride in earning their trust, and I continued to educate myself further about the world of good beer in an effort to protect and enhance that trust.

Joshua and I wanted to take our love of beer to the next step, so we decided to brew our own. We located the one shop in all of New York City that sold beer-making equipment and ingredients and began what would be my first of many batches of beer.

For this first batch, I began by sterilizing two dozen large beer bottles by baking them in the oven for 20 minutes. Then, I took them out, piping hot, and placed them on a cheap rug, which promptly melted, permanently affixing the 24 bottles to it. While still attached to the rug, I filled the bottles with beer, capped them, and dragged them into a dark corner. After the requisite week had passed, I cut each bottle out of the rug and placed it in the refrigerator. Other than the odd packaging—a small chunk of area rug melted to the bottom of each bottle—the beer looked pretty good. It was a pale ale made with cherries. I called it Cherry Brew since it was my virgin batch and all.

We threw a party for the inaugural tasting, assembling a motley crew of taste testers to sample the batch. In addition to my two roommates, Mariah drove down from college and, oddly enough, Ricki Lake, of talk show fame, joined us for the festivities. I had been subsidizing my Nacho Mama's income with infrequent acting gigs and just did a spot on her show.

Once the beer was chilled, I pulled the bottles from the refrigerator and opened them to share with roommates and friends. As I handed out glasses of beer, people began commenting that it tasted fantastic and looked at me in wonderment. I wasn't exactly known for my cooking abilities or my cleanliness, but somehow the beer came out really well plus it had a subtle red hue and fragrance from the cherries. The recipe did not include cherries but my great grandmother who was known in her town for making the best sausage using only pinches and handfuls to measure. I felt comfortable trusting my judgment and it actually worked out well. I was dumbfounded to recognize this latent, hereditary skill.

As I watched my friends kick back and enjoy something I had made, I experienced a sense of pride and accomplishment on a level never felt before. The beer was the hit of the party. More than that, I had created something unique that people enjoyed. I had given people something that, at that moment, they really needed. That evening I spent as much time as my friends could stand talking about all the different beers in the world, the ingredients used in making them, and all of the small breweries that were popping up around the country. My buddy Joe listened, sipped, and said, "Dude, you're obsessed." He was right, and, instead of being embarrassed by his comment, I was actually quite proud.

As we sat there drinking, I could not help but begin planning the next batch to brew. I began considering new ingredients and different methods, but I decided to keep my signature bottles for the time being. I also started thinking that, while maybe I would never actually write the great American novel, I might be able to make the great American beer. That evening I stood up and, with Ricki Lake as my witness, told everyone in the room that I was going to be a professional brewer. They laughed at my bold and unlikely statement, and I laughed at myself, but I woke up the next morning, left the apartment with a fuzzy head, and camped out in the public library to research just what it would take to open a brewery.

I suspected starting my own business wouldn't be easy, especially considering I had zero practical business experience. What I knew for sure was that I had a good head start because I had an idea I was passionate about and solid, people-oriented values.

As you consider opening your own business, try to condense your reasons for wanting to do so into one main idea. What is it that is so appealing about the business you want to open that you are actually ready and willing to take the big step of doing so? If you can successfully complete this exercise, congratulations, you have a firm grasp of your big idea. Not that the hard work is behind you. It is one thing to have big ideas. It is a whole other thing to actually execute them.

THE VALUE OF EXECUTION

After continuing to research the brewing industry for a number of months and brewing more batches of beer in my kitchen, I came to the conclusion that, since I was young, inexperienced, and broke, I would need to start small. In my research I learned there were essentially two kinds of small breweries: microbreweries, where beer is brewed then packaged into kegs and bottles and sent out the door to be sold in bars and stores; and brew-pubs, where beer is brewed within a restaurant and sold primarily on tap within the restaurant itself. The start-up costs were relatively similar, so I decided to open a brewpub. I figured I could reduce my risk of failure if I had revenue streams coming from both a brewery and a restaurant. My parents were supportive of the idea and were actually impressed when I came home for a holiday with a business plan that was nearly half complete.

While in Maine taking a short brewing class at a small commercial brewery and completing my business plan, I decided to name my brewery Dogfish Head after a small peninsula off Southport Island, Maine. My parents have a summer cabin on Dogfish Head where I spent a lot of time as a child, so the name has sentimental value. I also thought the sound had great rustic connotations that would work well for the brewery I imagined I would someday build. I returned from my Maine trip ready to make the leap. It was time to seek out a location and financing.

I decided to open the brewpub in Mariah's hometown of Rehoboth Beach, Delaware, where we had spent a few summers together. The coastal towns of Delaware are absolutely beautiful with wide beaches, pretty harbors, and a thriving commercial community. I needed a location where the little capital I had would allow me to get the doors open and commence brewing. I had to find a leasable building that was already a turnkey restaurant. For a small, seasonal town, Rehoboth has a ton of restaurants and a sophisticated, varied clientele that includes locals, transients, and vacationers from the surrounding cities. The lack of choices for potential sites made me nervous, but I also realized it said good things about the community's support of the local restaurant scene. If there were a lot of abandoned restaurants ready to rent I would have wondered about my decision to open in that area.

So I only had a couple of choices; there were two buildings that fit within my parameters. I decided to focus on the one that was farthest from the beach but had its own parking lot. Since rents were relative to proximity to the beach, every block you moved back cut up to 30 percent off the price of rent. The building I decided on was a good number of blocks back; farther away than any of the successful restaurants in town. To put it in

Monopoly terms, if the beach were Boardwalk and Park Place, the building I hoped to rent was the equivalent of a light blue property. While the rent was fair it wasn't cheap, and the best move I made in signing the lease was the ability to have 20 percent of my annual rent set aside toward an option to buy the building at the end of 5 years. I think the landlady allowed that section into the lease because she realized the odds were very much against my business surviving that long. The place had been rented in previous years by a series of fly-by-night party animals. The most recent tenant left town very quietly at the end of the last summer without paying rent or notifying any suppliers. Not only did the restaurant have all of its equipment in place but there was still booze on the bar shelf and a couple of random onion rings floating in the fryer. We even found a few bras, a pair of boxers, and a random stiletto. The building had a room attached to the main bar that used to be a take-out kiosk. I realized that if we put a picture window into this wall, which overlooked the main dining area, this room would be the perfect spot to install the brewing equipment.

Now all I needed was a brewery to install.

INNOVATION: TURNING LEMONS INTO LEMON-FLAVORED BEER

I contacted every manufacturer and broker of new and used small-scale brewing equipment in North America. I knew we would need $80,000 to buy and install even the smallest prefabricated system. At this point I had exhausted much of my capital renovating the building, upgrading kitchen equipment, and installing a wood grill. All I had left to build my beloved brewery with was $20,000. I recalled reading about a small rack system used by home brewers that might fit within my budget. While it would be a challenge to brew enough beer on such a small system, I figured I could buy it and just brew a lot more often than I would on a true, full-scale commercial system. Of course, I would need somewhere to store and ferment all of the little batches that would come out of the brewery. We bought a bunch of used kegs, cut the tops off, and installed sanitary ball valves at their bases. We then built an air-conditioned room full of racks where I could store my homemade fermenting vessels. The little home-brewing system finally showed up one chilly spring day. In addition to a few other packages we received from UPS that day there was a big box containing a little brewery on the back of the truck. I unwrapped it, rolled it into place, plugged it in, and began making test batches in the weeks before the restaurant opened.

In the months prior, I visited the few area breweries to take tours and learn more about the hands-on work it took to run a brewery. A number of the brewers I had met stopped by to see how I was progressing: I was pretty embarrassed to show them my brewery system. Brewers calibrate their world in barrels, which is also how the federal government taxes us. For every barrel brewed (31 gallons), brewers are taxed $7. Therefore brewing equipment is built in barrel increments. The average microbrewery system produces 30 barrel (930 gallon) batches. The average brewpub system in a restaurant produces 10 barrel (310 gallons) batches. My original brewing system produced 10 gallons or 0.3 barrels per batch. When brewers I had met while visiting other breweries would stop by the brewpub, I felt like a boy among men. I suffered from an acute case of brewery-envy, but I would not be discouraged. It's not the size of your brewing system that matters, it's what you do with it . . . or so they say.

Although brewing on such a small system really sucked from a labor perspective (it takes pretty much the same amount of time to brew a 5 barrel batch as it does to brew a 50 barrel batch of beer), it was great from an experimental perspective. To make enough beer for the restaurant, I had to brew two or three batches a day five or six days a week. I quickly got bored brewing the same beers over and over again so I started to wander into the kitchen of the restaurant for new ideas. I would grab some apricots or maple syrup or raisins and toss them into the beer. Like my great grandmother had, I worked on these recipes by instinct. I trusted my own palate more than any recipe I'd come across in a brewing book. I would change one variable each time I brewed and track the progress and evolution of that batch through fermentation and into the keg. From the beginning, I knew I wanted to experiment and find my own way. I was unaware of it at the time but Dogfish Head's reputation for experimentation and quality was born from the humble beginnings of that 10 gallon system.

OVERCOMING OBSTACLES TO BUSINESS: REPEALING PROHIBITION

With the brewery in place, I still had one small obstacle to clear before I could open the pub: My plan to open a brewery in Delaware was totally illegal.

I needed to rewrite state laws in order to do business. After Prohibition was repealed in 1933, it was up to each individual state to establish and regulate their own brewing laws.

One of the main reasons I decided to open the brewpub in Delaware was that, in 1995, there were only a handful of states that didn't have breweries yet. I recognized the marketing opportunity and curiosity factor that would come with being the first brewpub to open in the state. I drove to the capital of Dover and literally knocked on the doors of a few state senators and members of the house. They were helpful from the very first day and sympathetic to my situation. I learned there had been attempts to change the laws in previous years but the legislation never made it to the floor. The sponsors of the proposed bill just gave up.

My big idea was to make off-centered beer and food for off-centered people. Before I could do this the laws needed to change. Traditionally one would hire a lawyer and hand off the responsibility of navigating the bureaucratic process. I knew that unless I was very active personally in describing our intentions to the legislators our proposed bill might not be voted on in the spring session. It was imperative that this be resolved quickly enough to allow me to open for the critical summer season. While I worked with a great lawyer, I did a lot of legwork and lobbying myself. It was an off-centered approach that was in keeping with my big idea. I found an ally in a lawyer named Dick Kirk who was affiliated with a Wilmington-based law firm. He had worked with a man who owned a chain of liquor stores so he was already familiar with the state liquor laws. Dick and I went to work drafting a bill and then spoke for it on the floor of the state senate and house of representatives. We met with some resistance from a couple of neo-prohibitionists in the senate but our bill passed with an overwhelming majority. I was amazed and delighted by the support we got from the majority of the legislators. Before I could sell Dogfish Head to customers I had to sell it to legislators, and it proved to be a rewarding experience as they all got behind our company and saw us for what we were—a David in a brewing world full of Goliaths. They moved quickly to help the first brewpub open in the state. The story of that victory and the brewpub's impending opening hit the pages of the state and local newspapers simultaneously. I used the interviews with local publications as opportunities to further the community's education about us. I told the story of Dogfish Head, and our intentions to offer fresh food and fresh beer in a unique, rustic atmosphere. I talked about our values and our goal of teaching people to expect more from their dining and drinking experience than they had in the past. Days before the brewpub opened people began driving into the lot hoping to get an inside glimpse of the first restaurant in the state to brew its own beer. I hired a great staff of restaurant veterans from the area and trusted friends from college and home. We worked night and day painting and decorating the restaurant, hoping to open before the summer rush. I began to furiously pump out little 10 gallon batches of beer to stock up for opening day. Whatever challenges you may face in opening and running your business, use your big idea for a touchstone to keep you focused—it will serve you well. With each challenge that you put behind you, your faith in your idea will grow stronger.

EDUCATION + BODY + MIND = PERSONALITY

This equation proves true whether you are talking about a person or a company. The mind is the *who,* the body is the *what,* and the education is the *how.* My goals were to focus on the Dogfish Head brand (mind), to offer great unique beers and food (body), and to educate our customers about our values of making better things to provide a better experience for them (education). People don't want to just use a product. They want to like the product they are using. Your personality forms the basis for whether other people like you or not. The same philosophy holds true for a company. Consider the who, the what, and the how of your business. If you can develop and implement these three objectives in a way that shows your distinct approach, the personality of your business will shine through.

WE ALL NEED A LITTLE HELP...

Even though I was able to stockpile dozens of gallons of beer, and our chef and general manager were able to get the menu and bar ready, I had started the licensing process later than I should have. In addition to changing the law I had to get a business license, a fire inspection, a health department inspection, and a liquor control board inspection. We had stairwells to paint, lights to install, and fire extinguishers to mount, and we were running out of time. I looked out the window one morning and saw a man with a white beard peering back at me. Lots of people poke their heads into a construction site just to be nosey but I recognized that this was the third or fourth time I had seen this particular face looking inside from various windows. I took a break from my desperate, preopening chores and went outside to introduce myself. His name was Doug Griffith and he was a home brewer really excited that we were opening a brewery. He asked if he could see it. I told him not to expect much and took him back to the room. Instead of scoffing at our diminutive brewery, his eyes widened further in excitement as he asked me about the different gauges and pumps we had installed. He obviously knew and cared a lot about brewing. I told him I'd love to sit and chat but we had a bunch of stuff to get done before our next inspection and moved to excuse myself. He asked if he could help. I said sure, if he didn't mind being paid in beer and pizza.

Within 2 hours he had our back stairwell painted and was framing out some drywall for our secured liquor storage area. He had every tool you could think of and could use them better than any of us. Doug has truly turned out to be a guardian angel for Dogfish Head. He built the room where our second, upgraded brewery was set up, then he actually helped build the brewing system as well. He has installed stoves, load-bearing, steel I beams, and he built the copper bar at our Milton location. He has done so much for our company and asked for so little in return. For that reason, he and his wife, Patty, don't have to open their wallets when they come to the brewery or the pub. I don't know where our brewery would be if it weren't for Doug, but I do know we would not have passed our inspections in the days leading up to our grand opening without his assistance.

A good company is nothing more or less than a group of good people gathered around a good idea. If you can locate even one person in addition to yourself who believes in the who, what, and why that you plan to build your company around, you should trust that person to help you spread those beliefs to others. When you are just getting started in business, it can be easy to slip into a myopic, dictatorial mode. Your life is on the line, and you have the most vested interest in making your business work; but if you notice there are other people who share your passion, and if you can bring them on board and motivate them to help you move forward, you will gain momentum more quickly than if you try to do everything yourself. Once your idea is embraced by someone other than yourself, you have the basis of a new community.

MAKING YOUR IDEA A REALITY

It wasn't pretty but we were finally in business. I was a professional brewer. Three years earlier, if I had told my friends and professors that this was what I'd be doing, I'm sure they would have laughed at me just as my friends had that fateful day I christened Cherry Brew. I would have laughed, too. I had always been a creative person, but I hadn't always shown great initiative or follow-through. That's because I was never really passionate about anything until I decided to be a brewer.

The only reason to make that leap into opening your own business is the unwavering belief that you can make it work and that making it work will make you happy. So many people have great ideas: Some of them go into business, and some of them fail. It is not having the great idea that makes you a success in business, it's executing it.

Your faith in your idea will be challenged many times as you go into business for yourself and even after your business is well established. You learn not only to be undaunted by the challenges and obstacles you face but to be nourished by them as well. Every small victory should be recognized as a testament to your faith. Having confidence in your idea begins with having confidence in yourself. This confidence is born from the belief that your idea has a place in the world and that you can deliver your customers something they will value. You will encounter many hurdles as you make this delivery, and some will surely trip you up. It's okay to falter, and it's okay if customers or coworkers occasionally see you fall. But they will also see you get up, dust yourself off, and continue running toward your goal. If you truly believe in what you are doing, nothing can stop you.

So many emotions went through me as we counted down the days to our opening. I remember a monumental moment of truth that, while I can look back and laugh at it now, gave me great anxiety. Our big, spiffy Dogfish Head Brewings & Eats sign arrived a week before we opened. I drove my piece-of-junk pickup truck onto the sidewalk alongside the façade of our building to hang the sign. Mariah stood across the road ready to capture a historic moment with a disposable camera. However, before we could put up our new sign we had to remove the old one from the last business. We got a great picture of us doing this.

Behind that sign was yet another, older sign from the business that occupied the space before the last business. I asked Mariah not to take a picture of us removing that sign. As I pried it off the building, a flood of emotion came over me: *Oh, my God! What am I doing?* But I also remember that it was not at all a negative feeling. I remember thinking, *They are not you, Sam. Their ideas were not your ideas. If your ideas are as potent as you think they are, and you work your ass off to see them to fruition, nobody will tear your sign off the front of this building.* Execute your ideas well, and you will achieve your goals.

Opening day finally arrived and we put the finishing touches on the restaurant as we unlocked the door. I remember standing by the front door with my mother and staring at the throng of people that crowded the bar and tables before me. Mariah, my parents, sisters, grandparents, investors, friends, and new friends were there to celebrate with me. I remember thinking how much my family meant to me. How my family had successfully balanced a love for business with a genuine love of people. How I was blessed to now have the opportunity to carry on this tradition. I intended to work hard to expand my family to include the coworkers and customers I saw sprinkled throughout my relatives and friends that evening. In so many ways the birth of a business is equally as miraculous as the birth of a child. An entrepreneur who witnesses a vision come true and sees the reflection of that vision in the eyes of customers and coworkers is participating in the development of a magical, culture-transforming entity. Even if that culture never transcends a neighborhood or a strip mall, once it exists, it takes its place in history. I kissed my mother and went back to the cold room to put a fresh keg on tap. I sampled a bit before heading back to the bar. I silently toasted all of the people who had influenced this outcome, and I was very proud to have made something that people wanted to enjoy.

chapter 2

BUSINESS FROM THE INSIDE OUT

self-discovery, inspiration, passion

In Miles Davis' autobiography, *Miles,* he writes about his time at Juilliard and how it wasn't really that inspiring for him. In the evenings, after classes, he would sit in with Dizzy Gillespie and Charlie Parker and other greats of the nascent, modern jazz world. He would return in the morning to classes only to feel stifled and bored. He realized he would never learn how to create his own music by studying classical music at an establishment school. So he found his own teachers in Dizzy and Bird, and while he learned a lot from them he mostly learned how to be himself. He decided to quit Juilliard and concentrate on making new sounds with his idols who were doing the same. He worried what his father's reaction would be but was relieved to hear his father's reasons for supporting his decision.

> He told me something I'll never forget, "Miles, you hear that bird outside the window? He's a mockingbird. He don't have a sound of his own. He copies everybody's sound and you don't want to do that. You want to be your own man, have your own sound . . . you know what you got to do and I trust your judgment."

As a businessperson you have an idea that will change the world. The change might not be felt everywhere by everyone but it will be felt by your customers, whether you have 10 or 10 million. Before you can understand the world you plan to change, you need to understand yourself. Before you can look for inspiration from a book, a school, or a mentor, you need to be inspired by yourself. Every successful businessperson I have ever met has exuded self-confidence. The necessity for extreme self-confidence is apparent when you realize that most small businesses fail. The most successful businesspeople are those who are so confident in their opportunity to succeed that failure is simply not an option. Of course there is a difference between being extremely self-confident and being self-confident to the extreme. Hubris is not an attractive quality in anyone, but there is a distinction between being egocentric and egotistical; the former acknowledges that society starts with the individual, the latter revolves around the idea that the individual need not be concerned with society at all, only the self. If you intend to succeed in business, there is no room for egotism. To succeed you must create a community that starts with you and one customer. But before there is the company, before there is the community, there is just you and your idea, the two most important things—like Miles and the sound of his trumpet.

Before you can consider whether your idea will resonate with the world, you need to make sure it resonates within you. Believe me, you are going to hit some rough patches on your way into business and as you grow your company as well. Your success would mean less to you if you didn't have to make it through hard times, or if all you knew was triumph after triumph. Don't worry though; the odds of that happening are similar to those of winning the lottery. If the idea that you have decided to stake your future on is not perfectly aligned with your own values and beliefs, you will resent yourself when times get tough. Self-loathing is the polar opposite of self-confidence, and it has no place in the world of small business. Unwavering faith in your idea is unwavering faith in yourself. The self is made up of one's values. What do you value? Does your idea for business mesh with what you value personally? The all-important first step in opening your business is the inventory of your internal values. What your business ultimately becomes and how you manage it is determined by your values, your life experiences, and the people you meet along the way. . . .

DISCOVERING WHO YOU ARE

Believing in yourself is what it is all about. Sure, Miles Davis learned from Dizzy and Bird but what he learned most was to trust himself. By having their own sounds, they taught him to believe that he could find his sound, too. The only teachers worth listening to are those who realize that you might have something to teach them, too. Much of how I define myself has come from my family and my education.

While at Northfield Mt. Hermon, I discovered I was a creative person. Granted most members of the student body and faculty only saw me create havoc. But there were a couple of teachers who believed in me—English teachers who saw flashes of creativity in my writing and true enthusiasm for the novels we read (shouts to Bill Batty and Charles Hamilton). They encouraged me to formulate my own ideas and opinions that, along with those gleaned from my family, formed the basis of my values.

The school itself was inspiring as well. When you picture a New England prep school you might conjure up the image of a bunch of well-groomed, loafers-with-no-socks-wearing blue bloods throwing a football around a leaf-blown quad while skinny blondes giggle into their corduroy purses. Our school wasn't like that at all. Creative and unconventional expression was not only allowed, it was encouraged. The diversity in ethnicity, nationality, and socioeconomic background of the students was expansive from the day the school opened. The school's founder, D.L. Moody, was probably the most famous evangelist preacher of his time, and he established the Northfield and Mt. Hermon schools as places to grow the heart, the head, and the hands of young men and women. The head and the heart aspects are easy to figure out; Moody wanted to give the students strong minds and a strong faith.

The hands part of his holy trinity is where things get interesting. Since the school accepted students who weren't necessarily rich or who couldn't fully pay for their education, Moody put everyone to work to help defray the costs of running the school. In the early days this meant walking down to the barn to slaughter a dozen chickens for dinner after math class or shoveling coal into the school's power plant before heading off for baseball practice. In the late 1980s, when I was a student there, the work ran more along the lines of shucking corn in the dining hall or shoveling snow off the pathways. To this day the students make, package, and sell their own maple syrup every March.

When I met my future wife, Mariah, she was a 16-year-old sophomore standing in the dining room, filling 600 pastries with cream. I put down my paring knife and stepped to her. I believe I told her she looked good enough to eat, and then I learned that she was the girl with the heirloom brownie recipe.

One of the greatest things about NMH is how egalitarian it has always been. D.L. Moody instilled a D.I.Y., punk-rock work ethic into the core philosophy of the school before the parents of the parents of the Sex Pistols were even born. But there was more to it than that. Moody translated to the students a noble passion for work, for one's calling. As the school matured and evolved away from its fundamentalist roots, faith in Christ metamorphosized somewhat into a faith in one's self. The faculty at NMH relished not only the diversity of the student body but the diversity of our opinions, dreams, and passions. As students, we were made to feel like we could do anything, and asked to look at the students next to us and believe that they were capable of anything as well, as long as they had faith in themselves. Of all that the world has to offer, people are the most interesting.

EDUCATE YOURSELF

I first decided to open my brewery when I was 24 years old. I was very focused from the moment I made this decision. I read everything I could about breweries and restaurants. I worked as a brewer's assistant as I wrote my business plan. I wrote a menu and tested different pizza-grilling techniques on my backyard barbeque. I made pilot batches of beer and developed recipes and brand names. I met with countless banks and raised all of the money to open the business. I signed off on the loans and was personally responsible for the debt.

While researching the industry, I discovered the best way to gain insight into the kind of person you are and the evolution your company might follow is through reading. The insight you can gain from somebody else's experience is invaluable. You can sift through the things that apply to your brand and separate them from those that don't.

As an English major in college there was a lot of reading that I loved to do and some I just had to. The latter was usually the stuff that I unconsciously recognized had very little to do with my life. I was pretty disappointed when I discovered how little Simone de Beauvoir's *The Second Sex* had to do with actual sex, but I waded through it because I had to. There were other writers like Raymond Carver, Ernest Hemingway, Ayn Rand, and F. Scott Fitzgerald who, once I started, I couldn't stop reading.

Looking back I know the reason I was so passionate about these writers is that something of myself resonated in their words. I was learning about what kind of person I wanted to be and what kind of world I was living in through the eyes of their protagonists.

Since deciding to open a business I applied the same introspective analysis of exposition to business books as I did in college to works of fiction. The difference was that I was now trying to learn about what kind of company I wanted to build and what kind of business world I lived in. In time I learned that the experiences of businesspeople in industries other than my own were at least as valuable as those I learned about in the brewing industry itself.

As I began studying the world of small-scale commercial brewing, I was alarmed by how few titles I found on the subject. I was living in Manhattan when I decided to open a brewery. I would wait tables at a beer bar at night and then walk off my research-induced hangover on my way to the public library each morning. I would do Lexis-Nexis searches from all angles on all related subjects: beer, brewery, business, etc.

While there was very little written about small-scale brewing, what I did find proved encouraging. At that time, the microbrewing industry was only about a decade old and still, for the most part, an underground phenomenon. While the base of comparable companies was small, the growth was exciting. Microbrewed beer accounted for less than 1 percent of the overall domestic beer market, but the segment was growing at a rate of 40 percent annually. So while it wasn't common knowledge yet, I recognized that the microbrewing industry was expanding at an attractive, risk-reducing rate. All I could find was one book on the subject: Bill Owens' excellent *How to Build a Small Brewery*. It became a sort of bible for me, but it wasn't enough. My search for more knowledge led me to articles in local papers from around the country and marginal but progressive publications like *Mother Jones* magazine and the *Utne Reader*. I realized that it was probably a good sign that articles on small-scale brewing were appearing in these places as opposed to *Forbes* and the *Wall Street Journal* as it meant interest in the subject had yet to bubble to the surface.

In my research I learned that brewpubs had one-tenth the failure rate of restaurants that open without breweries. I knew this statistic would be critical in raising capital. I began to collect and record similar data into the notebooks that would soon form the basis for the marketing segment of my business plan. I began researching beer and food and where they overlapped. I learned from articles in obscure culinary publications about restaurants in Belgium and Amsterdam that used local beer in their food recipes and served beers from glassware specific to their region and breweries. I read a lot about barley and small-scale baking and recognized the similarities between the high-end baking and brewing businesses—the importance of freshness and high-quality ingredients that both share. In addition to all of the articles I was copying in the library, I was reading business books as well.

LEARNING ABOUT YOUR BUSINESS

I decided I wanted to own a brewery in a restaurant as opposed to a straightforward beer-production factory because I felt there was great brand-building value in direct interactions with customers. The bar in the pub would act as a barometer. In essence our customers would act as our de facto R&D lab. They were paying *us* and providing feedback on our beer, and yet they enjoyed a level of input into what we brewed that is unheard of in the world of large-scale commercial brewing.

The first business book that I really fell in love with was Paul Hawken's *Growing a Business,* which covers the social and ecological ramifications of starting a business as well as the commercial. I also read books on business-people and companies as diverse as Andrew Carnegie, Budweiser, Donald Trump, Coors, Starbucks, The Body Shop, L.L. Bean, Walt Disney, and Coca-Cola. I read publications like *Fast Times, Inc., Wired, Forbes,* and *Fortune* and began to get comfortable with the nomenclature of business. As busy as we were once we opened, I didn't stop reading. If anything, I read more.

Reading outside of your industry disrupts your egocentric view of your company and helps you to break out of patterns and ruts. People are always chastising each other for "reading into things," but usually it's the best thing you can do.

I read every local and national beer periodical and book I could get my hands on, but I realized I was learning more about what kind of company I wanted Dogfish Head to be from the stuff I was reading that had nothing to do with brewing—the *Wall Street Journal, Vanity Fair, Forbes, Rolling Stone, Entertainment Weekly,* and the *New York Times.* I also read less-mainstream publications, like *The New Yorker, Adbusters, zing, WoodenBoat, Art in America,* and *Interview.* I read the stories and articles through the context of how they relate to Dogfish Head. At home and at work, Mariah and I discussed the trends that cross-pollinated all of the different industries and cultural groups and looked into them for the reflection of our own company.

I do not consciously think while I'm reading something, "Gee, how does this relate to Dogfish Head?" I recognize the connections reflexively, and it's almost like I'm editing and analyzing everything I read from the perspective of my brand. Even the words in the thought bubbles above my head are in the proprietary Doggie font as I reflect on what I am reading.

In the same way that you can condition your body to become more muscular and agile, you can strengthen your business mind. Let's face it, the periodicals and books about your industry are instrumental in helping you understand what is happening in your little world but they are not always helping you figure out how your brand fits into the world at large. If someone is writing about something, that means it's been done. Reading outside of your industry is more effective in giving you a fresh vantage point. As you continue to absorb this new information you'll spend less time trying to figure out what your brand is and more time recognizing your brand in the world around you. If something innovative has been done in one industry, can you take that new idea to your industry?

LEARNING FROM THOSE WHO CAME BEFORE YOU

While your business endeavor must be unique to stand out in the marketplace, it is important to remember the successes of others to both inspire and motivate you. I learned a lot about the kind of leader I wanted to be while at Northfield Mt. Hermon. In opening the Northfield and Mt. Hermon schools (the two combined in the 1970s). D.L. Moody successfully created a community that nurtured the head, hands, and heart of its members.

D.L. Moody's name is essentially synonymous with evangelism. An evangelist is someone who believes in something so strongly that he becomes consumed with a passion for convincing everyone around him to share in his belief. Isn't this pretty much the definition of an entrepreneur? Of somebody committed to bringing a vision to fruition even (especially) when that vision does not reflect the consensus of the day? In his essay on self-reliance, Emerson wrote, "To believe in your own thought, to believe that what is true for you in your private heart is true for all men—that is genius. Speak your latent conviction and it shall be the universal sense; for always the inmost becomes the outmost, and our first thought is rendered back to us by the trumpets of the Last Judgments."

Moody once said, "I have done one thing, and the work is wonderful. One thing is my motto." Our motto at Dogfish Head is "Off-centered ales for off-centered people." I like to think that Moody would approve.

By the time I got to NMH there was no longer a course specifically on D.L. Moody and the history of the school, but a number of teachers incorporated that history into their lessons. In addition to what I learned about Moody while I was there, I have read books about him, and about him in other books. President Woodrow Wilson once described a memorable encounter he had in a barbershop:

> While sitting on the chair I became aware that a personality entered the room. A man had come quietly upon the same errand as myself and sat in the chair next to me. Every word he uttered showed a personal and vital interest in the man who was serving him. I was aware that I had attended an evangelistic service because Mr. Moody was in the next chair. I purposely lingered in the room after he left and noted the singular effect his visit had upon the barbers in that shop. They talked in undertones. They did not know his name, but they knew that something elevated their thought. And I felt that I left that place as I should have left a place of worship.

Woodrow Wilson was no slouch in the charisma department himself, but he recognized a passion for life in the man next to him at the barbershop that was singular and infectious. Before becoming a preacher Moody was a shoe salesman in Boston and Chicago. He was so good at it that a year before he quit to do the Lord's work he was earning a salary over 100 times the average of his day. Moody was a gifted salesman because he was able to concentrate, distill, and direct his passion to the people around him. This is a skill that every businessperson needs, and it only comes with an honest and wholehearted belief in the work. As evidenced in his encounter with Woodrow Wilson, Moody took his house of worship with him wherever he went. As a businessperson, you need to do the same.

Miles Davis believed in the greatness of his own musical talent but he believed equally in the greatness of the talents of Dizzy, and Bird, and many other gifted musicians. The best role models and teachers are the ones who you admire to such an extent that you lose any aspirations of emulating them; the greatest lesson you learn from them is the value in being yourself. There are great lessons to learn from other business leaders throughout history who also believed in themselves and made their ideas into reality. As a businessperson you have a lot to learn even once you wholly believe in yourself and your idea. Take the time to learn about the people you admire. Find worthy role models in your community and spend time getting to know them. If it is time well spent, you will also be learning about yourself through them. Understanding the lengths someone went to on the road to success, and the goals that were able to be achieved, can help you maintain your perspective on all that is possible from a single individual, and how much it takes to achieve the goals that are most worth achieving.

KNOW YOURSELF

It is essential to define who you are when embarking on a business venture. At the same time that you write a business plan for your company, it is helpful to write a values plan for yourself. This plan should revolve around a list of the values that are most important to you in descending order of importance. It should also include a list of the things you hope to personally gain by going into business for yourself. Of course this list will include money or financial stability, but if that is all you have on your list you may want to rethink your plan. This exercise sounds corny, but it can be really effective in letting you know if the company you plan to open reflects the kind of person you want to be. It is the adherence to your view of yourself that will dictate the standard you hold yourself and your business offering to, how you treat people, how you handle difficult or challenging situations, and how you define success.

BEING ABLE TO ROLL WITH THE PUNCHES

After the brewpub was up and running, I went on a family vacation in Big Sky, Montana. The week got off to an inauspicious start when my morning call to the brewpub brought wind of a disaster. An absentminded brewer forgot to put a pressure-release valve on a sealed tank of fermenting beer. The pressure built up in the tank to the point in which the door blew off in one direction and the tank barreled across the room in the other. The tank door pierced through two double doors and the side of another brewing vessel. The tank itself knocked down two load-bearing support beams on its way to crushing our ice machine. What's worse was that the batch of Chicory Stout that was in the tank was now in every nook and cranny of the two rooms it flew through—including the nooks and crannies of our computers and fax machine. Thankfully, nobody was hurt, but there was a lot of conversation about who was responsible for the disaster. I spent a lot of time on the phone that day with our insurance company, which was suddenly a lot less warm and friendly than they were when they were soliciting our business. Lots of finger-pointing and displacement of blame. I turned on the TV to try to clear my mind of the day's events only to learn that we had gone to war with Iraq. More finger-pointing, blame, and bad blood. My son, Sammy, came into the room looking at the pictures of a dinosaur on the outside of a DVD case. I told him I needed some cuddle-time stat and asked him to put in the movie. We watched the movie together on the couch and raced each other to shout out the names of the dinosaur species appearing on the screen before the announcer named them. I usually lost. The movie came to a section that dealt with plate tectonics and continental drift, and I was reintroduced to the concept of Pangaea—the supercontinent that existed before all of the continents separated.

I had an idea.

I thought about that concept the next morning as I read a book to my son, and then I thought about it some more as I skied the deep, fresh snow that afternoon. I was at a moment in my life when I was feeling pretty dislocated. Everyone at the brewpub and insurance company was shirking responsibility for the damage. The television was reporting that every country was blaming each other. The only thing that made me feel better was family. But in a broader sense I started to think about the family of the world. About how we are all too similar to have such pervasive differences. I am not a raging peacenik by any means, but on that day I felt the world needed a little healing and a reminder of the greater family that we are all members of. I decided that Dogfish Head would make a beer called Pangaea. It would be an effort to bring all of the continents back together (at least in liquid form).

Pangaea would be brewed with an ingredient from every continent, packaged in a cork-finished wine bottle, and available for sale just in time for the family holiday dinners. I dropped this idea on the brewers once I returned from vacation and they were psyched. Another off-centered beer from our off-centered brewery. Sourcing ingredients from every continent that would work in harmony in a beer proved to be a challenge. You can't imagine how much a bucket of water from Antarctica costs. I mean, whose idea was it to even make Antarctica a continent, anyway? The beer was made with crystallized ginger from Australia, an exotic grain from Asia, an obscure sugar from South America, and a bunch of other natural ingredients from all over the world. It was brewed to pair well with food in the hope that people would drink it during meals together. Pangaea has a great cult following among fellow beer geeks, and it sells out before we even make it each winter. We never market it in the context of bonding a fractured, warring world. We never advertise it as a peace-inducing, cure-all elixir—just a beer made from stuff that grows in places all over the world that we hope families will enjoy drinking together. I never would have thought of making Pangaea if I wasn't watching movies and reading books with my son. The books had nothing to do with brewing, but they sparked my imagination and allowed me to use our brewery to make something I could be proud of in a world and at a time when I was feeling pretty defeated.

A BUSINESS IS A REFLECTION OF ITS OWNER

It might sound cliché to say that I have business running through my veins, but I like to think it's true. Not business in the Forbes-400, Lear-jet-setting sense of the phrase, but I come from a line of big personalities who ran small businesses. My father is a country doctor, and my mother taught special education. My father grew his medical practice from one office to five to become the managing partner of a group of five doctors. So he was a doctor first and a businessman second. He taught my sisters and me to revere business and to respect people, which, in his mind, were essentially the same thing. My father's success was built on a path of loyalty that ran from his family to his friends to his patients to the community. When you build a path like this it is easy to navigate from the opposite direction, and that loyalty finds it way back to you.

I'll never quite understand how she did it, but my mother managed the lion's share of the day-to-day parenting. My father worked long hours and wasn't home until late evening many weeknights but on the weekends his children were his priority. Whether we were waiting in line for a ski lift at a mountain in Vermont or standing in the crowded grandstand of the demolition derby at the county fair, he would always ask us the same question, "What do these people need that they don't have right now?" We would look out at the crowd and consider the best answer. The people in line at the ski mountain might need lip balm, the people sitting in the dusty grandstand might need a cup of lemonade. I don't think he was as concerned with our answer as he was with sparking our thought processes. He never couched the question in a financial context. It was never, "How can you make money off these people?"

My father had an unusual method for collecting payments from some of his patients that was loosely based on the Native American tradition of wampum. Certain patients who didn't have the money to pay bills would pay in other ways. Maybe they sold skis or built stone walls, or sold fishing poles or trimmed trees. Instead of charging $600 for removing four impacted teeth, he would accept a pair of work boots that were one size too big for him or a bunch of left-handed hockey sticks when his children were all right-handed. My family used to laugh at some of the ridiculous deals he made, knowing full well that my father never expected those deals to work out in his favor monetarily. What mattered was that this bartering process allowed patients to keep their pride. This compassion brought my father a lot of loyal patients, and their families became patients as well. He made a good living and provided for us, but for him, satisfaction, pride, and success in life came from knowing he was providing a good and needed service for the community. This was a lesson he learned from his parents and grandparents. He never talked up or down to his patients but treated them as equals, and this is something I try to do every day at Dogfish Head. If a potential customer that I meet knows a lot about beer, I am comfortable and excited to get very technical and talk about the different hops or fermentation methods we use. If the person I am talking with is a newcomer to the world of full-flavored ales and is trying our beer for the first time, I work equally hard to indoctrinate them into the world of Dogfish Head. Always remember that you are your customers and your customers are you. To treat them any differently than you would expect to be treated just because you are the seller and they are the buyer would be a mistake.

My father's parents owned and ran a successful wholesale candy and tobacco distribution company, and they learned how to run their business from my grandmother's mother, Maria Iacovelli. Maria emigrated from Italy as a young woman shortly after the turn of the century, and her family, along with many others from the region in Italy where she grew up, settled in the town of Milford, Massachusetts. By the time she was in her early twenties she was married and had opened a small grocery store on the first floor of her home. In those days every neighborhood had its own store that sold dry goods and food for the community. Maria focused on the quality of the products she sold and made sausages from scratch using only the finest ingredients. Although each neighborhood grocer made his own sausage, people would not only come from the other neighborhoods to buy from Maria but many customers drove 30 miles from Boston to wait in line for a pound of my great-grandmother's sweet or hot sausage.

She never used measuring spoons or scales when preparing the sausage. It was always a handful of this and a pinch of that. Some weeks they would make over 400 pounds of it, sold mostly a pound at a time out the front door. Maria kept meticulous books and, as my father tells me, always had her pencil-marked ledger book at the ready in her apron. She was stern and exacting and expected hard work and obedience from her children, who helped in the store, but she was also compassionate and altruistic and set a great example for her children to live by. She educated them about how the store worked, and this education also contained lessons on how the world worked. The lessons always revolved around respect for people. She relied on the profits from the business to support her family, but more than that she valued the customers who patronized her shop and recognized that it was they and not she who made her business a business.

Family meant so much to her, and her notion of family extended into every alley of her neighborhood. She would shut the light and close the shop's door at seven o'clock in the evening to feed, bathe, and tuck in her family of nine, but if someone knocked on her door looking for a quart of milk, she would reopen and sell them what was needed. Maria counted every penny, but she also understood each of her customers personally. She knew who had lost their jobs at the shoe mill but had mouths to feed, and she would forgive them their bills or throw an extra pound of sausage in their grocery bags. Her business was her customers, and taking care of them ensured that her business would thrive.

When I listen to relatives and acquaintances talk about my great-grandmother's store, it's as if they are reminiscing about their relationship with an old friend, and her personality lives on in these shared memories. Years after she had retired and closed her store up for good there would be knocks on the door of the house by people who had come to pay their bills. The people who journeyed to her door remembered all of the times that my great-grandmother put an extra loaf of bread in their bag or erased an overdue debt. Some of these people had counted the worth of every single item she had given them over the course of a lifetime and returned to make good. She would accept half of what they believed they owed her, see them off, and then bring the money to the old cigar box where she kept her ledger book. She would update the books of a business that had been closed for a decade to note the money that had come in for the goods that had been sold long ago. Her business was closed but her passion for business would never go away.

You will not succeed without passion: passion for your product, passion for your coworkers, and ultimately passion for your customer. If you care more about how much you make than what you make, you are bound to fail or at the very least create a negative workplace environment.

In business large and small, loyal customers are earned from trust, respect, and the consistent quality of products and services based on personal values. Prioritizing a dedication to people—both consumers and coworkers—is the first step toward running a successful business. Nothing will establish your reputation for integrity more than your ability to show respect for the people around you. My great-grandmother kept perfect books, but that is not the detail of the story that is important or memorable. It is the respect and generosity she showed toward the community that supported her. Profit is not evil but it is a means to an end and not an end in itself. When you are compassionate toward the people you interact with professionally, that compassion pervades the image of your company and resonates within all of the people you do business with—your coworkers, customers, suppliers, and your community. You will see that your leadership style can reflect these values. Return on investment isn't just about money. Consider your investment in your coworkers' happiness and in the vitality of your community.

I learned lessons about values and integrity from my great-grandmother, and I learned about fulfilling a need by providing a hypothetical value to potential customers on the ski hills and fairgrounds of New England from my father. But, like every person who goes into business for himself, I had to figure out on my own what my business would be and why it was worth my time, effort, and devotion. Your business venture will only be viable if you believe in it with everything that you have. So many external factors go into the development of your business that you must have the internal aspects of your own beliefs well established before you do anything else. Believing in yourself is the first step toward creating a successful business. Consider your likes and dislikes, and your skills and shortcomings, as you formulate your business around your idea. Cultivate your own unique perspective and incorporate that perspective into the philosophy of your company. In this way your company will reflect you. Do what you are good at, do what you love, and do what you believe is worth doing. If you can align your own values with those that you champion at your business, this alignment will give you the strength to overcome any obstacles that might be in your way.

chapter 3

KEEPING YOUR BALANCE

creating a harmony between work and life

As Dogfish Head moved forward though the start-up phase and into a period of sustained but hectic growth, there were more moments to catch our breaths and look into our past at lessons learned the hard way. It has not been easy to transition from a bootstrapping little brewery, hand delivering hand-bottled beer in a pickup truck, to a brewery distributing to 26 states and 4 countries. But it has been fun. As the president of this growing company, I find that my role is constantly changing. It has been quite a challenge to build a great brand, but that is what we are aspiring to do. It takes strong leadership, commitment, and passion to persuade the rest of the company to follow your vision. You must have a clear understanding of who you are, and what your business goals are. I still do not have 20/20 vision when it comes to the business, but I am a lot less blind than I was in the old days. Living through inevitable mistakes provides clarity. Living through the wrong way to do things teaches you the right way. Starting a business can be Sisyphean: Sometimes you crush a toe as the rock lurches back at you, but when you love your job those instances only give you more conviction to push the rock forward. This is a story of one of those instances.

NOBODY TOLD ME THERE'D BE DAYS LIKE THIS

It was the end of the summer, early September 2002. I was scheduled to face another physically impossible workday. As our bottling crew loaded our undersized delivery truck with pallets of beer, I stood at a worktable constructing tap handles.

Most of the big breweries opt to order generic tap handles out of a catalog, but to be consistent with our off-centered motto, our brewery produces an off-centered tap handle. First a local blacksmith bangs out a metal rod and welds bolts to the base of it, then a friend of the brewery who is a guitar maker designs and whittles a few dozen foot-tall wooden fish. The rods and fish make it to the brewery in paper bags and land on my workbench. Then I put them together by drilling a hole in the fish, filling the hole with epoxy, jamming the rod into the hole, and affixing a metal badge onto the fish that describes what style of beer is on tap. I then take these tap handles to potential draft accounts in the surrounding cities along with cold beer samples and try to convince them to put Dogfish on tap. When I'm making these tap handles, I always feel like a Zulu warrior, sharpening his spear before a big hunt. I'm thinking about nailing a few new accounts and the thrill of the chase more than the incredible inefficiencies associated with making tap handles this way.

On this particular day, after completing the tap handles, I had to deliver a truckload of beer to Friedland Distributing in downtown Philadelphia, check in with a few existing accounts, drop off samples at a couple of potential accounts, and end my day hosting a beer tasting at a hip-to-be-square art gallery in downtown Philly. Since we first began distributing our beers in 1996 I had been playing the role of delivery guy-salesman-president-brewer with blurry and varied results.

Believing this to be a great way to kill a whole mess of birds with one heavy stone, I would schedule other appointments while in the city to drop off a delivery. I drove the truckload of beer into the city, unloaded the truck by hand, headed out into the city to solicit new business, patronized an existing account for an early dinner/happy hour tasting during rush hour, then drove back to Delaware to be home in time to tuck my children in.

The first time I delivered to Friedland's (our Philly distributor located in the absolute worst, crack-addled neighborlesshood in all of Philly,) I got lost. Like a man with a death wish, I rolled down my window to ask some guy standing guard over a burning car for directions. He said he knew exactly where I needed to go but wouldn't tell me until I bought "something" off of him. I did as I was told out of fear and arrived at Friedland's 10 minutes later. When I described the freakish scene I just lived through,

Eddie Friedland calmly informed me that he knew exactly the person I had run into, and quite frankly, the shit he was selling wasn't nearly as good as that being sold three blocks in the opposite direction. Welcome to the beer business.

On this particular day, I had to load a few cases of Midas Touch beer into the cab of my truck along with a bunch of posters and coasters for the art gallery event we were sponsoring later that evening. I had been contacted by a partner in a thirtysomething-run self-described "edgy" and "young" PR firm. His company was putting together this extreme sport/skateboarding/art throwdown that was being covered by major magazines and cable networks. All we had to do was provide some product. How could we lose? It was the perfect demographic for us to showcase our over-the-top, edgy (that word again) beers, which, he added, he happened to love himself.

And love himself he did. But it sounded like a good opportunity, so I said what the heck and committed eight cases of beer and my presence to the event. I called my college buddy Tom, invited him, and asked if I could crash at his downtown apartment if we had too much fun. He was on board. The plan was set. The truck was loaded. I hit the road.

As usual I was multitasking—driving, writing down a phone number in my Palm Pilot, and talking to the production manager, John, on the cell phone—as I came to the intersection for coastal Route 1, the primary road bisecting east and west Delaware. As I prepared to stop, my brakes failed and the box truck coasted out into oncoming traffic. I was composed enough to inform John what was about to happen. "Holy shit, I'm about to hit this car!" were the words he later informed me I used before he heard the sound of breaking glass. I threw the phone down and braced myself as a Ford Escort station wagon bore down on me from the southbound lane. I could see the driver's face clearly and his posture mirrored my own. White knuckles on the steering wheels, our wide eyes met. He was already braking and his 60 mph speed was dropping. I thought if I sped up he would pass right behind me. Boy was I wrong. As I accelerated he fishtailed into me. He nailed me right below my driver's side door. My window shattered, and I took a little glass shrapnel in the cheek. He had just missed my gas tank but took out my hydraulics and my electronics at the point of impact. So now, thanks to my brilliant decision to speed up, I'm doing 30 mph over the median and into the northbound lane unable to turn or brake. The first thing I noticed as I looked south at the oncoming traffic was that there were no cars within striking distance. My sigh of relief was choked by a fearful gasp in the next instant as I realized I was headed directly for a telephone pole on the shoulder of the road. I turned the wheel instinctively, which of course did nothing, but the impact of the accident had altered my course so that I was turning almost as much as I needed to. The telephone pole sheared off my driver's side mirror and scraped down the side of the box truck. More interesting I suppose was the way the telephone pole support cables sliced through the top of the box truck and opened it like a giant can of tuna. As I jammed to a stop to the sound of metal cutting metal, I looked out my nonexistent window and noticed the Escort had landed safely in the median and the driver was blinking in shock at the fully inflated air bag before him.

The engine was killed when I lost electric and as the symphony of destructive sounds faded from my ears I heard my name being called. It wasn't God. It was John. He was still connected on my cell phone. I picked up the phone and put it to my one un-bloodied ear. First he asked if everyone was okay. He then informed me that the scene he just heard unfold—shattering glass, shearing metal, and lots of meaty cusswords—was more exciting than any episode of *Cops* he had ever watched. I promptly thanked him, hung up, and dialed 911 to fill them in on what just happened and where we were. I climbed out my window and ran to the median to check on the guy I had just hit. Thankfully he was alright. His nose was bleeding from where his eyeglasses met the air bag, but otherwise he was not hurt. As I was apologizing and explaining what happened to him the police arrived along with an ambulance. They gave me a ticket and called a tow truck. The dealer from which I bought the truck was only 10 miles up the road. I called to inform the guys at the brewery that they should rent a moving truck and meet me at the dealership in half an hour. At the dealership they informed me that the frame was bent beyond repair, the electric and hydraulics were shot, axle ripped, and that the box on my box truck would never look like a box again. The guys from the brewery showed up, and we backed the U-Haul flush with the rear of our useless truck and unloaded and reloaded 350 cases of beer by hand.

Two and a half hours after the moment of impact I was ramping onto the highway, back on course. I was sweaty, dirty, a little bloody, but back on course. I called my friend Tom to inform him of what had just happened. He asked if I was sure I still wanted to come. I stiffened my upper lip and blurted, "You can't hurt steel," an old rallying cry of immortality from our college days. He responded, "Game on," as I had hoped he would. I hung up and called Friedland Distributing to inform them I would be a little late. The U-Haul I was driving was basically a glorified van with a box-truck back that was made to carry sofa sets and coffee tables, not multiple half-ton pallets of beer. It was doing this swervy dance all over the highway anytime I went over 52 miles per hour. Each time I hit a pothole, the back tires would bottom out and scrape the underside of the wheel wells in a cloud of smoke and burnt rubber stench. This happened until I was just north of Wilmington, at which point a back tire blew out and I careened off the highway. I managed to do a controlled dive onto an exit ramp and into a gas station at the base of the ramp. I jumped out and went to the gas station window to ask the attendant where I was. The first thing I noticed was that he was yelling at me from behind a wall of bulletproof glass. Not a good sign. He told me to move my truck away from the pumps, that he didn't fix tires, and that I should buy something or fuck off. Nice. I bought some gum, moved the truck, and called AAA. They told me they wouldn't handle rental truck tires. As I asked them politely for advice, my cell phone died. I then went to a pay phone and dialed U-Haul. They said they would call me right back. I called my friend Tom, told him what had happened, and reminded him that they still couldn't hurt steel. He laughed at me and hung up. The good folks at U-Haul called back and said they hoped to have someone there in an hour to change the tire, but they needed my rental information. I went back to my truck to get it. The information was inside my wallet, which was inside my locked truck along with the keys. That was it: the last straw. My spirit was effectively broken. Turns out they *can* hurt steel. I called my friend Tom and told him to please send lawyers, guns, and money ASAP. I gave him my coordinates. The sun was going down in the land of bulletproof glass, and I had a broken truck overflowing with mind-altering substances. It was like a robbery-scenario equivalent to *The Perfect Storm*. Tom left work and headed my way on a life-saving mission.

To make a long story a little less long, I was back on the road a mere 3 hours later. I paid one company to unlock the truck, another to replace the tire, and purchased more gum than a bus full of sixth graders on a field trip for the right to stand my ground. Tom arrived to help me through all of this, ever mindful of the desperate eyes fixed on his late-model Audi. I headed back onto the highway in a truck that was still way overloaded. I was covered in sweat, grime, motor oil, and exhaustion. It was enough to drive a man to drink.

I called Friedland Distributing and told them where I was. They said there was no way I was going to reach them before they closed and could I come back tomorrow. I laughed a little too maniacally into the receiver of Tom's cell phone (mine was long dead) and asked them if they were kidding. They weren't kidding. They felt my pain but would not acquiesce. I called my friends at Philadelphia's Yards Brewery. They were gracious enough to let me leave the beer at their place and have Friedland pick it up the next day. I dropped the load and raced to the art gallery. My contact there was antsy when he greeted me because the party was set to start in 10 minutes. He wondered why the beer wasn't cold yet and if I was really going to wear *that* to the party as he pointed to my dirty, bloody shirt. I started to describe my day to him as his eyes glassed over and he interrupted to say that while I iced the beer he would get me another shirt.

I was now wearing a too-small skater shirt, and I looked like an extra from an Avril Lavigne video. I was standing behind a Red Bull bar in a graffiti-stained art gallery preparing to serve beer made with grapes to a bunch of green-haired, multi-pierced trustafarians. I found myself wondering what August Busch III was doing at that very moment.

Tom and I went out to retrieve the last two cases of beer from the truck. When we returned, the pansy-assed PR guru got in my face and started waving a bloody middle finger at me. He had broken a bottle while trying to remove its cork and boy was he pissed. The corks weren't coming out of the bottles, and he didn't have time for this. I looked down at the empty beer cases and noticed they were marked "recork." These cases, I now realized, were from a batch we bottled with corks that were one size too big. Most of these cases mistakenly were distributed, yet their reception was a great indication of our customers' loyalty. The corks were supposed to pop out a la champagne, but since they were too tight you needed a corkscrew. Unfortunately, if you screwed down too far the bottle exploded in your hand, which, according to the number of irate phone calls and e-mails we received, happened quite frequently. We instituted an aggressive policy in which anyone who e-mailed us a picture of their hand bleeding received a Dogfish Head T-shirt. Anyone who e-mailed a picture of their hand with stitches received a hat. Our lawyer was more dumbfounded than impressed with this policy.

So I explained the situation to the PR guy, and he continued to give me the finger. I really wanted to pick this little wuss up by his overquaffed hair and shake some backbone into him. In the last 12 hours I had lived through a car accident that totaled two vehicles, hand-loaded and reloaded 350 cases of beer, swerved off the highway in my second runaway truck of the day, survived a lockout in one of the scariest urban combat zones outside of a third world country, and continued on to Philadelphia in the very same death mobile only to make it to his little party on time.

But that's not what I did. Instead I walked around him to the bar. I opened up every bottle of beer that I brought with me except four. I told him his problems were solved and that I would send him a T-shirt. Unless he required stitches, in which case I would send him a hat. At the end of the evening I lay awake on the sofa at Tom's apartment, alone with my thoughts and bruises. I couldn't really be upset with the bloody-fingered PR pansy. On a basic level he was right. I promised him the beer, and I had an obligation to make sure his patrons got what they expected. Before leaving the art gallery I shared a beer with a guy who hadn't tried Midas Touch before. He usually drank wine, and I explained the winelike character of this beer to him. I described the day the recipe was discovered in King Midas' tomb in Turkey. How the 2,700-year-old tomb was so perfectly preserved that, as the last rock obstructing the entrance was removed, the archeologists on hand literally watched the colors fade from the tapestries on the walls. He really liked the beer and asked where he could buy it in Philadelphia. I wrote out the address of the closest store as I walked out the door. As I lay there on the sofa thinking about this new Dogfish convert, I polished off the last glass of Midas. I thought about what a career-affirming moment it must have been as the archeologists walked into that tomb staring at the fading walls. I thought about my day and all of the work that I had in front of me. I shut my eyes and fell sound asleep, looking forward to the next day.

IT'S ME AGAINST THE WORLD

This is what it sometimes feels like to be an entrepreneur. When you are a one-man start-up, this feeling is even more immediate, but, as you grow, you will continue to encounter the resistance of the established business world around you. There are lots of people out there representing the status quo, and you must fight for your niche. Hopefully, for all our sakes, many people out there respect the healthy fight against the status quo. With all of the bureaucracy, red tape, consumer apathy, entrenched competitors, and general barriers to market that we face, it can be a difficult task to get a foothold.

One of the most difficult tasks we face is equipping the business and its employees so that it is possible to maintain a life outside of the business. When you open your own business, everyone from employees to customers expects you to be available all the time. In a lot of ways, your constant presence is truly necessary during the start-up phase. If the business is to be a reflection of yourself, you need to make sure your self is present at the business. Before you can entrust coworkers to make decisions that will best reflect the company's philosophies, you need to make sure you spend the time necessary to present those philosophies, fully formed, to your coworkers and customers.

People learn best from watching, and you should never underestimate how much coworkers learn about the company by watching how the leader goes about a typical workday. Once you have established the philosophies that you believe are most intrinsic to your company, and you have instilled these philosophies in the people you work with, then you need to make time to occasionally step back in an effort to see the forest for the trees. While your coworkers depend on you to guide them in the day-to-day aspects of the business as the company gets on its feet, you need to direct the company in a way that allows you to leave the premises to gain perspective on where the company should go. If you want your company to grow strong, you need to realize that your coworkers depend on you to guide them somewhere beyond the completion of day-to-day tasks. If you allow yourself to be forever mired in the minutiae of your business, you can't possibly reach your potential as the leader of that business. Delegating to capable people is part of the solution. The other part is delegating some free time to yourself. Free time does not necessarily mean unproductive time. By my definition, it means engaging your mind and body in exercises that free you from the necessary tasks of your business.

I did the whole mattress-on-the-basement-office-floor, time-to-make-the-donuts thing during our start-up years at Dogfish Head. In fact, as I do the math now, I worked an average of 12 hours a day for the first 7 or

8 years we have been in business. At times I was exhausted and disoriented, but usually I was happy. I've heard the saying that you should work to live and not live to work. When you work for yourself, one doesn't take precedence over the other. However, you start to look like a socially challenged deviant if you do nothing but work. Regardless of whether you're okay with it, answering your home phone by cheerily shouting the name of your business to the caller doesn't go over very well with certain people who cannot understand such a thing as a healthy obsession. I realized that if I didn't want to burn out on the company that I created and loved I would need to have a life outside of work and develop some hobbies. The means to finding a physical release to the stress that comes with running a small company was easy. I played sports through high school and college and have continued to be physically active throughout my adult life. I had a rowing machine next to the mattress in my cellar office at the brewpub, and I would throw on my Walkman and row for 40 minutes every other day. Or I would take a jog along the beach in between brewing and working on the dining room floor at night. For me, the release of endorphins is equal to the relief of stress. My mind wanders as I exercise, and I often find solutions to business problems during a row or a run. While the time I spend exercising significantly reduces stress, it's not necessarily the most intellectually engaging use of my free time. I wanted to find hobbies that provoked my thoughts in ways that my normal business activities couldn't. To this end I have found a great release through artistic hobbies that challenge me to look at my business from a fresh perspective.

THE BUSINESSPERSON AS ARTIST

The artist and the businessperson each have the same ultimate goal: a desire to create something unique that might leave a lasting impression on the world. Both are productive activities of self-expression. You can create art by yourself but you can't create a business by yourself. At the very least it takes two people—you and a customer. The artistic approach relies on a passive, introspective process to achieve self-expression while the business approach involves a more active, inclusive process. That's why I see pursuing artistic hobbies as a perfect escape route for businesspeople. They can engage your mind in nontraditional yet productive ways.

I wrote short stories in college, but writing a business plan and recipes, advertising and marketing materials made me realize writing wasn't really an escape from business. But then I didn't really want to escape from thinking about business. I wanted to escape from thinking about the things I *had* to think about and into the things that were fun to think about. I have always enjoyed expressing myself through writing; even when those expressions were only interesting to me. I don't have a particularly evolved artistic knowledge or ability. I'm not sure I could tell a Monet from a Manet if my life depended on it. But I know what I like. And I know which art inspires me. My favorite artists are those who express themselves in multiple mediums. Warhol is the perfect example of inspiration for me. He painted, silk-screened, and photographed. He produced movies, bands, and magazines. And he completely melded his personal and professional lives into his art. In his 1975 book, *The Philosophy of Andy Warhol,* he expressed this intentional blurring of artistic lines.

> Business art is the step that comes after Art. I started as a commercial artist, and I want to finish as a business artist. After I did the thing called "art" or whatever it is called, I went into business art. I wanted to be an Art business man or a business artist. Being good in business is the most fascinating kind of art.

I have found a world of truth in this typically glib statement by Warhol. I understand his statement, "Business art is the step that comes after Art," to mean that business is a form of self-expression that can be interactive and engaging, not just emotionally but practically. Brewing has continued to be a great outlet for my artistic expression. But I'm proud to say I'm the least talented brewer of the five of us who work at Dogfish Head. I am better at conceptualizing recipes and beer ideas than I am at physically making a batch of beer. I still brew occasionally for two reasons: so I can call myself a brewer with a straight face, and so I can continue experimenting with new recipes, which is a strength of mine. I'm good at experimenting but not so good at repeating my experiments, so I usually make one test batch of something and then leave it to the technically superior brewers that I work with to find the best way of repeating that recipe and maintaining it in full production.

What I miss most about the early days when I was brewing every day at my pub, was how my mind would constructively wander as my body focused on the task at hand. Some of my best ideas for growing Dogfish Head came in those moments. Our business concept is centered around the idea that we approach everything as a craft. So I wanted to choose hobbies that could be used in my business, and to further the idea that Dogfish Head is a craft business. That was an easy image to convey in the days when anyone could look into the brew house window and see the president of the company actually making the beer, but as we grew and I left the brew house that image became a challenge to maintain. Once the brewery grew to a point where other people were brewing more of the beer than I did, I had to find something else to do with my hands. I couldn't find much inspiration in an Excel spreadsheet, and besides, my wife is better at constructing those than I could ever be.

So I began making wooden tap handles by hand and creating print ads and promotional material, too. As the business continued to grow, I couldn't keep up with the production pace necessary to satisfy the demand for the tap handles or the frequency of advertising updates. So we brought in professionals to make the tap handles and I continued to design the ads and write the copy but relied on a company to produce the digital artwork. Basically, two trends spoke well for the future of the company: (1) I was capable of creating a unique artistic aesthetic for Dogfish Head, but I wasn't always the best person to move forward with the actual production of this aesthetic; (2) I was capable of translating this aesthetic to key people around me who were better skilled to carry out the production.

The problem was that I received more personal satisfaction from making things than I did from running things. My company, however, needed me to run things more desperately than it needed me to be hunched over a drafting table shellacking homemade Dogfish Christmas ornaments. The only way I could make the transition from crafting tangible things to crafting the brand was to continue with hobbies that not only provided a creative outlet for me but fed back into the continued expansion of our brand identity. Again I think of Warhol as an inspiration. He introduced a production element into his work on a level never previously seen in the art world. He freely admitted and even boasted that other people helped him make his artwork. He recognized that embracing teamwork was the best way to make his art available to more and more people. He didn't call the place where the paintings were completed his studio, he called it the factory. This distinction infuriated the purists who believed the creation of art-work had to be a solitary pursuit, at the same time that it endeared Warhol to a new generation that realized art and commerce could cohabit peacefully.

REENERGIZING YOURSELF

The first years in any business are extremely demanding of both time and energy. Once your business develops a steady course of profitability, and if you are able to expand your company from a sole proprietorship to a staffed business, it is essential that you take a step back from the hands-on, author-itative leadership position. This simultaneously provides coworkers with the opportunity to develop a sense of responsibility and achievement while giv-ing you back your work–life balance. Competent people cannot rise above the fray and help relieve you from the daily minutiae of running a business unless you give them the opportunity to sink or swim. Once you see that you have picked the right people and have given them the tools they need to succeed, you'll be surrounded by a group of strong swimmers. You can be away from your business and not feel guilty.

Regardless of what kind of businessperson you are, I advise that you maintain at least one hobby. Having interests outside of your business allows you to gain some distance while allowing an alternative exploration of new meaning for your company. I realize that may sound like freaky, New Age psychobabble, but it is important. All parents think their child is a singular genius. Visit a friend with children and check out the door of their refrig-erator. There's bound to be a collection of crayon drawings and collages usually involving yarn and the tracing of a small hand. To you these items could seem as artful as a stick of gum but to the parent and the child the refrigerator door might as well be the main gallery at MOMA. These draw-ings represent the first few tangible symbols of individual expression for both the parent and the child. The drawings might depict a person that is three times as big as a car but that is how the child sees it and he has yet to be stifled by socialization that tells him his perception is wrong. In short, a child's perspective is purely and uniquely his own. It doesn't matter that a drawing of a fish looks more like a drawing of a ham.

Now back to the business world. Let's say you own a bike shop. If I told you to sketch a picture of your business, you might draw the outline of the building you work in and a realistic facsimile of the sign hanging from your awning. You wouldn't be any less or more right if you drew a picture of a little girl with a triumphant smile and two Band-Aided knees standing next to her bike. To you that image might represent the sense of pride that comes with learning something new and taking risks. You might sketch the view from the top of a mountain—a beautiful vista that you could ride to on a bike. To you that might represent achievement and reaching the top of your profession. None of these pictures is any more accurate than the first literal depiction. But taking the time to experiment with different perspectives will enhance and bring depth to your perception of the business. This exercise might even lead you in a new direction if you only thought literally, analytically, and practically about your business. Whether you end up incorporating the actual hobby into your business is less important than the journey that engaging in this hobby takes you on.

Business is all about risk. What's the worst thing that could come from making a sculpture that personifies your ideal customer? That it looks foolish to everyone but you? Who cares? I'll bet your customer would be impressed by your effort, would be proud to recognize herself in the artwork, and would leave with a new level of understanding and appreciation for the person she chose to do business with. Maintaining a creative activity separate from the day-to-day approach to managing a business enables you to expand your faith in yourself and your ideas and to amplify the identity of your company.

ROAMING

The best way to learn about your company is to get the hell away from it once in a while. Some time spent outside your workplace should have nothing to do with your company, and some time should have everything to do with your company and where it's going. You need to make sure you take vacations to recharge your batteries. If you are enslaved by your company, you will resent it. It might be 6 months or a year after you open before you and your company are ready to be separated for a week, but that should be one of the main things you work toward. It will keep you healthy, and, if you can do it, it means your company is finally stable enough to survive your short-term absence. I use all of my vacations and most of my weekends to just hang out with my family. Since Mariah and I work together, we get to spend a lot of time with each other. If you do not work with your loved one, you need to realize how much your commitment to your company wears on them in ways it doesn't weigh on you. You have the stress of running the company, but your partner probably has the stress of trying to maintain a relationship with a person who is way more obsessed with work life than the average nine-to-fiver. These loved ones deserve your time as much as your business does, and time away from the company is necessary to nourish your personal relationships.

Besides vacation and family time, a business leader benefits from spending time outside of the company working on the company. Previously I mentioned that one characteristic all good businesspeople seem to share is a high level of self-confidence. The next most obvious quality they share is great salesmanship. Salesmanship is really just an extension of confidence—it is the transference of your confidence to other people. If you start a small company, you are not in a commodity business. You are not selling a commodity and you are not selling to a commodity, you are selling to a person.

When you take time to leave your workplace and roam through your marketplace, that time will be best spent engaging with people who are relevant to your business. Whether it is a service or a product, you are in business to sell something. Your desire is to sell. But effective selling is not based on what you desire, it is based on what your customer desires. To understand your customers' desires you must have compassion. You need to understand what they care about and why they care about it. You will get only a fraction of this understanding by interacting with your customers on your home turf—in your office or store or on an official sales call. You will gain a better perspective of your customers by observing and interacting with them outside of these traditional forums.

Once you've figured out who can mind the store (a huge task, really), it's time to get out and meet your brand through the eyes of the world. You should try to talk to the people who come in contact with your brand at every step that it takes through the marketplace. In the case of the beer business that means I spend time with my distributors, retailers, and my customers. But the key is to find out where to get the important information from every step of the way. When I go to the distributors, I meet with the owner and talk about sales volume, product mix, and budget planning. But I also go down to the warehouse loading dock and talk to the people who actually load the trucks. I ask how much of my beer is going out the door compared to other brands. I ask what styles of beers sell best in which neighborhoods. I ask a bunch of questions and I learn a lot.

The beer industry is heavy on festivals. We get invited to pour our wares at over a hundred festivals a year. This makes sense because we sell a fun, social product. I doubt the guy who makes paint thinner is loading his van with T-shirts and samples every weekend on the way to another paint-thinning festival. These festivals are great because we get to catch up with other brewers who have made their way through the pitfalls of the industry alongside us. We get to meet and thank existing customers, and we hope-fully turn a few new customers on to our beers. The people that come to these festivals are passionate about beer, and if I can get them to talk about what they like and what they don't like, whether it's our beer or someone else's, I can leave with a wealth of information. Thankfully, the most com-mon negative feedback we get is that some of our beers cost too much. Once they've told us this we have an opportunity to explain that some of our beers are made with 5 times the ingredients and age for 10 times as long as those brewed by bigger breweries. We remind them that we make beers at a few different price points and we hope that we have beers in our port-folio that would appeal to almost any drinker. The important thing is that we are communicating with and learning from our customers and our potential customers.

Every time I interact with distributors, retailers, or consumers on their own turf, I get a better understanding about what Dogfish Head means to them. I learn what things we are doing well and the areas where we need to improve. I see not only how our brand is positioned and perceived in the marketplace, but how it compares to our competitors, as well. If you take the time to roam constructively, you will learn a tremendous amount about your company and its place in the competitive environment. You will be able to gauge your company's successes and failures through the eyes of your customer. In this outside environment your thoughts won't be clut-tered with unjamming the fax machine or paying the electric bill, and you can think freely. Call it proactive free time. However, gathering information while roaming is only half the battle. Once you have this information, you must translate it and use it to grow your company in the right direction—toward your customers' desires.

RHYTHM

Your hobbies may involve creating something, or they may simply be activities that allow your mind to focus on things other than business for a while. The most important thing is that your head escapes the business and the bottom line. Ultimately, whatever your hobby, it will in some way impact your business, either by directly contributing to it, or by giving you some time away to recharge and gain a clear perspective.

I have always loved music—I remember waving my magic Wiffle ball bat and chanting hexes on my parents' radio in an effort to get it to spit forth Laura Branigan's "Gloria." I remember being embarrassed to cry tears of joy in front of my sisters one Christmas upon opening my LP copy of *Doctor Demento's Funky Favorites.* (I didn't say that I always loved good music, just that I always loved music.) As I got older my tastes developed, diversified, and intensified, but my love for music goes back to my earliest childhood memories. Like many lovers of music I longed to create music of my own. Being an entrepreneur, I wasn't willing to let my lack of tone or talent get in my way.

A few years ago the lead brewer at Dogfish Head, Bryan Selders, and I formed a group called the Pain Relievaz. We bill ourselves as "Probably the finest beer-geek, hip-hop band of our generation." Of course we are also the only beer-geek, hip-hop band of any generation. Bryan is actually a talented musician and we have set up a pretty sophisticated little recording studio in his house. He lays down the tracks, and we both write our lyrics.

Obsessive as I am, I could not entirely separate my love of music from my love of Dogfish Head. So we sing songs with names like "Brewer's Bling-Bling," "Worst Brew Day Ever," and "I Got Busy with an A-B Salesgirl." We wrote the songs for the same reasons we make the beers and cook the foods that we do. It is basically off-centered music for off-centered people. We have used the band as a promotional asset for the company. We did a multicity tour of great beer bars, and we set up our mics and amplifiers and sang our songs and served our beers. We drove from city to city and lived out our rock and roll dream. One of the highlights was playing the book release party for Ken Wells' *Travels with Barley,* a great social history of brewing in America that includes a whole chapter about Dogfish Head. We cut a six-song disc on our own Dogfish Records label called *Check Your Gravity,* of which we have sold over 500 copies. As I've said, a sense of humor is central to the brand identity of Dogfish Head. Here's a sample of the Pain Relievaz new jack philosophy:

> I've been rockin' phat beats since the boys in Mendocino
> were sellin' all their ales from a Chevy El Camino.
> And when I rock the mic you'll know that I'm serious
> 'cause my rhymes are more fruity than the beers of New Glar-e-us!

This probably means nothing to you unless you know that Mendocino is home to one of America's earliest microbreweries and that New Glarus, a small Wisconsin brewery, makes a world-class cherry beer. But we didn't make this disc for the people who don't care about beer. We made it for ourselves, the true believers, and the people who are just getting into good beer and want to learn everything they can. The Pain Relievaz aren't exactly in the middle of a multilabel bidding war, but we're not that bad, either. And I don't think the level of professionalism matters as much as the message that comes from such a project: Our off-centered brewery has found another off-centered method to promote what we do. There's nothing wrong with taking a risk and experimenting. Especially if you don't take your experiment too seriously.

The Pain Relievaz are hard at work on a follow-up release. It will be the first beer-geek concept album featuring samples of beer jingles, beer ads, and sales motivation mantras interlaid with goofy lyrics and Bryan's melodic backing music. It ain't Jay-Z, but I hope it will represent the authentic, audacious, ambitious, exploratory image of Dogfish Head.

In addition to music I've continued to paint—mostly designs for T-shirts, ads, and label artwork, which I do at the kitchen table next to my son and daughter as they work on finger-painted and crayon-based masterpieces of their own. Works of art have been accepted as commercial objects for hundreds of years, but commercial objects aren't always considered works of art. Warhol worked hard to change this, and as a small businessperson you can, too. As long as the work of art represents your company in some meaningful way, the level of professionalism is secondary. The further development of the image of your company should be the goal, not winning any awards at the local art league.

Everybody is different, it's true. But I think that businesspeople and artists have more in common than most people think. Every businessperson benefits from exploring the artistic side. Of course your company started as the ultimate blank canvas, but there are lots of other canvases you can play around with as you make your way through the world of commerce. You need to be adamant about blocking out and using free time for free thinking. The free thinking you do will help your company whether it is pro-active free thinking—roaming the marketplace to better understand your company—or passive free thinking—roaming a bowling alley to better understand your children. Either way, these activities outside of the daily rigors of business life will fortify and refresh you for the battles you face as you grow your business.

chapter 4

CREATING A BUSINESS OFFERING

developing goods and services

Around the time Dogfish Head brewpub first opened, I read an article about another Mid-Atlantic brewery that planned to create a national phenomenon around a beer brewed with hemp seeds. Made from the fibers of the marijuana plant, hemp was in the news quite a bit in the late 1990s as a novel ingredient with an outlaw-chic lineage to an illicit substance. There was little that hemp could offer as a beer ingredient other than the shock value of its use.

In the late 1990s small breweries were opening and expanding at an alarming rate. As it turned out the marketplace couldn't support all of the new beer brands that hit the shelves. I imagine that the hemp-beer brewery owners thought of themselves as the creators of a counterculture company that was going to make the ultimate counterculture beverage. They rolled the dice and built an $8 million brewery based on a business plan that showed the nation falling into a veritable hemp craze. Hemp turned out to be a short-lived fad. In fact the FDA ruled that hemp seeds could no longer be used in many consumable products. This brewery is still reeling from their mistake. It has gone into receivership, lost money every year since it opened, and still flails aimlessly to grasp a meaningful brand identity.

KEEPING YOUR FINGER ON THE PULSE OF YOUR INDUSTRY

Alternative brands need alternative products and markets to reach the alternative consumer, but as you make your marketing decisions you need to recognize the difference between a fad and a trend. Trends will last, and fads will fade. While you should never alter the course of your marketing because of a fad, doing so in acknowledgment of a trend is only slightly safer. Let's say you are an electronics company and you recognize the trend of personal digital music players like the iPod. You could capitalize on the trend and release a slight variation, or a me-too product. You could try to differentiate your product on price or style, but the technology remains virtually the same. This might work because it's a safe bet that this electronics segment is not a fad. However, what works best is to recognize the trend and not just assimilate it but actually influence it. If you create a legitimate, distinct point of differentiation while still acknowledging the trend, you can drive the trend toward your service or product.

Belgian ales are becoming a more popular segment of the high-end beer category. Considering the growing interest of the American public in these beers, it's fair to say the Belgian beer segment represents a trend and not a fad. There are some fantastic, small American breweries that focus on authentic reproductions of existing Belgian styles like Wit beers and Tripples. Dogfish Head began making a beer called Raison D'Etre in the late nineties. Being a Dogfish Head product we were uninterested in brewing to authentic style so our beer was fermented with a Belgian yeast, Belgian beet sugar, and raisins. In the last few years, as Belgian ales have become more popular in America, Raison had been accepted as a representative and yet distinct American-brewed, Belgian-style beer. It is now one of our three best-selling year-round brands. We made our own interpretation of an off-centered ale while still acknowledging the Belgian trend.

We recently released another Belgian ale called Au Courant—a tart ale brewed with currants. The currant puree that we use during fermentation turns the beer bright purple. The stuff is really potent. Our brewers' hands are stained for a week. At first consideration we were worried that purple beer would seem like a fad, but then we tried the beer and it tasted perfect. We could have used less expensive, currant-flavored extract that would have given a similar taste without the color but that would have been inauthentic and not in keeping with Dogfish Head's ideals. We were confident that our off-centered customers would look at this purple beer and judge it by how it tastes. They would know that we wouldn't have made the beer purple unless it made the beer taste the way we hoped it would. We're not as concerned with whether the general public perceives Au Courant as a fad or a trend or an irrelevant novelty. We only care that our key customers like it, that it represents the off-centered Dogfish ideal, and that it's unique and good enough for them to turn a few other beer-loving friends on to it. We won't market it as a purple beer, but as an off-centered Dogfish Head beer made with black currants. Marketing is less about what your product is or does than what it stands for.

FIND A NICHE AND SCRATCH IT

After researching the brewing industry and gaining an understanding of the contrasts between the big players, the small players, and what I envisioned Dogfish Head to be, I was ready to develop my product. The big breweries were so successful in maximizing efficiency, marketing, and distribution that their beers got pulled through the marketplace every step of the way. They had created mass demand for their brands, and their pricing structure was such that they were guaranteed a high volume of sales. My brand did not even exist and held no meaning to my customers on the day I brewed my first batch of sellable beer. To find my niche I basically had to create a business model that was the absolute opposite of the one employed by the giant brewers. I wrote the following statement in the product section of my business plan long before we opened:

> Dogfish Head will focus on producing a wide range of beer styles using a wide range of ingredients. While we will make the standard, more accessible styles like Pale Ale and Golden Ale, we'll focus on stronger beers made with fruits, sugars, and even pumpkins in an effort to establish a unique identity in the brewing community.

When developing a new product, it is essential that the product clearly communicates how it relates to and intensifies your brand identity. Every aspect of the product must speak to your company's motto. At Dogfish Head, "Off-Centered Ales for Off-Centered People" influenced every aspect of product development. As I developed designs for our bottle labels, it would have been very easy to look at what other brewers were doing and assimilate those ideas into my design, but I knew such an approach would do very little to differentiate my brand. I also knew that the kinds of beers we intended to bottle would be very different in composition, alcohol content, and price from the other beers on the shelf. I saw more similarities between the wine world and Dogfish Head than I did between the beer world and Dogfish Head. So I shopped high-end wine stores and read publications like *Wine Enthusiast* and *Wine Spectator.* We bought rich and rough estate paper to print our labels on rather than smooth, thin beer paper. We paid a premium to design a metallic bottle cap that mirrored the foil wraps you see on some wines. We put a lot of descriptive language on our bottles as opposed to a giant logo. These were all lessons that I learned outside of my industry. All of the research I have done on wine informs the development of our brewery. If you are willing to absorb this new kind of information, you'll spend less time trying to figure out what your brand is and more time recognizing your brand in the world around you.

I knew that if I tried to bring my beer to a wide market immediately my business would fail. To succeed we had to build demand at the individual customer level, which would lead to demand at the retail level, which would lead to demand at the distributor level. Since it was still an unknown entity, Dogfish Head beer had to be pushed through distribution as opposed to being pulled through like the beer of the larger corporations.

Since I wanted to make full-flavored, strong beers—something that contradicted all of the marketing by the big three—I knew our beers needed to be sold directly by people who understood them, me and the Dogfish Head employees. The best way to build an audience for our beer was to brew it ourselves, sell it ourselves, and pour it ourselves. In other words, I decided to open the brewpub—a restaurant with an onsite brewery, as opposed to a microbrewery, which bottles and kegs beer solely for distribution to outside retailers. Starting with a brewpub instead of a microbrewery presented a number of advantages. One was that we would have a built-in market. Our restaurant patrons would help us build demand for our beers every time they told a friend about us or came back for another pint. They could see us brewing; smell the barley juice as it boiled; watch us shovel out the grain by hand; and understand everything that goes into producing top quality, adjunct-free, fresh beer. Customers would receive an education while we served them their meals, and we would receive critical feedback. Another advantage was that by having a restaurant and a brewery under the same roof we minimized our exposure. We had two revenue streams—one from the brewery and one from the restaurant. As my company evolved, this became a critical factor in our survival. The biggest advantage to starting out as a brewpub was that we could make beer on much smaller brewing equipment than if we had opened a distributing microbrewery.

DEVELOPING A PRODUCT

Ralph Waldo Emerson wrote, "Who so would be a man, must be a nonconformist. He who would gather immortal palms must not be hindered by the name of goodness, but must explore if it be goodness. Nothing at last is sacred but the integrity of your own mind." These lines became the misssion statement of Dogfish Head, and the standard by which we measure our offering.

Nearly 80 percent of the restaurants opened today fail within 5 years, and in order to ensure our success we needed to create a distinct identity in everything we did. Our goal was to use things that were boring, prosaic, and taken for granted, like beer, pizza, and burgers, and put our own mark on them to expand the definition of what they could be. So we made beers that were ales instead of the common lagers (lager is what all the big, mainstream breweries make and accounts for over 90 percent of the beer consumed today), and we made a lot of these beers with nontraditional and natural ingredients and heightened alcohol contents to further distinguish them from the beers that were already out there.

We became the first brewpub in the state, so we were novel and newsworthy. We were the only restaurant in the state doing wood-grilled pizzas and one of the few that emphasized locally grown, fresh ingredients from small producers. Our ales are free of adjuncts or the preservatives and pasteurization methods used by the big breweries. In short our beers are distinct, natural, and fresh. We wanted to mirror this natural, rustic, fresh approach on the food side as well. So we developed a menu based around a wood grill. We developed recipes for pizzas that were cooked over oak and hickory logs and made dough from the "wort" of prefermented beer. We focused our live entertainment around original bands playing original music to complement our original food and beers. The other restaurants and clubs in our area focused on presenting cover bands because they were a known entity and reliable draw.

We spend a lot of energy not just making our beer and food but making

the atmosphere in which they are sold. When you walk into
you are met by the smell of the wood grill, the greeting of a frier
visual impression of the space's design and decor, the sound of people enjoying conversation over a background of rhythm, blues, and folk music. We
pay attention to the temperature, lighting, mood, and feeling of each room in
the building. We pay attention to everything in the context of a customer's
experience of Dogfish Head because every element belongs to the same
product—Dogfish Head.

THE SMALL-BUSINESS ADVANTAGE

As in martial arts, you can gain an advantage over a larger opponent by
using his own strength against him. The big companies are not nimble
enough to maintain and create new niches. From where they sit, way up
high on the business ladder, they cannot see the low-hanging fruit. And
even if they could, it wouldn't be worth their time to bend over to pick it
off. When you are small you can see the low-hanging fruit that big competitors don't care about. At least they don't care until a smaller competitor
proves there is a growing and viable market for it. Once there is enough
low-hanging fruit to make a small company grow bigger, the big companies become hungry for that fruit, too.

When small breweries were popping up all over the place in the mid-
1980s the big breweries didn't even notice. These new breweries were
treated more as novelties than a viable subindustry. But as the small breweries began to grow at rates as high as 40 percent per year, the big breweries
bent down and took notice. Consumers were actually willing to pay to have
more and better choices in beer. The low-hanging fruit moved up a few
branches and was finally within the big guys' view. Realizing they missed
the opportunity to create and develop their own brands within the growing microbrewing segment, they quickly bought major stakes in some
of the more high-profile, fast-growing microbreweries like Redhook,
Pyramid, and Celis. None of these alliances has proven to be a home run
for the big breweries because, even though they cared enough to bend
down and grab some of the low-hanging fruit, they didn't understand that
it took passion, knowledge, and commitment to effectively sell it. At that
point, supply had also surpassed demand in the microbrewing segment and

growth flattened out. The big breweries no longer had to worry about continued 40 percent growth from the segment and the erosion of their market share. In fact many of the small brewery–big brewery relationships initiated in the mid-1990s have since disintegrated. It all boils down to nimbleness. The big breweries are too big to effectively market unique beers that need to be hand sold. They are better at moving large units of commoditized product through well-honed distribution channels.

When you are up against big companies, it can often feel like it is you against insurmountable obstacles. Those obstacles signify the inertia of the status quo, and the creators of those obstacles want you to believe that they are too big and powerful to be tripped up by some anachronistic cottage industry. The only way to guarantee failure is to try to beat them at their own game: price and convenience.

It used to be that the manufacturer set the pace of commerce—the Rockefellers and James Hills of the world. Today the retailer is the dominant force in the chain of commerce. Stores like Wal-Mart and Costco constantly audit their purveyors to demand the lowest price. This business model thrives on low margins, low price, and high volume. Ours does not.

Anheuser-Busch is a huge corporation, but they are not resting on their laurels. Last year they achieved an amazing milestone by growing their market share of domestic beer sales to 50.01 percent. In other words, of every two beers consumed in America, one was made by Anheuser-Busch. How did they get to this position of dominance? The same way the major record labels did. By not listening to what the consumer wants but by actually telling the consumer what to want. They start with an efficiently made, consistent, but bland product (J.Lo anyone?), and then they distribute and market the bejeezus out of it. The big breweries are so proficient at marketing they have convinced consumers that beer is supposed to be watery, ice cold, and brewed with corn and rice because it makes the beer "refreshing and crisp." Nowhere in their marketing is it mentioned that corn is a cheaper crop than barley, thus making their beer cheaper to produce, thus leaving more profits to spend on marketing to convince people to drink watery, bland beer. And the cycle begins again. They make their business model work. They have created demand for the product. They have capitalized on exploiting an effective business model. Their beer gets pulled through distribution because people ask for it because people know it because it is everywhere—on billboards, TV, radio, and on giant, convenient displays right next to the checkout counters in local supermarkets.

At Dogfish Head we use the big breweries' size against them. They wouldn't even know how to market a beer like our Au Courant, which is bright purple from the addition of pureed currants and nearly twice as strong in alcohol as their normal offerings. Besides, the limited potential customer pool for a beer this exotic would not make the launch of such a product worth their time and money. Maybe someday we'll brew so much purple strong beer that they'll sit up and take notice but by then they will have a difficult time diminishing the goodwill and identity we would have earned by being first in that category. More likely, the category will never grow to a level that interests them. We're fine with that, too. Either way we have used their strength and size against them. This is something every small businessperson is positioned to do.

Look at your biggest competitors. What are their strengths? Is there an opportunity to create a strength for your company that is diametrically opposed to that of your biggest competitor?

YOUR COMPANY'S IDENTITY IS YOU FIRST AND YOUR OFFERING SECOND

The map to success in small business boils down to this: create a product, create a brand, create a company that delivers higher quality at lower volume for a higher price, and your creation will be valuable to your customer.

Therefore, the products you develop or distribute must appeal to customers and fulfill their needs while also remaining faithful to your personal standards and the core of your brand identity. As fundamental as bringing a unique product or service to the marketplace, it is equally imperative that your product is sound and enduring, not based on unsubstantiated theories or fads.

You must also take pride in your role in creating and selling your merchandise. Whether in business for yourself or working for a company, you have a business card that conveys to consumers your skills and ability to provide the product or service they need. Your business card doesn't completely tell the recipient who you are, but it lets them know what you do—at the very least it summarizes your professional identity. This exercise oversimplifies my point, but, if you have a business card, pull it out and read it. What do you do? Are you proud of what you do? Does it give you a sense of purpose?

The most important goal in life is finding satisfaction and enjoyment in what you do. Since a greater percentage of waking hours are spent working than doing anything else, a profession that brings personal satisfaction is your ideal career possibility. Whether you own a business with only yourself as an employee, have 50 employees, or are an employee yourself, what matters is the enjoyment that comes from performing your job well. The closer your business reflects your personal and professional aspirations (who you are and what you do), the happier you are in your work life, and in life in general.

If you own a business or plan to, your product or service is your business card. It exemplifies both the quality of your business and the character of its owner. In addition to designing a business card that reflects who you are, you must consider each of your products to determine how effectively they reflect your company's mission statement. Your products are just a different format of a business card that work to tell the story of what your company is all about. If you do not have pride in the products you offer, it will affect your ability to sell it successfully.

I feel this sense of fulfillment when I look at my business card. Dogfish Head's production manager, Andy Tveekrem, also feels that way when he looks at his card. You can see the confidence on his face as he hands out his business card.

Andy has been in the brewing industry for over 15 years. Early in his career, he worked at a small microbrewery in the Midwest. While there, he helped the brewery grow into a regional powerhouse, and he speaks fondly of those days. In the years that followed, he was lured away by an opportunity to run a larger brewery and earn a bigger paycheck. Once there he realized that his new employer cared more about money than beer. Andy wasn't given the freedom or resources to do his job to the best of his ability, and it stifled his excitement about the brewing industry and, ultimately, his own level of personal fulfillment within the industry.

As the production manager at Dogfish Head, he is given the respect and responsibility that are due to a person of his ability. He is finally happy again, and it shows in his commitment to Dogfish Head. At the Great American Beer festival last year I saw him give his business card to fellow industry vets and it was obvious he was proud to do so. His name, title, and the name of the company on the card tells the full story of who Andy Tveekrum is; not just to the recipient, but also to himself.

KNOW WHAT YOU AREN'T

Before you know how your product or service is going to be perceived by potential customers, you must clearly perceive it for yourself. Perception is all about contrasts. You can't truly judge the quality or value of your product or service until you compare it to another. Starbucks is a great coffee company. That is an easy statement to make, but it's great in comparison to what? To give the statement meaning it needs to have context. Starbucks is a great coffee company compared to competing coffee companies. We can compare and contrast Starbucks with other coffee companies to quantify the perception of their product. You are only ready to launch your product once you fully understand how it compares and contrasts to the others in your industry. This starts with knowing your industry. Knowing who you are starts with knowing who you aren't.

As an entrepreneur you are most likely part of the same alternative commercial world that Dogfish Head is part of. You are not General Electric, you are not Procter & Gamble, you are not Anheuser-Busch. You are the alternative to the commercial status quo—hence, you are alt-commerce. Welcome to my world. It will be difficult to get your message heard over the din and roar of Wall Street and Madison Avenue, but it can be done. First you have to understand what you are up against. You have to learn everything there is to know within your chosen industry. If perception is all about contrast, then it's as important to know your competitors' (big and small) weaknesses as well as your own.

SIZE MATTERS: SMALL IS BEAUTIFUL

Anytime anyone anywhere is starting a business she stands the best chance to succeed if she dreams big and starts small. If you are able to open the business that you always hoped you would, regardless of its size, then you are exercising your biggest dream. But it's easy to be overwhelmed by the costs associated with start-ups. Undercapitalization is the number one reason small companies go out of business.

When I was preparing the business plan for the Dogfish Head brewpub, I knew my limited budget and my limited commercial brewing experience would factor into the scale of my initial brewery. As a 25-year-old English major with no real business experience, banks weren't exactly stumbling over each other to lend me large sums of money to open a brewery. The decision to put my brewery in a restaurant was an important one in terms of developing and launching my product line. In the grand scheme of things it can be said that smaller companies take smaller risks, no matter how huge they seem when you are taking them.

TURNING DISADVANTAGE TO YOUR ADVANTAGE

The average brewpub utilizes brewing equipment that makes about 10 barrels or 310 gallons of beer in every batch. That yields about 20 kegs per batch. Brewpubs usually serve about six styles of house-brewed beer. In addition to the tanks necessary to make the beer (boil kettle, mash tun, and hot liquor tank), one serving tank is needed for every beer on tap and roughly one fermenter for every two beers on tap. This means a 10 barrel brewery needs six serving tanks, three fermenters, three brewing vessels, and all of the support equipment (pumps, hoses, boilers, etc.). While there are a number of companies that make small-scale brewing equipment both in America and abroad, the average cost of a new brewing system of this size is roughly $200,000.

By the time I finished painting, furnishing, decorating, and outfitting the restaurant, I had about $50,000 left in my budget. I still had to buy ingredients and have enough working capital to open my doors and sustain us until we generated steady cash flow. This left me with about $20,000 to buy and install the actual brewing equipment. The equipment manufacturers laughed at me when I inquired about buying a commercial brewing system for this much money.

My limited funds forced me to be creative, and I'm glad they did because the brewing system we built not only allowed us to be in business without being overburdened with debt, but was perfectly designed to experiment with the different beers I wanted to brew. I saw an ad in a brewing publication for a glorified home brewing system that was essentially three kegs propped on a welded steel frame. I bought this little system, and then I bought a bunch of used kegs at a scrap yard, ripped the tops off these kegs, and made lids so they could be used as fermenting vessels. If we left room for the yeast head in every 15 gallon keg, we could get 10 gallons of beer out of each one. I bought 30 kegs, some to ferment the beer in and some to carbonate and serve the beer in. With everything in place, we were able to build a brewery that produced 10 gallons per batch as opposed to the industry average of 310 gallons per batch.

There are essentially two kinds of beer in the world: ale and lager. While lager is what the big, mainstream breweries make (which accounts for over 90 percent of the beer made in the world), our equipment could only make ales. We would be completely inefficient, have no economies of scale, and have no way of filtering or pasteurizing our beer. We were officially the smallest commercial brewery in the world, and we couldn't have been happier. We understood our strengths and our limitations as we did the strengths and limitations of our competitors large and small. We got to work creating demand for Dogfish Head beer 10 gallons at a time. Thinking globally, and drinking locally.

While making beer this way seemed insane from a labor perspective, it was absolutely perfect in terms of experimentation and diversity. In order to keep up with demand I had to brew 2 or 3 times a day 5 days a week. It would get really boring brewing the same beers over and over again so I would wander into the kitchen and look through the chefs' supplies. I would head back into the brewery with a handful of raisins, a cup of maple syrup, or a bucket of apricots. I would change one variable every time I brewed and monitor how well each beer was received in the restaurant and at our bar. We were fortunate to have some really savvy, beer-drinking regulars who were more than happy to give us their opinions on which beers worked and which ones didn't. We would tweak the recipes to satisfy our own palates and those of the customers who understood the kinds of beers we were trying to brew. They shared with us what they were looking for in a beer, and we tried to educate them on the kinds of beer we were hoping to brew. These regular customers and the staff and Dogfish Head learned a lot from each other, and we still use a small brewery at our pub to do test batches and sell seasonal beers that can only be enjoyed at our original location.

While many brewpubs have a handful of recipes that they make with some degree of regularity, we brewed over 30 different styles of beer in our first year in business. Most of these were stronger than your average beer and most had at least one ingredient that was not traditionally used in the brewing industry. By starting small, we were able to do exactly what we set out do and reduce the risks associated with overly ambitious start-up costs.

EDUCATE YOUR CUSTOMER ABOUT YOUR PRODUCT

Once you understand your core brand identity and can identify who your key customer is, you are ready to deliver your service or product. However, if you are a small company committed to emphasizing quality and distinction over quantity and convenience your strongest weapon is knowledge. How will you answer the most basic consumer question, Why is your product better than your competitors'? You deliver your answer by educating your customer on the elements of your offering that give it distinction and quality. And you do this by getting as much information into the hands of your customers at the same time they experience your product.

The descriptions of our beers on our labels are more verbose than those of the big breweries. That's because the beers they sell are remarkably similar to one another and the beer we sell is very different. If our beers have nontraditional ingredients or higher than normal alcohol content, that is exactly the information our key customers want to know. These are the features of our products that justify a higher price tag than those of our competitors. The most effective sales tool that we have at the brewery is the sell sheet that describes each of our beers. Like most sell sheets it contains a list of our products, a description of how they are made, and pictures of the labels. In addition to this information it tells the reader which of our beers would age well in a wine cellar, what is the appropriate glassware to serve each one in, what types of food to pair them with, and which style of wine each beer would replace if it were to be served with a meal. The more information the better. On our restaurant menu, under sandwiches, it doesn't just say "Salmon Sandwich" and the price. It says, "*Wood-grilled Salmon Sandwich: A fillet of Atlantic Salmon prepared in a Hawaiian-barbeque glaze topped with Saga Blue Cheese and served on a grilled French baguette.*" Our salmon sandwich might cost 30 percent more than the one made from a preformed patty served on a white-bread bun at the chain restaurant on the highway. The description that accompanies the product gives the customer the information she needs to decide if our salmon sandwich is a better value than the one offered out on the highway even at its higher price. Of course once the decision to buy the sandwich has been made, to ensure customer satisfaction, it must meet or exceed the expectations formulated on the basis of that description. Knowledge gives the customer the power to make a decision; the quality of the experience gives them the power to decide if the experience was worth the price.

In the same way that we have a captive audience in customers that visit our brewpub, we encourage visitors to coastal Delaware to visit and tour our production brewery as well. We give samples and tours to educate them and let them experience our products. I knew that a significant increase in our advertising budget would be the wrong way to grow our brand. Our key customers are pretty skeptical of advertising messages. What they care most about is education and experience.

We didn't always understand exactly what our key customer was looking for. When we opened our brewpub we served a few light beers because we didn't think a person that was not interested in full-flavored beers would want to drink a beer made by Dogfish Head. We learned to have faith in ourselves and our customers and removed items on our menu that had nothing to do with the unique experience we were trying to create. We listened to our customers and developed our own light beer that was brewed to the same high standards as our full-flavored beers. We knew our customers would expect more from our salmon sandwich than from a similar item served at a chain restaurant on the highway.

When you are deciding what products to specialize in, the process starts and ends with knowledge. Knowledge is gained through education. At the beginning of the process you must educate yourself on your marketplace and how you plan to fit inside or outside of it. Once you have that knowledge you are ready to formulate products that must be based on both quality and distinction. Not only should you aim to develop products that are *different* from what is already out there but products that are *better*. Different alone isn't going to cut it with today's consumer who has more choices than the consumers of previous generations. After you make your product choices, the education process starts all over again. You need to begin the second phase of the education process by making sure everyone within your organization understands how what you are selling is different from and better than what is being offered by competitors. The final stage is working together to transfer that knowledge from the company to the consumer—when you spend the time, effort, and money to educate your consumer about who you are and what you do, you are arming them with the knowledge they need to make a purchasing decision. This knowledge is a powerful weapon to bring you immediate sales from the enlightened and future sales from the people these loyal customers will go out and enlighten on their own.

You should have more faith in the intellectual capacity of your potential customers than the big companies have in their existing ones. Just watch an hour of prime-time television commercials to understand how big companies market their wares. They are obsessed with putting their brand identity message above any message of the quality and distinction of what they offer. Is Sears really offering anything different from Kmart? Not really; that's why they merged. Now their combined brand identity might have the critical mass to compete with the brand identity of Target and Wal-Mart. This is an approach that small businesspeople cannot afford to take. You are not in a position to buy brand awareness on any major level. Let your products and services earn your brand identity for you. Spend the time to explain yourself, and your customers will appreciate your effort as much as they do your offerings.

...AND LET THEM, IN TURN, EDUCATE YOU

We have always used our customer comment cards to find out not only what existing Dogfish Head brews our customers like but what types of new beers they would like to see us make. In 1999 we made our first light beer in response to this feedback. Since our brewery has always specialized in off-centered, strong beers we knew that those styles were well represented. From our regulars at the bar and the input we received via the comment cards we learned that, while our customers appreciated the big brews that we make, they wanted us to make something light so that their non-beer-geek friends could enjoy coming to our pub as much as they did. Not only did we listen to this request but we held a contest that allowed the customers to choose the name of the beer. The staff chose from the names the customers submitted and Lawnmower Light was born. It is usually the fifth best-selling beer of the 12 that are on tap at the brewpub.

Because there are so many well-made light beers available on the market, we have no interest in trying to sell this beer beyond our local market. But it has served a great purpose at our pub as a training-wheel beer. The customers involved with the R&D and naming components of this beer are proud of their involvement and let new customers know how they were involved. It allows people who wouldn't normally try microbrewed beer a lower-body, lower-alcohol alternative to our flagship offerings. We hope they will see that great light beer can be made locally, gain confidence in our brewing prowess, and start trading up to our better-known and more full-flavored beers.

Any small business can incorporate an R&D element into their business plan. If you ask your customers what they want from you that you are not currently offering, you will learn a lot. And if you act on their suggestions you will gain their respect by actually taking the time to listen to and react to their needs. Research your customers' desires and develop the products and services that will fulfill those desires. Every big company has a customer support department. They field countless calls and e-mails of complaints and suggestions every single day. At what point does a company see enough interest in repeated feedback to take action? I'm willing to bet that the bigger the company the slower they react. When you are small you can react a lot more quickly. Your reaction will show your customers that you care.

REMEMBERING QUALITY + DISTINCTION + EDUCATION = VALUE

The world of alt-commerce that we work in is also the world of alt-consumers. Just as we know that our beers are not going to be for everyone, whatever your product or service might be, there will be consumers that are within your reach and those that are not. Some people will always prefer the very light and inoffensive taste of the beers made by the big breweries. Some of these people are my best friends. I don't hold it against them, and I'm not one of those beer snobs who refuses to drink Bud if it's the only thing in the fridge (although I prefer Miller as it has a slightly more noticeable hop character). I know that for a lot of people our beers are going to be an acquired taste, but I also believe that once a beer drinker develops a taste for full-flavored beers she is not likely to revert to the less challenging and less interesting offerings of the big breweries. Dogfish Head will never make beers with the inexpensive ingredients or the efficiency as the big breweries; therefore, our beer will never compete with theirs on price. But we are capable of competing with them on value.

BIGGER, FASTER, AND CHEAPER VERSUS SMALLER, SLOWER, AND BETTER

Whether consciously or unconsciously, customers analyze your products or services and decide whether your business or brand name fills their needs. The number of products and services consumers have to choose from today is overwhelming. The amount and scope of marketing along with increasing economic and population diversity means small businesses need a broader range of offerings to appeal to a continually diversifying and far-reaching customer base. This crowded marketplace makes it difficult for a company or brand to stand out.

The good news is that consumers are trading up. Whether it's from basic to cable, dial-up to high-speed Internet service, or jug wine to a decent merlot, customers everywhere are recognizing additional value in spending additional dollars on the products and services they buy. They are customizing the material aspects of their lives to better suit their individual desires, and beginning to recognize that the turn-and-burn efforts of the fast-food, big-big-box consumer culture no longer satisfies their needs. Just because they can get something generic, cheap, and fast doesn't mean it will provide satisfaction. While it is true that many people feel this way, it is certainly not true for all people. If everyone appreciated the fact that better products take longer to produce, are harder to find, and cost more, Wal-Mart wouldn't control over 15 percent of the consumer marketplace.

Small companies must find a niche and focus on developing brands, products, and services that don't cater to the Wal-Mart consumer mind-set. Small-business owners need to seek out customers who are developing more discerning tastes. These are the consumers who will keep entrepreneurialism alive. They value quality and distinction over price and convenience. In other words, if what you are selling costs more than what your competitor sells, it should be worth the extra money. Pricing, and selling at higher prices than the competition, is discussed in Chapter 9, but for now we need to remember that it's important to charge what the product is worth. If what a small business offers has more value than what the competitor offers in the eyes of the consumer, it is worth the extra money. If you charge more for it and are careful about pricing at a level that allows you to make a fair margin, and the customer perceives their purchase to be a better value at the higher price, then it is a mutually beneficial relationship.

chapter 5

CRAFTING A BRAND IN A COOKIE-CUTTER WORLD

embracing your inefficiencies

A few months before Dogfish Head Brewing & Eats opened I was still trying to decide what brewing equipment I should purchase for the pub. Despite my lack of finances, I had delusions that I could open my brewery with a full-sized system, and so I shopped around to find one I could afford. There was an equipment broker in Texas with a line on a good used system, and I spent an hour or so on the phone with him going over all of the details and features. As we wrapped up our conversation he promised to send some pictures and spec sheets on the equipment, so I told him where to send it. When I told him I was in Delaware, he asked as nice as can be, "Delaware? Now, what state is that in again?"

Being in a small business is like being in a small state. It is difficult to get the larger world familiar with you. You might say Delaware has a branding problem. Branding is the process of moving beyond what your company does and onto what your company stands for. Delaware has beautiful beaches, corporate law advantages, and tax-free shopping, but that doesn't necessarily mean it stands for anything greater than the sum of those parts. I don't want to get started on all of the reasons why I think Delaware is a great state, but I remember taking it personally that this guy didn't even know Delaware *was* a state.

I felt somewhat vindicated almost 10 years later when the *Wall Street Journal* ran an article with a map titled "Beer Nation," which showed a cartoon of North America. In St. Louis, Anheuser-Busch's hometown, there was a drawing of a Clydesdale horse; in Sam Adams' hometown of Boston, it showed a drawing of a patriot. Further down the eastern seaboard it showed a horribly disfigured, mutated dog with a fish head next to the words "Milton, Delaware." Whether the guy from Texas would ever know it, Dogfish Head was doing its best to put Delaware on the American brewing map. It's not exactly the map they hand out with your car rental, but it meant a lot to me. Next to the picture it called our town the "home of extreme brewing." Dogfish Head had been making off-centered beer for off-centered people for nearly a decade when this map was published. But that is probably the first time that many people outside of the craft beer community recognized Dogfish Head as a brand. That is because the map illustrated what we had set out to do—make beer—and what we stand for—extreme brewing.

MAKING YOURSELF A HOUSEHOLD NAME

Each and every small business faces the challenge of establishing a brand identity that stands for something distinct from what is already out there. A few components go into the building of brand identity. Consistency of message, quality and distinction of offering, inclusiveness of message, and timing. To succeed, you must be constantly focused on every one of these aspects of brand building.

Branding is the way you differentiate your products from those of the competition. Your brand is not simply the product you create, the service with your name attached to it, or the store in which you sell a product or service. Your brand is all of these things and more. It's every tool and technique you use to translate your company's philosophy to the consumer. In part, your brand consists of your company's name, logo, and mission statement. While the name and logo are tangible, defined elements of a brand, the mission statement is something intangible, but must be present and consistent in all aspects of your business. It must be conveyed to the consumer through the product or service itself, communicated in all packaging and marketing materials, and subscribed to by you and any coworkers you may have. Every business decision you make reflects the image of your brand.

QUALITY

After brewing for about a year on the little 10 gallon system at the brewpub, we realized it was time to say enough is enough. There was a reason no other brewery in the country was using a system that small—it represented the absolute opposite of economies of scale. Besides, I always knew I wanted our beers to be distributed in the markets beyond our Delaware borders. Starting out as small as we did allowed us to experiment to an extreme degree without devoting a large investment to experimental ingredients, which would have been necessary if we were brewing on a larger system. However, we all agreed that we needed a bigger brewery. We were also in agreement that we still did not have the money to buy a true, commercial brewery. We caught wind of an auction being held at a local canning factory that had been driven out of business by larger competitors. While the food-grade, stainless steel vessels used in the canning process aren't built for making beer, we figured they might be close enough to meet our needs.

On the day of the auction I loaded my pickup with half-gallon jugs of beer and headed to the cannery. The people that showed up to bid on the equipment were mostly local farmers and small-scale cannery operators. There were four 150 gallon stainless steel tanks up for auction that were used to hold cleaning solutions for the cannery. As the auction began I broke out the jugs of beer. As the farmers came up for a sample I shared our intentions of buying those four tanks and impressed upon them the limitations of our budget. When the tanks came up for bid we were the only ones to raise our hands and make a bid. We were able to buy all four tanks for $900.

The auctioneer probably knew something was up when, upon announcing that the tanks were ours, the farmers hooted and hollered and slapped our backs as they helped us carry the tanks to our truck.

To fill the bottles, we bought a used, two-head tabletop bottle filler previously owned by a winery, and then we hand-capped every bottle. Three of us were able to bottle 100 cases in 10 hours before we'd load up my pickup truck so I could deliver the beer to the surrounding cities of Philly, Baltimore, and D.C. We were finally distributing Dogfish Head beer outside of the restaurant. It was hard work, but it felt great.

We were now able to brew two batches of 5 barrels each (150 gallons) to yield 300 gallons to the bottling tank. This allowed us to experiment with the beers without having to worry about costs, and without having to brew beer every single day. The new cobbled-together brewery looked more like the bride of Frankenstein than a traditional brewing system, but it made damn good beer.

The people that purchase small company beer and the people that make small company beer have a lot in common. They believe it is possible for a small company to make, market, and sell a product better than a big company. They respect the tradition of the craftsman. By craftsman, I'm not only referring to the blacksmith wearing a pirate's blouse at the renaissance fair. There are craftsmen who run bakeries, hair salons, copy stores, and most certainly small breweries. They work in many different fields, but the successful ones share a few similarities. They have a genuine passion for their work. They believe what they offer for sale reflects their own high, individualistic standards. They swim upstream against the big business current that emphasizes selling as much of something for as cheap as possible. They craft their brand identity with those same high standards with which they craft their products or services. They can recognize similar values, and their standards are upheld within and by their customer base.

LESSONS ON WHAT REALLY MAKES A BRAND

When we first started bottling our beers, I was naïve and idealistic enough to think that as long as we made good beer that was different from the other beers out there we would be successful. We weren't very good at quality control in terms of presentation and consistency. Yes, we always made good beer but sometimes one batch would taste a little different from another. Or our labeling machine would go haywire and affix labels to the beer bottles every which way but straight.

Once when the machine ran out of glue I decided we could affix the labels to the bottles with rubber bands. I subscribed to a snowflake philosophy of small business. Snowflakes are beautiful and intriguing in part because each one is unique. I assumed that since we weren't Budweiser, people would not only forgive the inconsistency of our beers and packaging, they would welcome it with open arms. The typical craft beer drinker is usually promiscuous, going from one brand and style to the next in the name of experimentation and the quest for new sensations. I thought these customers would appreciate the fact that sometimes our pale ale was a little lighter, and sometimes it was a little darker. We learned that our customers were forgiving of these anomalies to a point. I took a lot of calls from confused loyalists. It turned out they held us to a standard expected in every aspect of the product.

One customer told me that he was so amazed by the complexity and quality of our Immort Ale—a brew comparable to a single malt scotch that would later be named "Beer of the Year" by *Beer Philadelphia*—that he brought it to a whiskey tasting club only to be embarrassed by sharing a six-pack that contained four labeled bottles and two bottles covered in glue. I agreed that we needed to work on the labeling, but I guaranteed the beer inside the bottle was still first-rate. He reminded me that while that might be true, our presentation was less than professional. I apologized and hung up. I thought about what he said for a while. Part of me was proud that our product wasn't perfect; I felt it reflected the experimental initiative of our company. It showed that we weren't a giant, polished, aseptic brewery. But the more I thought about it, the more I realized the validity of the customer's disappointment. He was willing to make three times the investment in a six-pack of Immort Ale than he would have for a mass-produced six-pack. He was willing to personally identify and be associated with Dogfish Head, and we let him down. Dogfish Head reflected poorly on him.

A principle essential to the success of small business is that, since you cannot compete with big business on price, you must be sure that the value of your product over the competitions' is apparent in all aspects of your offering. If the customer is willing to *spend* more for your product, then he should *get* more from that product in every way possible. This includes the packaging, the customer service, and the product itself. As the business owner, you must set the standard of quality, and enlighten both customers and employees about this standard so they understand the value they are receiving.

DISTINCTION OR EXTINCTION

I am usually on the road selling our beer, attending brewing festivals, and hosting beer dinners a couple of days every week. I have a terrible sense of direction so I spend some fraction of almost every day that I'm traveling completely lost. I end up getting directions from the distributor or retailer I am trying to meet with. It's amazing how frequently the same landmarks are cited to help me navigate the roads between major cities and towns on the East Coast. It seems like every single direction-giver I talk to references passing a shopping center with the Gap/Big Box Books/Bed Bath &

Beyond/Ikea/Starbucks/Kinko's/etc. The frustrating thing is that I've usually passed two of these identical shopping centers in the time I've been lost and I can't even figure out which of the two centers the person on the phone is referring to. The sheer magnitude and sameness of mass-produced and mass-marketed goods that Americans have grown to expect can be really disorienting.

The central, nation-defining point that Alexis de Tocqueville kept returning to in his groundbreaking book *Democracy in America* was ". . . the general equality of condition among the people. I readily discovered the prodigious influence that this primary fact exercises on the whole course of society . . . the more I advanced in the study of American society, the more I perceived that this equality of condition is the fundamental fact from which all others seem to be derived and the central point at which all my observations constantly terminated." The central, nation-defining point that de Tocqueville saw us moving toward morphed into a railroad track within a couple of decades. His vision of a nation driven by mass consumption soon became a reality. Andrew Carnegie and the first generation of American industrialists honed and perfected this business model. The hard-line consensus boiled down to this: If you can cut costs, you can lower prices. If you can lower prices, you can generate higher-volume sales. If you grow sales, you will grow market share. Increased market share leads to market dominance, which is synonymous with success and influence.

This is the big-box retail reality that the alt-commerce businessperson is up against: the awe-inspiring, ubiquitous presence of these stores and the homogenizing effect they have on the consumer landscape. As a businessperson, when you consider these giant stores and the variety of products they offer, it can be pretty intimidating. You can't help but ask, What can I possibly offer as an alternative to this? But if you look closely you begin to see that while these stores are hugely successful and their inventories are massive they are also identical from store to store, town to town, state to state. People patronize these businesses because they are easy and predictable. While many people wish to simplify their lives on some level, you must have faith that some people are not always looking for what is easy and predictable to bring joy to their lives. The humble success of Dogfish Head specifically, and the craft brewing industry in general, is a tribute to this faith.

Just like the big retail stores, the big brewers focus on cutting costs and being as many things to as many people as possible in an effort to gain market share and volume sales. For the most part, their efforts have been fruitful. The brewing industry underwent a massive consolidation in the 1960s and 1970s as smaller players lost the economies of scale necessary to compete. The breweries that shut their doors were not always the ones making inferior beers. Often they were merely less financially driven and aggressive compared to the breweries that dominated them. They may have lacked the marketing savvy of the big breweries who threw all of their energies into producing the most homogenized product, branded in the most powerful way. The ambition and aggressiveness of big breweries and big companies in general may lead to market dominance and overwhelming brand presence at the cookie-cutter shopping center but that doesn't mean the small independent company has to go bust. The rise of small regional brewers in the 1980s and 1990s coincided with a growing consumer trend of supporting artisanal, more-expensive but more-exciting producers from countless industries. Think of all the small-scale ice cream makers, soda bottlers, wineries, bakeries, and coffee roasters that have popped up on a regional basis in the last decade or so. It may be less convenient (because of price or availability) to buy a product from a small producer, but it may also be more satisfying.

Today's consumer is much more self-aware and self-educated than previous generations. She recognizes and even embraces the dichotomy and hypocrisy in the simultaneous pursuit of material wealth and inner virtue. This consumer may buy a prefab bookcase from Ikea one day and a set of shelves built without power tools by an Amish family the next. The question is, How can you as an entrepreneur satisfy both the material wants and virtuous urges that today's consumers experience at the same time? The answer—give the consumer a choice that only you can provide. Use your small size, inefficiency, and individuality to your advantage.

The reality of American, class-blurring, consumer urges that de Tocqueville cited presents a double-edged sword to the small businessperson. On one side you have the very real economic benefits of efficient, volume production, and on the other you have the equally real, negative perception that comes with mass production, fast growth, and hypercompetitiveness. People want to see a small business succeed when taking on the giants, but the backlash against that growth can be detrimental. How big you are capable of becoming is only one piece of the puzzle. How big will your key customers be comfortable with you becoming is an equally relevant question. At what point did the perception of Bill Gates move from wunderkind innovator to bullying misanthrope? At what point did Nike's all-informing, competitive corporate culture lose its romantic luster? Probably right around the time that people noticed the company was moving manufacturing jobs off-shore in the name of improved efficiency. The challenge is well summed up by Nike CEO Phil Knight in the book *Just Do It:* "As you get bigger, you have to tone down your entrepreneurial instinct. But you have to do it in a way that doesn't put out the fire."

The fact that Phil Knight recognizes this challenge doesn't necessarily mean Nike will be able to maintain its entrepreneurial fire. However, I believe they will be successful because of their attention to a detail that can be summed up in one word: price. For Nike, on some level, price equals distinction. Nike continues to expand their market share, but they also continue to innovate. They may use cheap, third-world labor to produce the bulk of their shoes, but they pay a high premium to maintain research labs and employ top engineers in the name of improving their technology. When they discover a technological advantage, like their Air or Shox projects, they incorporate those innovations into their highest-priced (and highest profit margin) products. Small companies need to recognize the competitive advantage that comes with this expensive innovation and how it can further a reputation for innovation. For example, smaller shoe companies like New Balance and Simple created their respective niches by concentrating on different modes of innovation. New Balance has focused on tech-forward, runner-centric high-end shoes, while Simple has maintained a cult following for their retro, anti-tech market position. Innovation in itself, and the products created as a result, can differentiate you from the crowd.

Basically there are two kinds of corporate inefficiencies: those that hurt your bottom line, and those that help it. A straightforward, production inefficiency, like a broken bottling line that shoots out unlabeled bottles, is obviously hurtful. But an inefficiency like incorporating more costly, natural ingredients into a product than your competitor does in a similar product can have a positive effect on the bottom line if this innovation allows you to charge significantly more for your offering than your competitors can charge for their lower-quality, but more affordable, product.

Honing the good inefficiencies and culling the bad is the ultimate craft of the successful entrepreneur. The idea of beneficial inefficiencies would have been lost on the consumer of the 1950s who wanted the best marketed, most ubiquitous, and easily obtainable widget available. Today's consumer is a little more enlightened.

CONSISTENCY OF MESSAGE

Effective branding involves an emotional connection between the consumer and a company. To make this connection smoothly and seamlessly, you need to be consistent in everything you do. It may seem that big companies have the advantage in building a brand but, at a human level, a small company is closer to the consumer than a giant corporation. Recognize this fact and use it to your advantage. Celebrate your smallness in everything you do.

Before the age of the Internet, 20,000 magazines, and 100 television stations, consumers had fewer sources of information regarding their options. Since the consumer had fewer options, suppliers (companies) could get away with providing fewer choices. Those days are gone. The consumer not only demands more options but welcomes a choice between products from large industrial producers and small cottage producers. Today's consumer is savvy enough to know that there is a trade-off that comes with making that choice. They also know that the choice they make reflects who they are as a person and a consumer. They realize that paying less for something made by a giant, faceless corporation is often less rewarding than paying more for something made by a small company. The smaller the company, the closer the consumer feels to the producer. The transaction takes on a human element at this scale. Being a consumer yourself, think of how small you feel in a world inundated with billion-dollar advertising campaigns. You like to believe that you have higher standards and more control over your buying decisions than the marketing forces coming at you from every direction would lead you to believe. Of course you are smart enough to acknowledge that these marketing campaigns must work on someone or they wouldn't exist. But that someone isn't you. Or at least it doesn't dictate every buying decision you make. If the product of a small company is actually better than the one made by the giant, faceless company, then the consumer wins on both fronts. By better I mean beneficially inefficient. It cost more to deliver but was worth the extra money. The consumer feels better about the purchase because: (a) The company they are supporting is small like them; and (b) the product they are buying is better, like them. It sounds elitist but it's actually an authentic and self-respectful attitude.

The new American consumers believe in supporting what most purely and positively reflects themselves as individuals. They believe in buying the freshest, least-processed offering at the same time they are buying the most industrial, least-inspiring offerings, and they'll put them in the same shopping bag as a means of canceling out any guilt. They recognize that the choice made by the small businessperson to produce something more expensive is the same choice they make to buy something more expensive. A value in craft production is that it is consciously, beneficially inefficient. Small companies are not alone in recognizing and embracing this reality. Although there is a bit of a backlash about the fact that there is a Starbucks on every corner the company continues to grow and thrive. Of course they make great, predictable, consistent coffee. Of course they market themselves well and pay attention to the bottom line. But they also understand that assuring the highest quality sometimes conflicts with a superficial obsession in maximizing profit. Starbucks has a policy in which they dump out any batch of coffee that has sat for more than a few minutes. Starbucks would rather dump money down the drain than serve an inferior product. Of course Starbucks knows that if they pick their locations right and run each store efficiently very few batches will be poured down the drain. But by sharing this policy of beneficial inefficiency with their customers they are forgiven for growing so big. A company would show a glaring inconsistency of corporate philosophy if they paid lip service about how much they cared about coffee and then let it sit and get old before serving it. Starbucks recognized all of the subtle nuances that go into building a strong brand.

As a small businessperson, you need to focus on selling your special and considerable skills. If what you are selling is truly more special and extraordinary than similar products from bigger competitors, then you deserve to be paid more. This is the business definition of the word *crafty*.

There is, however, a great difference between being crafty and being unprofessional. Here is the poem I wrote that appears on the bottom of every six-pack that leaves our brewery. I think it summarizes the Dogfish Head definition of *crafty*:

Recipe:
Ingredients & Directions for
sampling, exchange, exampling,
and change.

The ingredients in our recipes come from
The earth and the oven,
They come from interfering
and letting be.

We use organic and natural
ingredients wherever possible
and our recipes are blissfully inefficient.

We spend premium prices on
the finest barley, hops, and herbs.
We use no extracts.

For us, brewing is not a process
of automation,
but of imagination and passion.

We wrap our hands around plastic
shovels to clean out our mash tuns.
We wrap our hands around sticky
clumps of whole leaf hops
and toss them into the boil kettle.

We wrap our hands around our work
because we are proud to make
something with our own hands.

We hope you enjoy drinking
Dogfish Head Craft Brewed ales
as much as we enjoy making them.

We want people to know we make our beer by hand. That real people add
the hops to our boil kettle, take the bottles off our bottling line, and load
the pallets onto trucks. Each of the people I work with is passionate about

beer and proud of the beer we make. You know that we make our beer in small batches using the finest ingredients when you taste it. The fact that we use expensive, hard-to-find ingredients speaks to our emphasis on quality. I also now know that a crooked label doesn't say handmade, it just says careless. Efficiency is an idea that comes up in business all the time. But you can define efficiency to your benefit.

Here is a story about Dogfish Head and a decision we made to push the boundaries of our brand identity to include a style of beer that many of our key customers would consider to be inconsistent with our brand identity. We punch out early one Friday every month for a company-wide meeting. Anyone who has an issue or a suggestion can bring it to the floor at these meetings, and it's also a chance to say thanks to everyone for working so hard. We serve pizza and beer at these meetings. But instead of just serving our own beer I try to get a case from a small brewery whose products aren't readily available in Delaware. We take these tastings pretty seriously and grade the different beers we try. For a change of pace we decided to taste 40 ounce bottles of malt liquor at one of these meetings. For those of you who aren't familiar with it, malt liquor is traditionally a much-maligned style of beer known more for its heightened alcohol content than any perception of quality. It is almost exclusively produced by the giant breweries and sold to the urban market on price and strength. To bump up the alcohol the big breweries use cheap corn or straightforward sugar. As we tried the different malt liquors we were underwhelmed by the distinction and quality of the samples and overwhelmed by the sense that we could do it better. Our malt liquor project became a study in beneficial inefficiency.

We knew that this particular beer style calls for brewing with corn, a cheaper crop than barley and one that traditionally contributes less flavor to the beer. We also knew that we didn't want to add plain cheap sugar to bump up the alcohol. We decided to make the beer with rare, exotic corns grown for the gourmet food industry. We located three styles that would work: Aztec red, blue, and hickory (white). We would release this beer in time for Independence Day, and it would be brewed with red, white, and blue corn. We added extra German pilsner barley to bump up the alcohol instead of sugar. Doing this would cost more money but contribute more flavor. We would bottle-condition the beer, which means dosing every single bottle with yeast and priming sugar so that the beer naturally carbonates in the bottle. It would have been much cheaper and easier to just force-carbonate the beer with CO_2 but bottle conditioning leads to finer bubbles and a more subtle texture in the beer.

Of course our big bottling line is only set up to run standard 12-ounce bottles so we set up a tabletop, gravity feed wine filler and a hand labeler next to the real bottling line. On one side of the room we had five guys bottling our 60 Minute IPA on our regular line at a rate of 300 cases per hour. On the other side we had five guys standing over a hand bottling line packaging 12 cases per hour. The labor cost for this project was insane as was the process itself. One guy would wash the bottles. The next guy would fill them. He would hand them to a woman who hand-twisted the caps onto each bottle. She would hand the capped bottle to another guy who would wash the bottle off and put it in the case. The last guy would ink stamp our logo onto 12 brown bags, put them on the tops of the bottles in each case, seal the case, and put it on a pallet. We figured 40 ounce malt liquor is usually drunk right out of the bottle wrapped in a brown paper bag so ours should be no different. We even put a hand-drawn comic in every case that provided instructions on how to use your brown bag on your bottle. Since our regular bottling line team was already hard at work, we had a motley crew running the malt liquor production line. Bartenders from our pub, the production manager, our head brewer, Mid-Atlantic sales manager, distiller, sales service manager, our CFO, and I all took turns rotating through the different positions. Nick, our CFO, just stood there mutely blinking at the colossal inefficiency laid out before us. But we all believed in what we were doing and knew that our customers would, too. By the end of our third straight bottling day we had 300 cases and blisters in the centers of our hands from hand-twisting the tops onto hundreds of bottles of malt liquor. We flaunted these blisters like red badges of courage and high-fived each others' injured hands as we counted the cases on the pallet. Then we noticed that the cases on the bottom of each pallet were making a strange hissing noise. Actually, it sounded a lot like they were laughing at us.

We soon learned that the plastic caps we used for the malt liquor worked fine as long as you didn't stack the cases on top of each other. When stacked, the pressure on the cap caused it to expand and the carbonation escaped. We couldn't send this beer out across the country without stacking it onto a pallet. It had taken us 3 days to bottle an amount of beer that usually takes us an hour, and it was now unfit to sell. The beer tasted great but we couldn't stack the cases. Instead of throwing it away, we hand loaded the cases into our truck one layer at a time. We sold some at our brewpub at a reduced price and most of it went out to the beer festivals that we attend every weekend in the summer where we gave them away as free samples for beer lovers to try. We went to work brewing another batch and found a source for better caps.

I served some at a festival in Massachusetts and was amazed by the response. People loved the beer. They loved the fact that a 40 ounce malt liquor could actually have a lot of flavor and be served bottle-conditioned and fresh. They also liked the hand-stamped bag that came with every bottle and the irreverent name that we gave the beer—Liquor de Malt—French for malt liquor. Again we proved that we could take our beer very seriously without taking ourselves too seriously. The beer was flying out the door at our brewpub and people were lining up at our booth to try it at all the festivals.

The next batch came out great and the new caps worked perfectly. By now all of the free samples of the first batch that we gave away had worked their magic. Beer lovers were calling their retail stores and our distributors looking to buy bottles of Liquor de Malt. Every case that we made was presold before it even came off our makeshift bottling line.

Normally, a 40 ounce bottle of malt liquor costs about $2 at the corner liquor store. We were selling Liquor de Malt for $7.99, four times the established price, and it sold out immediately. People recognized that the bottles exemplified our philosophy of beneficial inefficiency. They understood that we paid more for the exotic corn, we spent more time in the brewing process and in bottle-conditioning and then hand-bottling this beer than the big breweries ever would. They knew that we hand-stamped the brown bags that came with every bottle and that the person who designed the comic in every case worked at a liquor store in Madison, Wisconsin that named Dogfish Head their favorite American brewery of the year. We spent a lot of time sharing the glory of our inefficiency with our customers, and they believed in the choices we made.

A number of newspapers and magazines ran stories on our Liquor de Malt project. My favorite was from Kerry Burns of the *Boston Herald*. He wrote that Dogfish Head had "shown an ability to take something esoteric and abnormal and turn it into something special and coveted." We will make Liquor de Malt again next summer. This is not the sort of project a big brewery would take on. It wouldn't make sense to them in terms of efficiency, but it's what we are all about and we all know it: our customers, our retailers, and even our CFO. I went to a party at his house this summer where all he served was our malt liquor. All of his buddies were in town from Carnegie Mellon's business school. He went around to each person, handed them a bottle, and proudly showed them the spot where his blister had been. As they clinked their bottles together I stood there with a smile, trying to picture Andrew Carnegie rolling over in his grave.

THE INVESTMENT OF TIME INTO YOUR BRAND

I designed the Dogfish Head logo almost a year before we opened. I knew the nautical reference in the name needed to be represented graphically. I also knew I wanted to use a broken outer line on the shield to represent the rustic, comfortable, and casual elements that I hoped would be contained in the company I would one day build. I knew I wanted it to look like a hand-made stamp. I actually did make an ink stamp of the logo before we opened it and used it everywhere I could: on our stationery, on the borders of the framed pictures in our pub, on our menu. To this day I am maniacal about the Dogfish Head logo. We have little metal shields of the logo that we stick everywhere and 3-foot-wide metal shields that we hang in restaurants and liquor stores where we sell our beers. The logo has always meant a lot to me, and it seems to mean more and more to me every day. I now see that our logo means something to so many more people now than it did when I came up with it. All of the power of our brand is tied up in that reality. Once your logo means the same thing and as much to your ideal consumer as it does to you, then you are doing a good job of building brand equity.

I was recently paid one of the best compliments I have received in my professional life while pouring beer at a festival in Connecticut. A woman who obviously knew a lot about beer was asking specific questions about brewing with different yeast strains. We got off on a tangent talking about the retail stores in her area of New England that had the best beer selections. She told me that she and some friends are in a home-brewing club and at their last meeting they laughed at the shared realization that there was a definite overlap between the stores that had an impressive beer selection and the stores that hung our 3-foot-wide metal sign in their windows. At least to this group of home brewers the significance of our logo grew to contain not only our own brand but their perception of the business in which our sign was hung as well. That is the power of branding.

The highest level of brand equity is realized in the emotional relationship your consumer has with your logo. Ideally this relationship will be immediate and powerful—the consumer equivalent of love at first sight. What does your logo stand for? Does it mean the same thing to you as it does to your ideal customer?

Time is the brand-building factor that small businesspeople have the least control over. It's also one of the most important. Most of us who go into business do so with the intention of bringing a better idea into the world. It is an idealistic perspective whether it is motivated by ambition or altruism. Once your doors are open and you are doing business you learn just how far away your idea is from the reality of the marketplace. It's easy to be reactive to the existing marketplace instead of proactive about sticking to your idea, especially when challenged with making payroll and rent every month. Great ideas need time to take hold. Of course you need to do whatever is necessary to pay the bills, but if you have built a brand around a philosophy of quality, distinction, and a consistent message, strong brand identity will come in time.

chapter 6

MARKETING ON A SMALL-BUSINESS BUDGET

Promoting your business with little or no money at all

I remember reading the beer periodicals around the time we were opening our brewpub. I was awestruck by the success of some of the luminaries in our industry. Jim Koch at Sam Adams, Ken Grossman at Sierra Nevada—these guys were creating national brands on a wing and a prayer compared to the methodical plotting of the big three breweries. I knew that what they were doing was great but that there was no point in doing what had already been done. So I studied what was out there on the beer shelf and thought about what wasn't out there. I created new beer styles and sought input from my pub's regular clientele. I tracked which of our beers sold the fastest and which generated the greatest response. Then I would write down the description of the beer and all of the technical information that went along with making it. I listed the ways it was different from any other beer that was out there and the type of drinker I thought it appealed to. All of this information was compiled into a casual letter, put into a box along with a sample bottle of the beer in question, and sent off to a journalist. This was our version of a press release.

Initially these packages were sent to beer writers I respected. Most were soon returned to me with nasty messages from the Postmaster General threatening to put me in jail if I sent beer through the U.S. mail again. I soon learned to send "yeast samples" through private carriers. Some of the press releases finally got through and were met with enthusiasm. After a while I was searching the mastheads of publications outside of the beer world that might be appropriate forums for the news of our groundbreaking beers. This approach led to stories on Dogfish Head in periodicals as diverse as *Wine Enthusiast, Men's Journal, Jane* magazine, and *Esquire.* It also led to rejection or indifference far more frequently than it led to a story. I remember arguing for 20 minutes with a severely art-damaged intern at *Artforum* over whether beer can be reviewed as art. He hung up on me so I guess we'll never know. Each time I sent a release that got no response I would follow up with a phone call under the impetus of making sure the package arrived safely, but really to see if I could evoke an opinion about its contents over the phone. The feedback I received was as critical to the development of our brand as any reviews that might have resulted from my efforts. Their decision on whether our story was worthwhile was cut and dry.

Effective brand building, like effective writing, revolves around a few central ideas. Developing believable, interesting characters—these are your products. An effective and easy-to-follow narration—this is your advertising and marketing. Strong plot development—this is your business plan and budgets. Singular and memorable writing style—this is your brand identity.

If you are a small company and you hire a PR firm to do your press releases, odds are the press release will not be written in your company's voice but in the generic voice of most press releases. Most likely, the PR company will only tell you when someone is interested in a story and not try to follow up and find out why the people who weren't interested walked away. While there are many successful PR firms who have helped make companies successful, if you take the time to do your own press releases, even if they are a little unorthodox, at least they will stand out as something different. You can't be offended if they didn't see something worthwhile to write about from your pitch. But you can ask them why they didn't think it was worthwhile, and you can learn from that information. In fact, the reasons behind that no decision contained the information I was really interested in.

There is an element of fortune-telling in the journalistic process. These people are asked to write tomorrow's news today. Or, in the case of a magazine writer, what they write today needs to be relevant in 2 or 3 months when the issue hits the newsstands. Think of how challenging that must be. Journalists are tasked with discovering the new new thing on a daily basis. Of course they know that a person who is pitching them on a story has an agenda but that doesn't mean that the interaction has to be superficial or perfunctory. Journalists have the broadest, most objective opinions on what constitutes worthwhile news of anyone whom you interact with professionally. You learn from them what works and what doesn't in terms of presenting your brand to the public. You take the good feedback, incorporate it into your next press release, and cut out the bad. The important thing is to keep writing because you realize that as you write these releases you sharpen your message and start to learn more about your brand in the process. The exercise of sitting in front of the computer and writing down what is exciting *at this moment* about your brand can be humbling, but it forces you to keep your brand exciting. You hear writers talk about developing their voice. The only way to do this is to continue practicing the art—writing. Writing about your company is no different. As you continue to hone your message into something unique, you are creating the voice of your brand. Creating a brand is nothing more than bringing fiction, the idea for a product that you have in mind, into reality.

At Dogfish Head we have a voice that we speak to the world with. At times it's irreverent, self-deprecating, honest, respectful, artistic, and fun. This voice is most forceful when it's all of these things at once. A recent press release centered around the news that we were the fastest-growing brewery in America. That is big news no matter how you look at it. Granted we're small so a giant year of growth for us still makes us tiny in comparison to the revenue generated by the big breweries. So we wanted to share this news with the world without puffing our chest too much but still letting everyone know the facts. The press release was stapled behind a thick piece of tan construction paper that had only one sentence printed on it: "As you would expect, the fastest-growing brewery in America is located in rural Delaware." Whether the person reading this press release was familiar with Dogfish Head or not, in one sentence they received the news and the voice of our company. We don't take ourselves too seriously, but we do take our beer very seriously. Rural Delaware isn't exactly Milwaukee or St. Louis, but it is home to Dogfish Head.

MAKE YOUR MARKETING AS UNIQUE AS YOU ARE

About a year ago I was flipping through a magazine and read an article about the organization MADD (Mothers Against Drunk Driving). It detailed how the organization's agenda had changed over the years from bringing awareness about the dangers of drunk driving to stopping alcohol consumption. They attacked beer specifically and suggested that drinking beer leads to taking drugs, which in turn leads to the downfall of civilization as we know it. Meanwhile, government-recognized medical reports have shown that consuming two beers per day is actually healthier for you than not drinking at all. Of course drunk driving is reprehensible and should be strictly prohibited, but I thought they crossed the line when they categorized drinking itself as bad. I suspected that if MADD's recent marketing campaign vilifying drinking infuriated me it was sure to infuriate the people who care enough about beer to spend the extra money to buy better beer. I decided to create a guerrilla marketing campaign that addressed MADD's position, outlined the health benefits of moderate alcohol consumption, and reminded consumers to drink quality over quantity. Imagining the impact that spreading such propaganda might have on legislation, I was faced with the responsibility of bringing to task the organization, or at least bringing awareness to the broader, neo-prohibitionist goals of the organization.

Whether you are a small company that only does sales out your front door in your hometown, or you are the marketing director of a multinational corporation, marketing is marketing. It's all about defining and promoting the features and attributes of your product or service and relaying to the consumer what the inherent and unique benefits of your product are all about. Before you can construct an effective marketing campaign, you need to know who you are trying to reach. Once you know that, you need to decide what is the goal of your marketing. Examples of different goals would be: increasing sales of a certain product, expanding your customer base by focusing on broader geographical areas, increasing awareness of your brand in general, or differentiating yourself from your competition. Once you have figured out what aspects of your business you are marketing and to whom, the next step is figuring out how to effectively and affordably do it. Will you use traditional marketing outlets like print or TV advertising and direct mail, or guerrilla marketing tactics like flyers, special events, or free samples? A few truisms apply to any effective marketing agenda.

1. Your marketing should have a unique and consistent voice that is distinctly yours and plays off the brand identity you aspire to achieve for your company.

2. Your marketing should center around the benefits and advantages that your product or service offers, and you must truly deliver on these benefits in order for the marketing to have a worthwhile impact.

3. Your marketing should motivate your targeted customer to *do* something. In other words, it needs to have some value beyond entertainment.

The development of this Dogfish Head marketing campaign was born out of my reaction to MADD's neo-prohibitionist agenda, using the who-what-how and three-truism approach.

who

We wanted to get the message out to fellow beer lovers who would be as offended as we were to see something we love and respect—beer—be unjustly vilified and stereotyped in ways not based on fact or reality. We already knew that our success as a company was based on the interest and excitement for our beers resonating outward from a core audience of people who are truly passionate about good beer. Excessive alcohol consumption is bad no matter how you look at it. Drinking and getting behind the wheel of a car is even worse. But if MADD was going to sensationalize the effect of drinking *any* beer at all, then we would need to fight fire with fire and stand up for the community of responsible, mature beer drinkers for whom we made our products. Beer has been around since the dawn of civilization. In fact some historians believe that man evolved from a nomadic hunting and gathering existence into rooted communities as a result of the need to tend their crops of barley that they grew for sustenance and the production of beer. In short, beer may be the conduit of civilization as we know it. To have it lumped in with heroin use and rape as it has been in campaigns sponsored by MADD is just flat-out ludicrous. I believed that fellow beer lovers would be equally outraged if they realized how beer was being portrayed by this organization.

what

Our goal was to create a campaign that diluted the strength of MADD's message by showing it to be unfounded and ridiculous. I realize no one in their right mind would choose to make an adversary of such a noble and recognized entity. But, the way I saw it, MADD made an adversary of Dogfish Head first. Not that the people who run MADD have any clue what Dogfish Head even is. But their ultimate goal, through this irrational line of thinking, was to put companies like ours out of business. Our goal was to bring MADD's extreme agenda to the attention of our core demographic and arm them with the facts that could help all of us refute their claims. Since our goal revolved more around a general message than driving customers to buy a specific Dogfish Head beer, we recognized that the success of the campaign would not be measured by a spike in sales for a particular product, but increased awareness of a major movement in the alcohol industry and of Dogfish Head's stance on it. Therefore the campaign had to focus on enhancing our image as a proud, concerned, and responsible member of the beer community, and not around selling the benefits and advantages of our particular line of beers.

how

We knew we wouldn't be able to dedicate a budget for this marketing project that would allow for national or even regional advertisement purchases, so we decided to take a guerrilla marketing approach. We made a short film that presented our position in an entertaining way but with enough information about MADD's agenda and our own, with the goal of swaying the viewer toward our side of the argument. We planned to introduce the film at high-profile craft brewing events in Boston and Washington, D.C. Our hope was that beer writers and critics attending the event would cover the story of our film and expand the dialogue generated by the controversial subject matter. The film was incorporated into our Web site so people anywhere could watch it.

Your Marketing Should Have a Unique and Consistent Voice That Is Distinctly Yours

The tone and content of the film was in keeping with the rest of our marketing efforts. We use a combination of humor, irreverence, and passion in all of our marketing, which represents our philosophies about the work we do and the customers for whom we make our beers. We fought sensationalism with sensationalism. Our film was loosely based on the format of the 1930s extremist, anti-drug movie *Reefer Madness* that showed society overrun by a mass of zombie-like marijuana smokers. Our film is called *Lupulin Madness,* after the oil on the hop leaf that contributes bitterness and fragrant aroma to beer. In short, the film showed our brewers as a bunch of hop addicts. They were interviewed by a fake news correspondent about their varying degrees of hop addiction and how they came to be addicted to hops.

Your Marketing Should Be Centered around the Benefits and Beliefs Specific to Your Product

We made this film to promote the responsible, healthful attributes of our industry in general and not Dogfish Head specifically. In between footage of our out-of-control, hop-addicted brewers, we would incorporate text that outlined different points of MADD's neo-prohibitionalist position on beer drinking in general. At the end of the film we outlined all of the facts that refuted MADD's position and referenced the medical studies that showed moderate alcohol consumption is actually beneficial to one's health.

Your Marketing Should Motivate Your Target Customer to Do Something

Since the film did not promote any specific products, the effect of the campaign is more subjective. We hoped that our creative response to a sensationalist position would garner goodwill toward Dogfish Head from our core customers. But more important, it would get our core customers, who in a lot of ways are the opinion makers of the craft beer industry, to speak out. The facts outlined in the film could be the basis for opinions taken away by the viewer after watching it. The goal was to inform people about MADD's position and motivate those who are passionate about beer to take a stand against what we viewed as an irresponsible, inaccurate message by MADD.

the outcome

It is not cheap to make a short film, even one that's only 12 minutes long and shot in black and white as *Lupulin Madness* was. To defray costs we used production time to shoot additional footage of our brewers and bottlers performing their jobs with excitement and passion that would later become a 30 second ad to be shown on local television and our Web site. The film was welcomed by the beer community, and the humorous tone was effectively tempered by the serious nature of the message. The film did what we hoped it would do and started people talking.

I have great respect for and support the majority of the initiatives put forth by the MADD organization, and I recognized the inherent risk of calling out this esteemed nonprofit group. My hope is that this organization will refocus its efforts toward its original agenda of preventing drinking and driving, and away from the agenda of preventing the responsible consumption of alcohol by anyone.

As this example shows, the process is more important than the outcome. Any company looking to gain awareness for their products and services at any level can benefit from an organized approach to creating an effective marketing plan. There will be variations on this approach, and the methods by which you use these ideas must be specific to your company. But all of marketing boils down to expressing the interest of the producer to the interest of the consumer.

SEAMLESSLY INTEGRATING YOUR PASSION AND PHILOSOPHY INTO YOUR MARKETING

When you are trying to build a brand and make a name for yourself, it's critical that you don't completely farm out your marketing. When you place this task in the hands of a paid outsider, there is little chance that they can understand your company or your brand or be as passionate about it as you. That doesn't mean that the time will never come when you should seek professional help in marketing your brand. But in the beginning, the alt-commerce purist must recognize that if the image of the company isn't created by its founder, it will not ring true. It's too easy to assume that because you are sure of what you are trying to accomplish, the world will be, too. If you don't understand how you fit into your niche and how your niche fits into the bigger commercial picture, you will have a hard time creating something that stands out.

In the preindustrial commercial world, the art of selling was based on the belief that the person who had something to sell and the person who needed that something would inevitably find each other and come together naturally to exchange money for goods or a service. Today, between the constant media-blitz of advertising and marketing and the breakneck pace of production and distribution, it can be easy to overlook the passion of the person selling and that of the person buying. But it's this shared human passion that has always fueled commerce; this opportunity creates extraordinary circumstances for the production and procurement of something entirely new.

Big brands throughout all industries spend an amazing amount of time and money marketing and advertising themselves to maintain critical mass. They are trying to appeal to the lowest common denominator and hoping that it is also the largest amount of people. It usually is. This is actually a really encouraging fact for those of us who exist in the alt-commerce world. Most people who gravitate toward the mass-media–hyped brands are price conscious, and merely looking to quickly and conveniently fulfill their needs. Those who are more discerning, and more apt to decide for themselves what to buy, tend to spend time learning about exactly what products will fill their needs and are willing to spend more for something of higher quality. For this reason alone it makes the most sense to establish a company that is based on quality and distinction rather than price or a marketing budget. Battling a huge, nameless, faceless company by trying to undercut prices is a war of attrition. However, even if you lack the funds for a major advertising campaign, if your creation is special enough, it is capable of capturing the customers' imagination and perhaps that of the media as well.

For Dogfish Head, the single most important component to our success is aligning the passion of the people who make the beer with that of the people who care enough to buy it. This starts with defining who you are and to whom you are selling. Once you have found the people who share your passion you have to convince them of what makes your offering so special.

KNOWING YOUR MARKET

So what is your company synonymous with? Or what do you hope to make it synonymous with? As you define what your positively recognized ideal will be, it is helpful to envision the market you are entering as a great big organizational chart. At the top is the president of the company, below that are the vice presidents of each department, beneath that are the various levels of managers, assistant managers, and so on. There are usually solid and broken lines between different positions to denote how they relate to one another. If you work in a company, are ambitious, and want to move up the corporate ladder, you don't waste your time worrying about what the people at the same level or the levels below you are doing. You look at what the people above you are doing. You want their position so you try to do a better job than them.

Think of the industry you are entering as an organizational chart with the individuals as companies, and determine where you intend to fit into it. The giant players in that market, the presidents and VPs, are focusing on broad issues such as price, marketing, market share, mind share, and so on. Only a few companies are at that level. But down the ladder a bit is where things are more dynamic. This is where the companies responsible for innovation, development, production, and planning are. Think of the organizational chart of a whole industry with companies in the various positions.

Take the fast-food industry: You've got McDonald's as the president, and Burger King and Wendy's as VPs. They are bashing each other out over the big issues of price, market share, and mind share, trying to take the highest position from one another. They are using broad marketing strokes to capture mind share from the broadest customer base imaginable. Therefore, they aren't as nimble or nuanced as smaller, marginal players further down the org chart, such as Hardee's, for example, a company that markets a more expensive but higher quality burger. Or White Castle, a company that created a new segment for their mini-burger—the "slider." It's in these mid-levels on the industry org charts where things are interesting as all of the competitors jockey for position to figure out where they stand in comparison to the entities in positions above them.

Take the time to draw out all of the players on your industry's org chart. Where are the major players in relation to each other, and where do you want to be? What is each company fighting to be synonymous with (e.g., McDonalds: biggest/fastest; Burger King: flame-broiled, etc.)? Determine which company is associated with what ideal and formulate your goal-ideal based on a combination of what you want to stand for and what your marketplace will allow you to stand for. This can help keep you from making the decision to open a national burger chain that markets itself as home of the flame-broiled burger. It's already been done. This exercise will also help you to define your competition's market appeal so that you can decide what aspects of your offering to focus on, thereby better differentiating yourself from them. Creating an org chart also works on a local scale. For example, there are two Italian restaurants in town: One is known to be the high-end/white table cloth choice, and the other does primarily pizza and is known to be fast. As a result of this analysis you might see room on the chart to be the mid-level homemade pasta place. You will also recognize that your marketing efforts will be unsuccessful if you create a brand on par with or below that of your competition.

Once you understand the entire breadth and scope of your industry and the customer base it sells to, you can begin to notice opportunities to create a new segment or capitalize on an underdeveloped niche. Odds are, the big guys are so far up the org chart slugging it out for market share dominance that they won't even notice you until you are well established and have become synonymous with your chosen niche.

Obviously a strong and desirable market position is being first. That doesn't necessarily mean that your market share will become the biggest. When you are the first to provide a new product, it is immediately newsworthy and interesting to somebody. Hopefully it's interesting to enough people to make it worth producing or distributing. Being first has been an integral part of the Dogfish Head marketing philosophy since before we opened our doors.

CAPTURING YOUR AUDIENCE

When you are developing your product in a crowded marketplace, the question should not be, "How will I fit in?" but "How will I stand out?" This perspective works equally well in terms of marketing a product that already exists. There are a lot of marketing messages out there. How will yours stand out? In his memoir, *Chronicles,* Bob Dylan recounts his days breaking into the professional music scene: "Big time record companies were strictly for the elite, for music that was sanitized and pasteurized. Someone like myself would never be allowed in except under extraordinary circumstances."

Bob has nailed the marketing zeitgeist. The marketplace is saturated with a glut of bland, "me too" products that have homogenized the consumer landscape. The extraordinary circumstance that allowed Dylan to break into the music scene was the development of his own unique voice.

There's nobody else who sounds like he does, and there is no one else writing songs like he writes. In essence he created his own extraordinary circumstance by creating a product different from the rest.

When marketing a product or service, small-business owners are in the same position Bob Dylan was in. They are striving to make headway in a saturated, ultracompetitive marketplace. The best way to do this is to come up with something innovative so that there is nothing to compare it to. I realize that sounds a lot easier than it really is, but it can be achieved in any industry if you are willing to segment your market in a way that your bigger competitors have never considered. If the big companies have recognized this unexplored segment or niche, they decided it was too small to be worthy of their attention. In any case, segmentation offers strong opportunity for a small company. You begin the process by locating the people who believe in the same things that you believe in. Apple has done a great job of marketing their products toward design-savvy computer buyers. Yankee Candle broadened the market for heavily-scented, jarred candles that was underserved before their products became available. Each industry is different but all industries have unexplored paths toward innovation. As the leader of a small business your job is to keep exploring until you find yourself on the right path.

To understand what this group of people needs you must first understand who they are. Your customer is a reflection of yourself. You must offer the customer a product or service that has never been available before. That is the basis of a powerful business relationship.

If a segment doesn't exist and you make the choice to try to establish one, you will be taking a greater risk than trying to capitalize on an existing trend in an existing market segment. The good news is that along with risk comes opportunity. The bad news is that sometimes, when you don't play it safe, you fail. The more research you can do, the more time you spend roaming through your industry in search of the worthwhile path, the better the odds that your innovative product will be well thought out and appropriate to your target audience.

DEFINING YOUR MARKET POSITION

I decided to open the brewpub in Delaware mainly because it was one of the few states that hadn't changed their laws to allow for small-scale brewing.

By working hard to change the laws, I was able to be first. Delaware was the first state to ratify the Constitution so I am able to promote Dogfish Head as "The first brewpub in the first state." The category of Delaware brewpubs didn't even exist until we opened our doors. Now there are six brewpubs in the state. Dogfish Head will always be the first.

If the main category that your business falls into is overcrowded, then it's time to create and define your own subcategory. I knew that Dogfish Head could never be the world's biggest brewery, but I thought we could make the world's strongest beer. We did it, too. Our World Wide Stout was the strongest beer in the world for all of a month before Sam Adams reclaimed that title with their Millennium beer. We reclaimed the title with our Raison D'Extra before Sam Adams captured it yet again with their Utopias. Obviously being first is seen as an important marketing position to the Boston Beer Company, makers of Sam Adams, as well. We have not been able to recapture the title but in the time that we've been brewing these beers we've continued to create subcategories in which we are first. Dogfish Head makes the world's strongest dark beer (World Wide Stout), the world's strongest Belgian beer (Raison D'Extra), the world's strongest fruit beer (Fort), and the world's strongest bottle-conditioned beer (Olde School Barley Wine). *Bottle-conditioned* means that yeast and priming sugar are dosed into every single bottle of beer, which allows the beer to naturally carbonate in the bottle. It's not important that everyone knows that we are number one in this small category. What matters is that enough beer enthusiasts exist to recognize that the world's strongest bottle-conditioned beer represents an extraordinary circumstance to them. The more you can segment a mature market, the more you can level the playing field with competitors and gain recognition for the "firsts" generated by your company.

STAND FOR SOMETHING BECAUSE YOU CAN'T STAND FOR EVERYTHING

As Dogfish Head, Boston Beer Company, and a handful of other small breweries continued to push the envelope on strong beers, a new category was identified in the business lexicon—extreme brewing. We had been doing exactly this for nearly 10 years before the *Wall Street Journal* used the term in an article, but it took that long to bubble up to the mainstream media. As a result of our focus on these beers for a number of years, we had developed a substantial share of the extreme-beer market. Not that this market even represents 0.01 of 1 percent of the overall U.S. beer market, but a hundredth of a percent represents a massive number of cases to a brewery of our size.

In addition to being first, there are other ways to separate your brand identity from your competitors'. If you can't be first in a category be something else in that category. The idea is to make the name of your company or your product synonymous with some positively recognized ideal. Avis is number two so they *try harder.* Delta is the *friendly* airline. Trying the hardest and being the friendliest are positively recognized ideals that these companies have made synonymous with their names. It's not like Dogfish Head backed into the world of extreme brewing by chance. As I've said we've been doing this for years. But we never viewed what we're doing as being "extreme" to our customer. I guess you could say we like to think we make normal beer for an extreme customer base. At Dogfish Head we are at the epicenter of this customer base ourselves; we prefer the term *off-centered* to extreme.

TO ADVERTISE OR NOT TO ADVERTISE

When we opened our brewery-restaurant in spring 1995, the first print ad we ran in the local paper showed our logo, address, and three simple sentence fragments in our custom Doggie font: **Original beer. Original food. Original Music.**

Another one of our earliest ads showed a group of asymmetric cartoon people all leaning in different directions while sitting on a couch. Beneath the drawing was the slogan "Off-centered ales for off-centered people." We have since trademarked this slogan, and we incorporate it into the design of T-shirts, pint glasses, and key chains. But we use it in an even more fundamental way than that. As a company we strive to make this off-centered ideal synonymous with everything we do. Since expanding the product line to include everything from soda to soap, we now use the slogan as a lie detector. We simply pull out the word "ale" and fill in the blank with whatever product or service we are considering bringing to market. "Off-centered *soda* for off-centered people." That's true because we sweeten our birch beer soda with natural brown sugar and real vanilla beans, unlike the large soda companies that rely on cheaper, less-flavorful corn syrup. "Off-centered rum for off-centered people." That's true because we age our rum on wildflower honey and toasted French oak instead of the ordinary methods used by big distilleries. "Off-centered steak sauce for off-centered people." That's false. We were approached by a company that made sauces and asked if we wanted to do a custom Dogfish Head steak sauce. They wouldn't even use our beer in the sauce, so the association between the product and Dogfish Head would be inauthentic and we felt we knew our key customer well enough to know that this hollow approach would disappoint them and us.

While most small businesses have little or no advertising budgets to speak of, in some instances the right ad in the right place may be so well targeted as to get the attention of your niche market. Because ad campaigns and the ad dollars of small businesses cannot compete with those of big business, advertising the way big business does is not an option. Targeting the same media that your larger competitors advertise in will not catch your key consumer's eye, and blanketing numerous media outlets is not an option. Whether it's the local paper or a national magazine, you need to find the right people to advertise to before you waste your money trying to advertise to everyone. By preaching the gospel of your company in unlikely, nontraditional places, you allow your potential customer to glimpse a side of your company that doesn't even exist with your competitors. This should increase awareness for your company as it increases the complexity of associations to your brand image.

Advertising cannot build a brand because, odds are, your discerning customer probably, usually, and righteously doesn't trust advertising to begin with. There are a lot of people out there who don't trust the messages they are being force-fed. They resent being sucked up to. They resent the hard sell. They resent all the horseshit and hyperbole, and they don't believe the hype. They have higher expectations, and they want to make informed decisions about what to buy. They want this information from a source they trust. Therefore, this source should be independent from the maker of the product being considered. For a small company, nine times out of 10 this source is the print media, where publicity and journalism come in to play.

At Dogfish Head we spend a very small fraction of our revenue on advertising. In fact, we pretty much only pay for advertising in the beer trade periodicals. The reason we place our ads here has less to do with our hopes that the ads will sell our beer and more with our desire to support the publications and writers who support our industry. We spend far more money on PR and marketing materials than we do on advertising—not that we spend that much in those areas, either. By PR, I mean press releases more than public relations. Our press releases are expensive to send because they usually contain beer. Your company may be in an industry in which there is no equivalent to our beer periodicals—publications that address both the professional community you work in and the customers you seek to attract. Your choices for print advertising may be limited to local and national, general and specialized publications. There is no formula for deciding where the best place for spending your advertising might be. I would stay away from the publications where your bigger competitors spend their advertising dollars. You probably won't be able to afford similar ads in a similar publication, and even if you could it would place you in the shadow of your competitor.

Advertising is only one facet of marketing, and the amount you spend on advertising should only be a fraction of your annual marketing budget. Your marketing budget should always be a percentage of your revenue budget. That doesn't mean it has to be a big percentage. Dogfish Head has grown mostly on word of mouth about the quality and distinction of our beers, but we still dedicate 3 percent of our annual sales to all aspects of marketing, including advertising, press releases, special events, free samples, and so on. Of course as your company grows bigger, the dollars available to marketing will grow as well. You may be tempted to reduce the percentage of sales that you dedicate to marketing as you grow. However, to sustain incremental growth you need incremental marketing dollars. That doesn't mean that you shouldn't vary allocations within the marketing budget each year. One year, advertising might be a bigger priority and special events less important. You may want to attend a lot of trade shows one year and send out a large volume of free samples the next year. The important thing is that you spend a consistent amount of money in marketing to tell a consistent message. The biggest challenge will not be finding places to spend your marketing dollars—people who sell advertising and marketing will be beating down your door; the real challenge will be gauging which are the appropriate places for you.

Unlike your cost of goods sold or the efficiency of a new piece of machinery, you can't always quantify the return on investment of every marketing dollar spent. Remember, you are dealing with human beings; not all decisions can be rationalized. Sometimes people don't know why they like something; they just know that they do. I recommend that some fraction of your marketing budget should be spent on things that are quantifiable. You could take out ads in three local publications incorporating the same coupon that offers a free T-shirt with every purchase of $10 or more. Code the coupons so that as they come in you can tell which publication they were taken from. That will give you a quantifiable baseline for determining which publications your targeted customers read the most and therefore which ones to direct your advertising for. We have a discount coupon on our web site for our brewpub and we can track how often it gets printed, at what time of day, at what time of year. All of this information lets us gauge the ebb and flow of our web site traffic. There are lots of ways to quantify certain components of your marketing initiative, but you won't be able to do it with everything. The important thing is to think of your marketing as an investment and not as an expense and to adjust your spending each year toward the marketing initiatives that give you the best return on investment.

Public relations, the way I define it, is every single aspect in which a company interacts with a potential customer. It's whatever brand-building mechanisms you employ. Marketing is one facet of public relations. Examples of marketing materials employed at Dogfish Head include product packaging, signs, coasters, pint glasses, T-shirts, tap handles, and so on. We use our advertising and marketing materials as vehicles for delivering a more poignant, unsolicited opinion. Our coasters and signs have the quote: "America's most adventurous and interesting small brewery" (attributed to Michael Jackson, not the one-gloved alleged wonder but the world's foremost beer critic based out of London). Four-packs of our 90 Minute I.P.A. are adorned with the quote: "Probably the best I.P.A. in America"—*Esquire* magazine. Our posters simply state: "The Emperor of Beers"—the *Boston Globe*. Remember, people are smart. If they don't know you, they don't believe you. Everyone knows that we pay for advertising and we pay for our posters, but if we use those mediums to transmit an endorsement from a reputable and renowned source, that's the most powerful message we can send.

As you search for the quintessential ideal that is synonymous with your business, it's important that the chosen ideal represents the broadest definition of your brand identity. The better your choice, the less likely you will one day have to change it. Nothing will dilute your marketing message more than changing your main ideal in midstride. If your main ideal is based on something authentic, unique to you, and valuable to the customer, you will succeed. If it is based on a fleeting fad or a hollow, business-speak euphemism like *customer satisfaction* or *quality*, it won't work. Those concepts are either too ethereal or too generic to make truly synonymous with the identity of your company.

SUCKING AND HOW IT'S GOOD FOR YOU

The way a person experiences a product is much broader and more nuanced than merely how he consumes it. Every detail must be considered in your marketing, design, production, and advertising efforts. Every aspect of the presentation plays into your customers' experience of your product. Logo design, color schemes, typefaces, and advertising copy all play into the visual representation of your product. But what about the emotional perception? When you are small everything you put out there about who your company is, what it stands for, and what it sells counts. Energy and imagination are necessary to create a distinct marketing identity. You need to be bold, confident, and sometimes loud to get your message heard, but you should never be obnoxious or conceited. Buy my product because it's the best. That doesn't work unless you are in a position of market dominance. When you are small, your company is at a very human scale and your marketing should tap into the power of human emotion. Sometimes what you do works, and sometimes it doesn't. You should be as ready to market your failure as you are to market your success. That's called humility. It's a niche segment that the big guys are usually unable or unwilling to fill.

Think of the recent Enron and Martha Stewart scandals. People were outraged by the participants' arrogance and inability to admit wrongdoing more than they were disappointed by the actual crimes committed. To admit that you did something wrong is to admit you are human. The perception of a world gone mad with corporate greed and irresponsibility is fueled by high-profile businesspeople acting as if they are superior to the law and superior to the consumer. Small companies must be willing to go out of their way to say they are wrong and show how they will make up for being wrong every chance they get.

We have done a lot of things right at Dogfish Head, but we've done a lot of things wrong, too. Hundreds of customers eat at our brewpub in Rehoboth every day in our busy season. Our staff tries to think of every detail that will make the experience of Dogfish Head a positive one for everyone who comes to visit. Hopefully, we get this experience right 99 times out of 100 but that means there are probably a few people every day who have a less than perfect experience of Dogfish Head. We do everything we can to provide a forum for our customers to inform us of what we did well and what we could do better. We use the comment cards and responses to questions we ask customers about their visit to improve the experience of our brand. If there is a negative report on a comment card, we try to follow up by phone or e-mail to find out where things went wrong. If the customer had a legitimate gripe that can be corroborated by someone who was working at the time, we send them a gift certificate. We want them to come back and try us again. This gesture says a few things to the customer: We value your opinion, we admit when we are wrong, we are only human, and sometimes we make mistakes, but most important, we want you to visit us again because we think we can improve the experience based on your feedback. This process isn't just good customer service, it's good marketing.

SMALL BUSINESS'S SECRET WEAPON

I'm sure you've heard the adage that if someone has a good experience odds are they won't tell anyone but if someone has a bad experience odds are they'll tell a lot of people. We expect them to tell three people, but we are hopeful that we can reach a great number of these dissatisfied customers and turn them into believers by admitting when we've done something wrong and making it up to them.

Word-of-mouth marketing is key to the growth of small brands. More than anything, you want people to talk about your company. As already established, you cannot go toe-to-toe, dollar-to-dollar, or outspend larger competitors with more advertising dollars. Besides, once a product becomes a household name, it's not really worth talking about. The companies that

have the greatest word-of-mouth potential are those with abno
products. By abnormal I mean outside of the norm, not weird,
is what you are going for and has some realistic benefit. In other words you
need to give people something worth talking about and that something
better be the benefits and advantages of the products themselves. There
might be a lot of watercooler chit-chat about a funny beer ad with talking
gorillas or the ad for a car with that really cool song, but the chit chat is usually about how good the ad is and not how good the product featured in
the ad is.

The decision to make a purchase is an individual choice, but it's still
part of a social process. Knowledge is valuable, but it's only really valuable
when shared. What is easily transferable is the knowledge your company is
communicating and its ability to move from one excited customer to
another potential customer. Here, again, the tone of your company's marketing is so important. The more similar you and your coworkers are to
your target customer the easier it will be for you to communicate with
them and for them to communicate with other potential customers in their
peer group. As individuals, when we discover something that improves our
lives, we naturally want to share this knowledge with the people we care
about. Everyone already knows about the big brands; there's nothing new
to talk about there. The up-and-coming brands create the most word-of-
mouth excitement. Remember, people will trust the opinion of a friend
about a product's virtues more than they'll trust the company line touted in
a paid commercial. Peer-to-peer marketing has taken on a new level of significance in the age of the Internet.

MONITORING YOUR MONITOR

The Internet is the great marketing leveler. Small companies can have a big
presence on the web, and big companies can have a small presence. For any
company, some fraction of online presence can be bought in the form of
your own web site, banner ads on other sites, links, and so on. You'd be
amazed at how much of a company's presence is earned, good or bad,
through no effort of its own. The Internet allows people to share their
experiences about products with other consumers. It takes the local experience of your product and makes it universal. People want their opinions

to be validated by other, shared opinions. The quality of a product and the online information about the product are inextricably linked. I would advise anyone who is going into business to set up a web site before even opening the doors. There should always be some interactive element to the web site so you can collect customer feedback immediately. Google search your own company, and your competitors as well. This is where you will find candid, truthful, unsolicited opinions about your marketplace and the perception of your company within it. If marketing is all about building a brand that stands for more than what it does, the Internet is a great tool to check out how well you are doing at building your brand.

The Internet is probably the greatest forum for customer feedback that we have at Dogfish Head. Literally dozens of busy web sites specialize on the craft beer segment; chat rooms abound where beer and breweries are discussed; and detailed rating systems for judging and ranking beers by categories of style and region are shared online. Some of the most popular and best organized are beeradvocate.com, beertown.org, ratebeer.com, and realbeer.com. Anyone who wants a broad, informed impression of the brewing industry would learn a lot by visiting these four sites. We monitor them and participate in the events they sponsor because an educated consumer is more likely to appreciate the full range of great beer made in this country than the person who bases his beer-buying decision on which brand he most recently saw an ad for on national television. I'm proud that Dogfish Head is one of the highest-rated American breweries on each of these sites, but I'm also proud to say that we've received a fair amount of negative feedback from them as well.

Some of it we deserved—for example, we released a bottle-conditioned beer called Festina Lente prematurely, and it was undercarbonated. We issued a letter of apology and promised that anyone who could send us photos of their bottles would receive T-shirts from the brewery as compensation. It was amazing to see how many of the T-shirt recipients took the time to e-mail us directly and tell us that they appreciated what we did. They know we weren't bound by law to send them something free of charge. They knew that the beer may have been stored improperly and gone bad at the retailer or distributor's warehouse. But they saw us step up and take responsibility for the mistake. The beer has since come up in carbonation and is enjoying a renaissance in the online beer community.

Some of the negative feedback we didn't deserve. At Dogfish Head we are beer geeks, not beer snobs. This means we love and respect all good beer and realize that appreciating beer is subjective. We are too small to be all things to all people. If someone doesn't like our beer we are fine with that, but if someone uses our beer or our brewers as a punching bag or as catalysts to voice irrelevant, intentionally hurtful opinions we don't stand for it. Beer snobs are the people who want to prove how much they know about beer by bashing on a brewery. This has happened to us a few times. When they say our beer is bad because our brewer is an idiot for adding too much hops, we don't send someone like that a T-shirt but we take the time to clarify what we are trying to do by producing the kinds of beer that we make. We answer these missiles as much to defend our loyal customers as we do to defend ourselves, and we learn a lot about public perception in the process. Basically, negative feedback is good medicine for a company even when it is unfounded. If you are willing not only to apologize for your mistakes and make it up to your customers but also actively defend your customers when their taste in your product is brought into question, that sends a powerful message.

HELP FROM OUR FRIENDS

I'm fortunate to work in an industry in which mutual support has been the norm rather than the exception. I could write a whole book filled with instances of one small brewery helping another. In both the formal environment of our annual industry conferences and in informal Internet chat rooms and beer-soaked bull sessions, we share recipes, techniques, financial information, and general support. I share information about distributors with fellow small brewers who are seeking growth, knowing well that if their beer is sold by our distributors there is a chance their beer sales could overtake our own. But at the end of the day I also realize we are better off banding together than trying to make headway on our own.

Like many small businesses, our industry is one in which a bunch of small players try to make inroads in a market dominated by a few giants. We are not selling our products so much as we are selling the idea of an alternative. To buy into an idea the consumer must understand it. So we all share the same selling position—we sell knowledge. If a person understands why beer tastes better if it's made from higher-quality ingredients, she will be willing to pay more for it. Once the consumer understands the difference between our unique, high-quality products and the homogeneous products offered by the bigger competitors that brew with cheaper ingredients, this consumer is enlightened. How can we expect to find an enlightened consumer unless we are enlightened ourselves? Enlightenment means understanding the truth, whatever that truth may be—better beer or better business practices. For me enlightenment started when I realized Dogfish Head was not competing against other small breweries or independent restaurants.

There are so many different ways to work together and to locate potential partners. A good way to start is to see if there are any trade associations in your industry. The brewing industry has the Brewers Association, which represents small breweries in legislative issues, helps us market and promote our beers, compiles industry data, and acts as a central intelligence agency for all aspects of the small-scale commercial brewing industry. Usually trade groups represent an industry on a national level. Some local resources for finding small-business compatriots are your state's chapter of the Small Business Association and local and statewide chapters of the Chamber of Commerce. We have been participants and members of these groups and found them to be helpful to our company and in promoting small business in general.

Partnerships can also expand beyond your industry into related fields, and at times to industries not related at all. Rogue Brewery produces and markets two special beers with Morrimoto of Iron Chef fame. Garret Oliver of Brooklyn Brewery recently released the beer and food book *The Brewmaster's Table,* which has taken him around the world to promote the virtues of pairing high-end beers with meals. Realbeer.com stages an annual "Battle of the Beers" on their web site, which coincides with the March Madness NCAA basketball tournament. Each of these breweries and businesses does a great job of bringing the battle for the consumer back to the product itself.

EXPANDING YOUR OFFERING: THE 360-DEGREE DOGFISH EXPERIENCE

As we put together our budget for 2004, I recognized that, while we were growing strong, our ambitious revenue-growth projections would never be attainable without a refocused attention to our core constituent. If our key customers and coworkers were going to bear the responsibility of fueling this growth, I had to bring them together to learn and teach one another what Dogfish Head was all about more than I ever had before. Recognizing a key customer is easy at our brewpub—these are the people who walk through the door to sit at the bar or a table to have something to eat and drink. The definition of a key customer is a little broader at our brewery. The vast majority of the beer made is sold to distributors who in turn sell it to retailers who then sell it to consumers.

The idea for the 360-Degree Dogfish Head Experience comes directly from recognizing the overlap between the product we were going to launch and the brand we were trying to grow. If we believed that the ultimate desire of our key customers was to experience our full-flavored beers and full-flavored food in a five-senses, all-encompassing environment so that they could sample and learn more about Dogfish Head, we would create the ultimate atmosphere in which to have this experience.

The experience starts with the place. The brewery in Milton and the brewpub in Rehoboth are located on the same intercoastal canal about 20 miles from each other. This stretch of state-owned parkland and wetlands is beautiful and lined with rolling green marshes, beaches, fish, osprey, fox, and ducks. In the middle of this stretch is the first town in the first state, Lewes, Delaware. Lewes is a beautiful, historic town with a breathtaking, busy harbor. There is a building alongside the harbor that still has a cannonball lodged in its foundation from when the British Army invaded the harbor. The prettiest upscale hotel on this harbor is called the Inn at Canal Square. I decided this would be the perfect location from which to centralize the Dogfish Experience.

I met with the owners and managers and laid out my plan. Dogfish Head would like to redecorate one of its harbor-side hotel rooms, buy a small motorboat and kayak to keep on their grounds, and create a themed, weekend package around our brewery to the north and our brewpub to the south. Each weekend, guests would enter a room stocked with Dogfish Head beers and sodas. The room would be decorated with Dogfish Head artwork and beer memorabilia. They would have Dogfish Head pint glasses, bottle openers, and T-shirts on a table. The bathroom would be stocked with Dogfish Head soap & shampoo, and thick terry-cloth robes. The library would be stocked with books on beer and food, new and old. The TV would be paired with a serious stereo and a collection of CDs by national recording artists who have performed on the stage at our Rehoboth brewpub.

The weekend package would start with a Friday afternoon tour and tasting at our Milton brewery. Guests would drive from there to check into their room in Lewes. There would be chilled beers and good music playing for them as they entered the room. After relaxing in their room they would stroll through downtown Lewes and have dinner at one of the many local restaurants that serve Dogfish Head's beer with a coupon that would entitle them to a free dessert and nightcap. They could start their day on Saturday with a kayak tour of the harbor and then spend the rest of the day visiting the beautiful beaches, stores, and state park, all within walking distance. In the evening they would be treated to a sunset trip on the SS *Dogfish* motorboat down the canal to our brewpub in downtown Rehoboth. After dinner the guests would make their way back to the hotel. On Sunday morning they would be encouraged to sleep in with breakfast in bed before checking out to explore the area some more.

Dogfish Head would secure the room at a reduced rate for an additional 70 weekday nights, and invite retailers, distributors, brewers, writers, contest winners, perspective hires, and friends of the brewery to partake in the Dogfish Head Experience. A handful of our coworkers—the production manager, sales manager, lead brewer, CFO, restaurant manager, Mariah, and I—would use the SS *Dogfish* to take these guests on tours of the canal to visit our brewery and the brewpub. On these trips and over meals, tours, and beer tastings, we would continue to forge the relationships with the early adapters who have helped Dogfish Head get to where it is today and to better know those who can help us grow in the future.

Joe and Ted, the owners of the Inn at Canal Square, embraced the idea and decided to move forward with us. For both the inn and our company, the 360-Degree Dogfish Experience offers a unique opportunity to attract key customers looking for an exhilarating, value-adding, educational experience. The program would generate regional and national press coverage for Dogfish Head, the Inn at Canal Square, and coastal Delaware. Dogfish Head would pay the bulk of expenses associated with the conversion of the room, the purchase of the boat and kayak, and the free Dogfish goodies that came with each weekend package. The Inn would have guaranteed reservations for the room from the weekend-package guests and for the 70 nights that the brewery would pay to reserve the room.

The project represents the ultimate five-sense experience of the Dog-fish Head brand and hopefully energizes and excites our key customers to a whole new level. We believe these guests leave The Inn and coastal Delaware with a whole new level of appreciation and understanding for what Dogfish Head is all about and they can take this newfound knowledge to share with friends and serve as ambassadors for our company for many years to come.

The 360-Degree Dogfish Head Experience represents an opportunity to move our core brand beyond what we make yet closer to who we are. By initiating this program we weren't so much launching a product or a service as we were creating a lifestyle. To kick off the inception of this program we invited Michael Jackson, the world-renowned beer critic to be our very first guest. A number of years ago he called Dogfish Head "America's most interesting and extraordinary small brewery." We are confident that he will believe this is still true after the weekend he spends in coastal Delaware, commuting to our brewery and brewpub from the Inn at Canal Square. The 360-degree Dogfish Experience acts as a fully-realized business card for our company. It is distinct, delivers value, and revolves around furthering education. It presents a powerful, all-encompassing overlap with the core identity of the Dogfish Head brand. It is one of my favorite projects, and it seems very appropriate for our company. I am hopeful it will live up to our expectations.

TURNING FAILURE TO YOUR FAVOR

Our latest marketing challenge has been particularly trying. We are unable to brew enough beer to keep up with consumer demand. Sounds like a great problem to have, right? I'm sure in the long run we'll look at this period with perspective and see that the unfulfilled desire for our beer created a heightened level of excitement for our brand. In the short term, I must say it hasn't been very pleasant. When our customers run out of beer, that means our retailers run out, our distributors run out, and our brewery runs out. Everyone is frustrated. We have customers who drive across state borders to find our 60 Minute I.P.A. They ask at every store if the beer is available there, and when the retailer says they are out of stock these cus-tomers just go to the next store without buying anything. So then the retailer calls the distributor and yells at them for being out of stock. Of course the distributor calls us to let us know that we are costing them money by being out of stock.

We could have just said it wasn't our fault that our beer was selling faster than we can make it, or that we are working on it and they'll have more beer when it is ready. But we recognized our responsibility to everyone with whom the situation was affecting and tried to keep people informed on how we were responding. We sent letters to all of the retailers who complained, and we apologized. We asked them not to blame the distributors that they bought from, that it was our fault and we were in the process of buying new tanks to help us catch up with demand. After these bigger brewing tanks were in place, we e-mailed pictures of them being installed to our distributors and asked that they share them with their salespeople and retailers so that they could understand the investment we were making to rectify the situation. Between the letters of apology, the pictures of bigger tanks, and the empty shelves, we had a makeshift marketing program that cast a positive light on our failure. Our customers, retailers, and distributors were willing to stick by us and hold out for our beer if we made good on our word and worked out our production woes soon. Mariah and I collateralized the only property we owned that had any value against a bank loan that would allow us to buy the equipment we needed in order to keep up with growing demand. We did everything we could to correct the problem, but it took a long time.

From when we first recognized the situation, ordered the tanks, installed them, and had enough beer flowing to catch up, seven months had passed. We were missing budget, our salespeople and our distributors' salespeople were missing commissions, and our retailers were missing sales. Matt, our sales service manager, and Devin and Allen, our regional sales managers, spent the better part of their workdays calling and running from retailer to distributor apologizing and putting out fires. It wasn't pretty, but it could have been worse. It could have been a disastrous situation, but we took the responsibility not just to admit that it was our fault but to explain how we were going to correct it.

Once you have proven that you have a great product to sell, found a worthwhile niche to sell it in, and made connections to key customers who share your passion for what you're making, you are ready to throw some time, money, and energy into advertising. I'm not saying you shouldn't have some sort of money allocated to advertising right from the get-go, but you should plan to increase your advertising spending once you are somewhat established. You will not have a good grasp of where the best places to spend your advertising dollars are until you have been in business for a while. The aspects of marketing and product development covered in this chapter and in Chapter 5 need to precede any large-scale advertising campaign. In the start-up phase, spending any small marketing budget, along with time and effort, on free samples and educational events to introduce people to your products is more effective than advertising.

chapter 7
PUBLICITY STUNTS
(ARE POORLY NAMED)

A friend of mine who is a journalist for a highly respected magazine recently revealed to me an interesting story that put the awesome power of Anheuser-Busch into perspective. He was doing a story on the big breweries and wanted to get a quote from someone at A-B regarding a controversial tactic they employed to boost sales. The press representative from the brewery would not return his phone calls, so my friend left a vague but ominous message saying that if he didn't hear back from the brewery it was going to be a very one-sided article that wouldn't represent the brewery's best side. This tactic did provoke a return phone call but it had a similar effect to poking a hornet's nest with a beer bottle. The brewery rep proceeded to inform my journalist friend that the reason he didn't call him back was that he and the company could care less what the magazine wrote. The brewery didn't need publicity because it bought its publicity in the form of advertising. And then he pretty much hung up without waiting for an answer.

While I doubt this guy's attitude reflects the official company line, the fact that A-B now owns over half of the domestic beer market could be evidence of the validity of this theory. What they are doing is working. They are the king of the hill and all they have to do to stay on top of the hill is to continually remind everyone that they are indeed on the top of the hill. They're really good at this. Their voice carries very well from up there. When you have a huge, successful brand you can rely almost entirely on advertising to perpetuate your status. When you are trying to grow a small brand, you don't have this luxury. Number one: You can't afford it. Number two: Nobody would believe your advertised message even if you could afford it.

When I see a corner pizza store with some wrinkled banner hanging lopsided from its awning that reads "Ray's Pizza: The Best in the Universe," I think they have no respect for their customers. If they did, they would attribute the quote to somebody. Odds are the quote can be attributed to an egomaniac named Ray. Does anybody really read a sign like that and think, "Well damn, if it's the best pizza in the entire universe I better hurry up and order because there's bound to be a spaceship full of little green men flying in from Mars to clog up the take-out counter"? The other thing I hate is when you see an ad that says "award-winning." Exactly what award are they talking about? If the award is genuinely something to brag about, you should say what the award is for. If the award is for honorable mention in the biggest turd category at the county fair competition, then they need a new marketing angle and maybe a new product.

Big consumer brands rely on advertising because there is little intrinsic difference between what they sell and what their competitors sell. So they would rather just promote their logo as something synonymous with a desirable lifestyle (bikini teams, blimp, talking animals, etc.). But at the end of the day, Bud tastes a lot like Miller, which tastes a lot like Coors, and so on. The reason these products are mainstream is they are designed to be as appealing, or as inoffensive, to as many people as possible. And a lot of people want just that—bland. Not that these are bad beers. They are just really well-made bland beers. However, if you are part of the alt-commerce community bland ain't gonna pay the bills. Advertising usually works best when it's aimed toward consumers who have the lowest expectations. When you are small you need to be different in order to stand out. And you need to stand out in order to be heard over the cacophony of half-billion-dollar advertising blitzes. The washing detergent made by Procter & Gamble works pretty much the same way as the one made by Johnson & Johnson. But what if you made one that truly worked better or had a more attractive and longer lasting smell or used a patented, reverse-osmosis technique to recover long lost socks? Nobody is going to believe it when you tell them how great your product is if they have never heard of you. But if these potential customers are told about the merits of your service or product by someone they believe in, you have a fighting chance. This is why public relations is so much more important for a small company than advertising.

THE POWER OF PUBLICITY

Dogfish Head has been the recipient of a disproportionate amount of mass media attention compared to our relatively small size. I attribute the bulk of this attention to our willingness to take risks in pursuing numerous unusual and unorthodox brewing projects. From the outside looking in I can see where the source of the attention we have received could be perceived as a chicken-or-the-egg scenario. Do we make the off-centered beers to get attention, or do we get attention because of the off-centered beers we make? I can honestly say that we have never made a beer that we didn't believe was worth making for its own intrinsic value. But what I have to say in this matter will obviously be biased and therefore holds less worth than the reception our beers have received in the marketplace.

If any of our beers brewed with exotic ingredients or over-the-top alcohol content levels were simply a novelty or fad they would have eventually disappeared. There would be no demand for them and therefore no reason to continue producing them. Thankfully that hasn't been the case for any beer we have ever brewed. Doing something for shock value or to gain attention solely for the sake of attention is never a worthy business pursuit. To paraphrase the advertising legend David Ogilvy: Nothing kills a bad product faster than good advertising. This statement is even more true with publicity events than it is with advertising because publicity events are more aggressive and timely. I could set my hair on fire while juggling monkeys holding bottles of World Wide Stout in the middle of Times Square. That might get a story about World Wide Stout in the *New York Times.* The story might cause people to try World Wide Stout, but if the beer wasn't actually good and worth the price, you would have a lot of people talking about how disappointed they were in World Wide Stout. The media attention that we have received, like the publicity events that we have organized, has always revolved around the quality and distinction of what is inside the bottle.

A couple of years ago the *Today* show did a piece on Dogfish Head that brought the brand a lot of national attention. That piece begot another in *People* magazine, which begot an appearance for me on the NBC show *To Tell The Truth.* Now I'm not sure how many high-end beer buyers are tuning into this B-rated daytime game show. Its host was the actor John O'Hurley who had played J. Peterman on *Seinfeld,* and I had to grin and bear it as some flunky from the series *Designing Women* tasted our beer and informed the studio audience that it "ain't no Heineken."

On the flip side, the show's staff left me alone   a moment too long and I scored a really cool mullet w wearing to parties. But all of this attention certainly hel national interest in Dogfish Head and didn't cost us a cent. I rec calls from other brewery owners who congratulated me on the co and asked if I wouldn't mind sharing the name of the public relations co pany I use. They were a little surprised when I told them that we didn't use one and never did.

Picasso once said, "The creative act is first and foremost an act of destruction." As a small businessperson I couldn't agree more. When you go into business for yourself, you are destroying preconceived notions. You are destroying business as usual because your business is unusual in that it could only have been created by you. For small businesspeople, our greatest challenge is gaining customers. The way you gain customers is by gaining attention. The way you gain attention is by standing out from the other businesses you compete with. . . . If you can disrupt business as usual, you will attract positive attention while shifting the spotlight away from your bigger competitors.

SPREADING THE WORD

As small-business owners, we spend much more of our own hard-earned money, time, and effort making our products compared to the lenders from the giant corporations. If the consumer is aware of this difference, or if we can successfully educate them about this difference, then the consumer can make an enlightened decision about whether our more expensive products are actually a better value than the cheaper, mass-produced, highly marketed alternatives.

No matter how good a product or service is, it will remain irrelevant unless the buying public knows it exists. As stated in Chapter 6, major advertising campaigns are usually beyond the budget and scope of small, bootstrapping companies. The public presentation of your product can offer a great opportunity for winning over new customers. However, there is a fine line between a publicity event and a publicity stunt. A publicity stunt is a publicity event gone wrong.

A publicity stunt draws more attention to the person or entity responsible for its execution, or to the event itself, than it does to the greater idea

ing executed. A successful publicity event is something that falls within our budget, attracts the right audience for your product or service, and helps to educate that audience about the benefits of what your business is selling. If you are thinking of holding (not "staging") a publicity event, the first question you have to ask is, How will this event add value to my brand?

Any method you can use to educate the consumer in a way that brings attention to the actual product is worth the money. Focusing on publicity events is a great way to upgrade the profile and public perception of your brand with a minimum investment of actual dollars. Great examples abound of successful publicity events within my own industry, and if you raise your awareness to focus on finding ways to promote your business, you will be surprised at the number of opportunities.

For small businesses, it is important that the publicity event extol the virtues of the product rather than the spectacle of the event. In the world of big business, too much is made of the hyperbole—the smoke and mirrors around the product—and not enough is made of the virtues of the product itself. As small-scale brewers we need to use whatever tools we can think of to further this education and explain to consumers why this makes more sense than buying bikini teams and blimps. The education process starts with an interaction between the customer and the company. The publicity event, when executed correctly, can be the perfect forum for this interaction.

PUTTING AN INTERESTING SPIN ON YOUR MESSAGE

One of the main challenges of being a small business in a world dominated by giants is educating the consumer about the value and benefit of the product or service you have to offer. Education cannot be done in a magazine ad or radio spot as effectively as it can during promotional events where your customer has direct exposure to your business offering. This involves finding your customers, getting their attention, and making a statement about your company that is both interesting and educational, in a way that they will remember. The lesson should revolve around what differentiates your offering from what is already out there. Revisit the big idea that brought you to consider opening your business. What was it that captured your imagination to such an extent that it convinced you to move forward with that big idea? First your own imagination must be satisfied, then you move toward capturing the imagination of a small base of customers. The novelty of your idea should then in turn capture the imagination of the media (local first, potentially national down the road). This media attention should serve to broaden your base of customers.

People are inquisitive by nature and knowledge is infectious. If you spend the time and effort involved in hosting a publicity event, the goal should be arming the attendees with knowledge about your brand and your position in the marketplace. Yes, you want them to buy what you are selling, but more than that you want them to leave the event with enough enthusiasm and interest to spread the word. If they tell five friends about what they learned at your event, think about how powerful that transfer of information can be for your company. For the friend it's an unsolicited endorsement from a trusted source. For the person telling the story of your company to the friend, it is the gift of knowledge.

WHAT TO DO

Jim Koch, the founder and CEO of Boston Beer Company, makers of Sam Adams, was one of the earliest entrepreneurs to see the opportunity for selling better, more flavorful beer in an industry inundated with too-similar products that focused more on advertising their logo than on producing a superior beer. In the early days of his company, Jim Koch would fill his car with cases and travel door-to-door from bar-to-bar preaching the gospel of better beer. His hard work began to pay off, and his company was soon at the forefront of the microbrewing revival that slowly took shape in the late eighties. Throughout his company's history he has recognized the pivotal role a well-executed publicity event could have in helping to differentiate and promote his company and his beer. He has staged some very successful events, but he also has been enmeshed in events that backfired.

One risky—and therefore memorable—event occurred as Jim Koch undertook a marketing campaign to educate the consumer that fresh beer is better beer. People take it for granted that a can of Brand X beer today will taste exactly like a can of Brand X beer a year from now. Not many people realize that the large breweries use additives, preservatives, and pasteurization to extend the shelf life of their beers. Basically these beers have the shelf life of a Twinkie and all the wholesome goodness of one as well. While his products might not have the shelf life of those from the big breweries, the trade-off is an uncommon freshness in his beers and a distinct full-bodied flavor. He works closely with his distributors to ensure that only fresh Sam Adams beer is sold. He tours his distributors' warehouses, checking the self-imposed freshness codes printed on cases of his beer. If a beer is out of code, he quarantines it and delivers fresh beer to be sold. He does not expect the distributor to contribute to the cost of replacing the old beer as a value-added statement, and he takes that statement one step further.

To drive the point home Jim staged a publicity event where he set up a dunking booth in his hometown of Boston. Instead of filling the dunking booth with water he filled it with stale Sam Adams beer, manned the booth himself, and allowed passersby to try their luck at hitting the target and dunking Jim Koch in his own beer. Of course the press was alerted and invited to pay witness to this spectacle.

This event truly embodied a risky proposition. Not only was he being dunked in his own beer, but it was his own *stale* beer. He was admitting that there was such a thing as stale Sam Adams beer, but he knew exactly what he was doing. By staging this event he was creating a forum in which he could tell people about the merits of fresh beer. He could emphasize the way Sam Adams was brewed as opposed to how the big breweries make their beer. He could convey the high standards of his company by relating his corporate policy to buy back stale beer. This event also served a secondary purpose of giving his company a human persona. He was humble enough to tell the world that stale Sam Adams beer existed. He was humble enough to be dunked in his own beer. He turned the fragile nature of fresh beer into a marketing strength and successfully portrayed himself as a David among Goliaths. The event was all about the product. Of course the press and the public loved this, and Sam Adams' sales continued to soar.

DON'T PASS UP THE CHANCE TO PROMOTE WHAT THE COMPETITION IS DOING

If you are building a brand your biggest challenge is convincing the public that your product is a better value than your (usually much bigger and better funded) competitors. The easiest way to convince potential customers about the value of your offering is to present it in contrast to those of a competitor. Choose the competitors you want to focus this contrast against wisely. The bigger the better for a number of reasons. First, their products are likely to be established and accepted in the marketplace. If you can present an argument for why your offering compares favorably to theirs, then the consumer can make an associative leap of faith as to why your offering deserves similar attention in the marketplace. It's also important to remember that people in general (and the media especially) love a David and Goliath story. It makes no sense to set up your contrast to someone of a similar size and in a similar position to you. Remember the smaller competitors within your industry are facing the same hurdles that you are and are usually equally oppressed by the bigger competitors. When you take on a big company, you subvert their brand equity. When you take on a smaller player, you may not only subvert their brand equity but yours as well by antagonizing an equally challenged small company. Also, when you contrast yourself against a company approximately your size it will only serve to bring more attention to that smaller competitor. Good or bad, attention is attention and if your story is going to be picked up by the media you are better off centering that story around a contrast to a bigger player than a fellow small player. Let the other small companies fight their own battles—don't bring them into yours.

If it's possible, spend time in the marketplace. Roam. Ask questions. When someone in your target audience doesn't buy your product, what are they buying instead? Use this feedback to structure your marketing in general and your publicity events in particular in a way that shows your product to be a better value in contrast to the most relevant competitors.

WHAT NOT TO DO

More recently Jim Koch was involved in another publicity event that didn't pan out so well. In an effort to regain market share with a younger, hipper demographic, he signed on to appear on a shock-jock-hosted radio show. The theme of the segment was "Sex for Sam." During the show, listeners called in and described for the host and the listening public the most provocative place they had ever had sex while drinking Sam Adams beer. In an epic example of being in the wrong place at the wrong time, Koch was in the studio for a live promotion when a call came in from a couple who were in the process of doing the wild thing in the shadowy corner of a Catholic cathedral.

Within a day the news was out and the protesting began in earnest. Boston Beer's corporate offices are in, of course, Boston, a Catholic city if ever there was one—where Irish pubs outnumber Starbucks locations something like 20:1. In the tumult that ensued, Irish bar owners in Boston were photographed dumping kegs of Sam Adams beer into the sewers and quoted in television and radio interviews vilifying the local company that supported the desecration of a symbol of their faith. Shortly after the show, Jim Koch publicly apologized for the bad taste of the event and the disc jockeys were fired but the damage was done.

In the long run the event was only a minor bump on the branding road similar to those experienced by any plucky company willing to take risks. However, you can consider the nature of this event compared to the stale beer event and see where one was bound to succeed while the other was bound to fail. The stale beer event was all about the product. The "Sex for Sam" event was all about the hype. The first example was a publicity event, the second was a publicity stunt that went beyond the control of the company funding it.

From these examples you can see the importance of planning and forethought in promoting your business. You must analyze what you are trying to accomplish by holding an event and focus on that objective. It costs time and money to pull these things off, and you want to make sure it is time and money well spent.

THE BEST THINGS IN LIFE...

One of the functions of hosting a successful publicity event is creating an opportunity to give away free samples. Regulations in your industry may dictate when and how you can give goods away, but it's safe to say that if it's legal, and you have a gathering of potential customers you should give away free samples.

While it may seem expensive and counterintuitive to give away the product you are promoting for sale, in the long run it's one of the cheapest ways to acquire new customers. It's important not to think of a unit used as a giveaway in terms of its lost retail value. Instead apply the cost of producing that unit (hopefully significantly less than its retail value) toward your publicity or marketing budget. This approach will help bring the true cost and value of the samples into perspective.

At Dogfish Head, 20 percent of our marketing and advertising budget is allocated for giveaway samples for the public and the press. If a big brewery were to allocate a similar portion of their budget they would be passing out thousands of cases every day in every major city. Big companies cannot afford to shift such a large fraction of their budgets away from advertising. Nor do they need to, since they are a known and established entity in the mind of the consumer. Small companies must get their products into the potential customers' hands any way possible—even if it means giving them away for free as a means to shift their views away from automatically buying from the bigger competitor.

Giveaways work equally well if you are selling a service instead of a product. Have an event where attendees can sign up to receive 1 hour or one unit of service for free. If your offer has true value, the customer will experience this upon receiving the free service, and gladly return with money in hand the next time. It's also important to realize that a customer will be more open-minded when trying a new product that was given for free rather than when paying a premium for a sample. In the same way that unsolicited press coverage resonates more strongly than paid-for advertising, if you are not soliciting money from a potential customer to give your product a try for the first time, their opinion is going to be more honest and less clouded by the exchange of money. Of course this can't happen all of the time or nobody would stay in business. But searching out the right opportunities to give free samples to the right people is also a powerful tool for building a brand. I say the right people for a reason. I have been at random, non-beer-centric festivals or done tastings in stores where I knew the second I set up my booth I was wasting my time. The demographics of the festival or those at the store were so far different from that of the ideal Dogfish Head consumer that the samples I gave out weren't appreciated and therefore were wasted. The people who tried it were not interested in buying it. My message fell on deaf ears and my samples fell on numb tastebuds. When you have an event make sure that the invite is set up to appeal to the type of people who would most likely purchase your offering once the event is over.

Assuming you've nailed the quality and distinction elements of your offering, nothing is as effective in marketing as free samples. If what you make or do is truly good, every sample you give away will lead to some multiple of that single sample in new sales. By offering a potential customer a free sample, you immediately negate the risk they take when buying something they haven't bought before. If your product exceeds their expectations, it will replace the competitors' offering they used to buy. If the free sample does not impress them, or isn't what they are looking for, they can't have buyer's remorse (since they didn't purchase the sample) so they will be more likely to try something else that you make instead of walking away frustrated that they spent money on something that didn't fulfill their needs. The more samples you can afford to give out to appropriate, potential customers, the more you will see sales grow. This aggressive tactic of attracting customers is part of the unflinching drive inherent in every successful entrepreneur.

Picture Anita Roddick in the early days of opening The Body Shop. She worked long hours mixing, bottling, and selling her hand creams and shampoos. In the evenings she would prowl the streets in her van full of samples, giving away the hand-printed bottles to potential customers. Everywhere she went she educated people on the superior, natural, fresh ingredients used in her products. During the day she would promote her product in her store, and at night she would hit the road.

LOCATION, LOCATION, LOCATION

When you organize a publicity event, you should locate the event at your place of business so you can control more elements of the presentation. And you should consider every single element of this presentation. How does your display table look? What music is playing? What smells pervade the air? How is the lighting? The more you can control, the better, and if the participants are in your place of business then they are experiencing your brand from its natural source. Wherever you hold the event make sure you have an abundance of written materials about your products or services for attendees to take with them. While people love free stuff, and a free calendar, matchbook, or magnet with your company's name and contact information can be great tools for getting your brand into someone's home, the most useful take-away item after the product itself is the sell sheet or information sheet. You need to get down on a single page of paper what your company does, what products it makes, some quotes from respected sources touting the quality of your products, and directions toward where to buy and learn more about your products. A proper sell sheet can be a potent sales tool and the perfect giveaway for publicity events. Spend as much as you can afford to make this item look as professional and attractive as possible. This sell sheet will play a bigger role in explaining who you are to a potential customer than a business card or bio.

In our second autumn open at the brewpub we were still struggling to increase revenue and keep the brewpub moving forward. We were doing great as a restaurant, featuring a wood-grilled menu, people were really into our homemade beers and touring our little brewery, and our weekend singer-songwriter series of original, live music kept people around for a few more beers after their dinners. Our focus on original beer, original food, and original music was mostly paying off. The weekday nights, however, were a different story. Rehoboth Beach, Delaware, was a seasonal town when the brewpub first opened 10 years ago. In the early days, business slowed down considerably right after Labor Day, as vacationers left the resort town. Many restaurants in town held different events on different weekdays to attract the local late-night crowd. It would be dollar drafts on Tuesday at this place, and free half-time buffet on Mondays at that place. Like Jim Koch's motivation in the "Sex for Sam" debacle, I was interested in attracting the younger late-night crowd to my pub. I decided we could get the word out to that particular crowd by having a DJ upstairs and promoting it with a local radio station. We promoted it as B.Y.O.L. night— "Bring your own log." We also unveiled our Boothbay Barley Wine beer that night, which was brewed with juniper berries and oak chips in keeping with the wood theme. Those who brought a piece of wood for the woodstove received a half-price pint of our new beer, and my hope was they would hang out, listen to music, and have a couple more beers. I paid a few of my younger coworkers to get the word out with flyers and their friends, and did the same with the DJ. On the inaugural night only one writer showed up from the local paper. I was happy to see a bunch of young people show up with logs. However, they were all there for the DJ and not our beers and asked if they could get half-price mixed drink instead of that "crap that tastes like pinecones."

The music was horrible and loud. More young twentysomething customers were coming up the stairs touting pieces of wood. As I looked around the room I noticed nobody was drinking the beer and there wasn't a single face that I recognized as a regular from the restaurant. Something was wrong. I looked out the window and confirmed my suspicions: People were ransacking the woodpile behind our kitchen that we used to feed our wood grill. Essentially they were redeeming logs at our bar that were ours to begin with. What's worse, these people couldn't care less what they were drinking. In fact, I noticed groups of them slouched in the shadows of our parking lots downing cans of cheap beer that they brought with them. So essentially they were having a B.Y.O.B. party with their friend the DJ that had nothing to do with Dogfish Head.

I swallowed my pride and canceled B.Y.O.L. night before it really got off the ground, and I'm glad I did. As with the case of "Sex for Sam," my event had very little to do with our product. Yes, I had made a special beer for the occasion (Boothbay Barley Wine is still produced and bottled as Immort Ale) but I focused on the wrong people. I forgot what Dogfish Head was all about in my attempt to increase our late-night business. For the most part, the people that go for the cheap-beer-and-drinks promotions that happen in Everytown, U.S.A., are not the people that would appreciate an 11 percent alcohol beer made with juniper berries. I lowered my standards in an attempt to grow my brand in an unnatural direction. I vowed to never again discount our beer except for our normal happy hour promotion. It was hypocritical to expect people to pay a premium for our beer everywhere else we sold it yet not treat it with the same respect in the place where we made it. Today, our original location in downtown Rehoboth is one of the busiest restaurants in town and we have people who make pilgrimages from all over the world to try our beers at the source. These are the people who understand that a great beer can be a fair value at nearly twice the price of a cheap beer. I'll never again underestimate our customers' expectations.

IF AT FIRST YOU DON'T SUCCEED

You may not achieve a successful publicity event that increases sales or expands a customer base right out of the gate. It may take a few attempts, tweaking your approach and the elements you use before your efforts translate into increased customer interest or higher sales. Publicity events may not always give you the results you expect, but sometimes attracting the attention of a single influential individual can be more worthwhile than capturing the attention of hundreds. Depending on your industry, attracting media should always be thought of as a secondary goal of good publicity. Attracting one reporter or one local anchorperson can have a tremendous ripple effect and your story could reach more consumers than the meager publicity budget of your business could ever reach through traditional advertising.

A year after hosting the B.Y.O.L. event, we decided to separate our restaurant from our production brewery and build a new bottling plant in Lewes, Delaware. I wanted to kick off the opening of our new brewery with a big publicity event, but I also knew that every cent we had was tied up in the build-out of our new brewery. Although the brewery and restaurant were 3 hours away from the New Jersey border by car, they were only 20 nautical miles away from the New Jersey border. Knowing we planned to sell our beers in New Jersey, I decided to build a rowboat in which to hand deliver the first Dogfish Head export of our handmade beer from Lewes, Delaware, to Cape May, New Jersey. This publicity event was loosely based on George Washington's crossing of the Delaware. I bought a kit out of the back of *Wooden Boat* magazine and began assembling my ocean-going rowing skiff in the upstairs dining room of our pub. This seemed to be a better use for the underutilized space than throwing late-night DJ parties. I did some research on the New Jersey shore and found a bar that was located right on the beach in Cape May. I contacted the owner, sent him some promotional posters, and he said he would help me get the word out about the event. We also made 10-inch replicas of the boat into which we stuffed samples of our new location's first bottled beers and sent them out with press kits to a bunch of newspapers and beer periodicals.

Once the real boat was completed I did a few practice rowing sessions in the canal where I learned firsthand just how top-heavy a keg of beer can be in a rowboat. After almost drowning and losing a full keg of really good beer to an outgoing tide, I downgraded my cargo to a six-pack of beer.

The date arrived, and I loaded my boat with the six-pack, some grapes, and some Gatorade. A local reporter and my father-in-law sent me off with a push and a prayer. It was a little disorienting once I was in the middle of the canal and couldn't see land on either side, but my compass and a guide boat kept me headed in the right direction. Soon, the Jersey shore was before me and I looked for the landmark water tower that the bar owner had described. I arrived on the beach 5½ hours after shoving off from Delaware. I was probably hallucinating with delusions of grandeur on my trip over because I expected a welcoming committee of at least a couple dozen boating and brewing enthusiasts. Three people walked down from the seaside bar: the owner, my New Jersey distributor, and George Hummel, a writer with a beer newspaper called *Barleycorn*. I hid my disappointment as George snapped a few photos of me and my six-pack next to the boat. My wife and a friend had come over from Delaware on a motorboat and joined me on the outside deck of the bar. Nobody else showed up for the event. I saw my posters, still rolled up and gathering dust by the cash register behind the bar.

Things went from bad to worse when my distributor asked me where the keg was. I told him that I left a message explaining that he needed to bring a keg from his warehouse as I would only be rowing a six-pack across the canal. So we sat there, eating jalapeño poppers and nursing the six warm beers that I rowed over as I wondered what went wrong. I was exhausted, but I talked with George about the brewery, our beers, and our plans for distribution before throwing my rowing scull onto a guide boat for the ride back to Delaware.

I tried to forget about it when I returned to work. I told my coworkers that everything had worked out fine. Obviously, it hadn't. I thought about all of the things that I had done wrong. I didn't check in with the bar to make sure they were promoting the event. I didn't follow up on the press releases to make sure people would attend. I didn't make sure there would actually be any beer present at my brewery event. I called it a learning lesson and went on with the chores of selling and making beer at the newly opened brewery.

A few weeks later a number of interesting coincidences came to light. George's article came out in *Barleycorn* with a very positive review of our warm beer. Also, the reporter whom we sent the story to at *USA Today* ran it without ever contacting us. We received a flurry of calls as a result of both of these stories from people looking to buy our beer. We then received a call from someone in the marketing department at Levi's. They had seen the picture of me rowing across the bay and asked me to send them more information on the press release and our company. Within weeks they decided to use me and five other young entrepreneurs to launch Slates, their line of casual business clothes.

Two months after rowing across the bay I found myself in a fancy photography studio in Manhattan. There must have been 10 people running around getting everything ready for the photo shoot. I was kind of nervous so, to break the ice, I asked the photographer if he had been doing this for a while. Everyone looked at me with shock and disgust. The guy with the camera was the world-renowned photographer Richard Avedon. As we spoke, he said he owed his longevity to the glass of beer he had before going to bed each evening. The Slates ad ran in major publications like *Rolling Stone, GQ,* and *Sports Illustrated* and led to stories in *Forbes* and *Businessweek.* A rough calculation estimates that if Dogfish Head bought the ad space we received from the Slates campaign it would have cost us nearly $500,000.

Whether you host a publicity event on your own or team up with an appropriate partner, a lot of planning must happen before a successful publicity event can take place. Because the public is involved, the human element brings an unpredictable variable to the event. It will not go exactly as you imagined it would in the conceptual phase. That's not a good reason to wing it though. You should spend a lot of time constructing an event plan that details what is involved in putting on the event, who will be responsible for each element, which and what number of people you intend to attract to the event, how you will promote it, what added value you hope results for the company, and how you will follow up to ensure you got the most out of holding the event that you could have.

TEAMING UP FOR PUBLICITY EVENTS

If you can't do a publicity event at your own place of business, hold it where people who care about your kind of product are likely to congregate—someplace with a similar customer profile and demographic to your own place of business. You don't want to sell Bibles at an atheists' convention. In the beer business this means I do a lot of events at restaurants that are known to have adventurous beer lists or wine and beer festivals where everyone is there to sample and experiment. Similarly, if you cannot host the event by yourself you should team up with others in your industry who share your passion and present themselves professionally. One publicity event in particular brought more positive attention to our brewery than I would have thought possible.

I had just been stopped by airport security as I tried to board a plane to Chicago. Things were looking pretty grim. Of the five people in the room I definitely held the minority opinion on whether a full-scale cavity search was really necessary. But I was also the only one in the room without a gun so I did a lot of listening. We were in a special room somewhere in the bowels of the Philadelphia International Airport, sitting at a table covered with whole-leaf palisade hops and a two-foot-long, fresh-hopping contraption called "Randall the Enamel Animal." The officers made some valid points about how much Randall resembled the bong to end all bongs. Their dog did not like me or my bag of sticky hop buds, but he was German and probably partial to Hallertauer (a German hop variety).

They sent the dog away after my impassioned speech on dry-hopping and the need for more bitter beers in America. One of the officers was from Wilmington, Delaware, and had heard of Dogfish Head, another drank Sierra Nevada regularly. Calmer, beer-friendly heads prevailed, and we all decided to forgo the cavity search. In fact, all of them were beer drinkers and found the story of Randall the Enamel Animal pretty interesting.

The hops were put in a special new bag. Randall was given a special new box. Each was plastered with very cool and highly collectable "Inspected by the Department of Homeland Security" tape. We were released from custody and loaded onto the next plane for Chicago. I was in the comfortable cabin and Randall sat in the cargo hold among the suitcases and snowboards. As craft brewers, we learn that educating people on the importance of fresh, quality ingredients isn't always easy but it is really important to do.

The story of this event starts with a Dogfish Head invention called Randall the Enamel Animal. The whole premise behind Randall developed a couple of years ago when I was asked to captain an East Coast team of craft brewers against a bunch of West Coast breweries. Dogfish Head, Old Dominion, and Capitol City anchored the East, while Pizza Port, Oggi's, and Avery hailed from the West. The event, called the Lupulin Slam (after the flavoring oils in hops), was set for back-to-back nights at RFD, or Regional Food & Drink, the sister location of the Brickskeller, which is the bar that holds the *Guinness Book of World Records'* title for most beers available in the world. RFD is located in Washington, D.C. I knew the brewers from the West Coast would bring some seriously hoppy ales from Boulder and San Diego. The West Coast is where most of the American hops are grown today. For the Lupulin Slam, we featured a giant version (120 minutes-20 percent alc. by volume) of our India Pale Ale. I knew it was hoppy enough for most occasions but that it could use a booster shot for the big event.

I got to thinking about an alternate use for a stainless steel filter I bought at a scrap yard, and I designed some fittings and a flowchart that outlined my intentions. I shared this diagram with our brewers, and they went to work modifying the filter. As usual, they were up to this unorthodox challenge; these are the kinds of projects that remind us what Dogfish Head is all about. The night before the contest we packed this reconstructed filter that we named Randall with whole-leaf Cascade and Willamette hops and flooded the chamber with 120 Minute I.P.A. Randall did exactly what we "hopped" it would. The alcohol in the beer strips the oil off the hop leaves on the way to the tap. The beer comes out the other side of Randall soaked in hop flavors and aromas not previously available in beers hopped only at the brewery and not at the point where it is being served. The "Enamel" in the name comes from the gritty feeling of hop resins on your teeth—when hopping is done right and to the extreme the first sip almost feels like the outer layer of enamel is being dissolved from your teeth. To a hop-head this is actually a very pleasant sensation.

Over two nights, 400 plus people voted between 12 entries for their favorite hoppy beer. The West Coast beers were pretty amazing as usual and the Old Dominion and Cap City beers were stellar. But a Randallized keg of Dogfish Head 120 Minute Imperial IPA took the belt and hipped the West Coast beer folk and hop-heads to the reality of hard-core East Coast IPAs. Maybe not better, but certainly equal in quality to the West Coast counterparts. Dozens of voters came up to me over the course of the two nights to tell me they had never tried such a flavorful, freshly hopped beer. Nearly every beer-centric publication in the country covered the event and Randall got his 15 minutes of fame with a front-page story and picture in the Dining Section of the *New York Times*.

So Randall was a hit and Dogfish Head's beer won the title, but the story of this publicity event doesn't stop there. We thought we would only use Randall for this event and then put him out to pasture. But upon seeing Randall in action, Dave Alexender, RFD's proprietor said, "Holy crap! Make me two of these things right now so I can install them here and at the Brick." Tom Nickel, one of the West Coast brewers and proprietor of O'Briens, a premier San Diego beer bar, ordered one as well. He now has "Randall Nights" where he lets his beer-savvy customers pick a specific hop variety and beer that they want Randall loaded with, and they change it every week. "I can't wait to get dueling Randalls at O'Brien's so we can try the same beer through different hops side by side," said Nickel. Dave at RFD uses Randall for special occasions as a way to let customers experience hops firsthand and in real time. Since that event a couple of years ago we've now made and sold over 150 Randalls at cost to bars and breweries throughout the country and as far away as England and Sweden.

In a way Randall represents the democratization of the hop leaf. But it also represents the perfect ingredient in a successful publicity event—a focus on the product and its uniqueness in the market. Randall is really nothing more than a tool to educate people on hoppy beers and to allow brewers to show off and describe their beers. Hopefully it will continue to be used as a tool to educate consumers on the importance of hops in beer—something the big three brewers could care less about doing. It's pretty amazing to realize that many beer lovers have never even seen a real hop leaf before, much less watched the pint of beer they're about to try flow through a see-through filter full of hops. Dogfish Head has decided to sell Randall at cost. We have no desire to make a profit for something that we think will benefit the whole beer industry (open source hopping). Kind of like the Linux scene, Randall is an evolving experiment. If brewers or bar owners have ideas on how to improve the design or suggestions for events to use Randall, they can e-mail them to us and we'll get the word out in online updates.

CREATING PROFITABLE PARTNERSHIPS

I wasn't always enlightened in my approach to helping other small brewers. I used to think that it was every man for himself. I wouldn't care if Dogfish Head replaced Coors on a tap handle at a local restaurant or if it replaced the tap of another small brewery instead. I only cared that we got a new account. As our microbrewery struggled in the early months after it opened

I was desperate for success because we were not yet profitable. There are definitely a lot more breweries making extreme and strong beers today than when we started to in 1995. It used to frustrate me when a brewery would come out with a beer very similar to ours or use a marketing slogan that we had come up with. But the more I thought about it and the more I interacted with other small brewers the more I recognized that I had a warped view of reality. First of all, it's not like Dogfish Head invented strong or extreme beers; the Belgians have been brewing them for centuries. In America, breweries like Sierra Nevada, Anchor Steam, and smaller ones like Hair of the Dog have brewed these kinds of beers long before our brewery ever did. While we have come up with some unique recipes and expanded the category, it isn't ours alone. I finally realized that having five $10 six-packs next to mine on the shelf actually helped our sales more than if our six-pack was on that shelf by itself. The consumer is more likely to be enlightened if there is more than one source of enlightenment.

As small brewers we have had great success promoting one another's beers at festivals, beer dinners, and tastings. We've let other breweries borrow grain, hops, filter pads, and equipment from us. Iron Hill, a chain of brewery-restaurants in Delaware wanted to bottle their Christmas beer in cork-finished champagne bottles but lacked the equipment to do so. We invited them into our brewery and helped them set up our bottling line so they could get their beer packaged. The way we look at it, their customers are our customers, and they will help spread the word of good beer, which will hopefully lead their regulars to purchase the occasional six-pack of Dogfish Head beer. We are working together toward the goal of enlightening the consumer to the world of good beer. The 2005 Brewer's Association conference, held in Philadelphia, motivated us to make a special beer to celebrate the event. Every year a brewery in the city hosting the conference makes a Symposium Ale. Our offering truly symbolizes the comradery of our industry. Seven local breweries' flagship beers are blended together into a single tank to make a seven-thread ale combining the best of what we each do. Can you imagine Coors, Miller, and Anheuser-Busch combining their resources and blending their beers to promote the solidarity of large breweries? It would never happen. They are fighting each other separately, while we are fighting against their dominance together.

We work just as hard to be a positive member of the restaurant community in Rehoboth as we do to be an asset to the greater microbrewing community. I'm proud to serve on the board of the Delaware Restaurant Association, and I volunteer time and beer at every event we hold. We have gained so much more than we have given through this involvement. I have spent time with some of the most successful restaurateurs in our state, and learned so much from them. The spirit of altruism, social responsibility, and community are the cornerstones of the association's agenda. We do monthly beer dinners at our brewpub, where we invite local producers and purveyors in to showcase their products. We work with other independent restaurants to promote tastings and at street fairs where the proceeds go to support local nonprofit groups. We make donations to special events held at other restaurants nearly every time the opportunity presents itself. The highway that leads to Rehoboth Beach has one of the East Coast's largest retail outlet centers and is blanketed with national chain restaurants that benefit from far-reaching, multimillion-dollar advertising campaigns. So the restaurants in downtown Rehoboth have banded together to promote one another in order to get the people who visit the area to make the extra effort and come into our town, visit our beautiful beaches, and support our local economy.

It's possible to work with other companies within your own industry and still maintain your unique identity. There are countless innovative ways to interact with your community that will actually further your company's distinction rather than blurring it. We realize the importance of supporting the community that supports us. When you are just starting out, the first priority needs to be becoming profitable so that you can be a contributing member of your community. Now that our company has achieved a sustainable pace of profitability I try to spend more time promoting the craft beer segment or the independent restaurant segment than I could have before. There are different definitions of community. If you have a flower shop, you may be working in your local town's community, a national association of independent florists, and a collective of independent farmers simultaneously.

Each business community is different, but, odds are, the community that sustains you is a lot broader than your immediate customer base. Recognizing these communities that support you and returning that support is a key to success. There's no way to qualify our own success or to quantify the fraction of this success that is due to the attention we pay to the communities in which we operate; all I know is the more time and energy we spend focused on the world beyond Dogfish Head the better our company does. There is definitely a karmic element to this phenomenon. You won't succeed in your communal efforts unless your interest is genuine. The merit for doing good deeds isn't in the result but in the mind-set from which you do them.

DEVELOPING ALLIANCES TO INCREASE SALES

There are numerous examples of strong and successful alliances in the world of big business. Ford Explorers are outfitted with Eddie Bauer interiors to enhance their standing as rugged yet comfortable, upscale vehicles. Ben & Jerry's capitalized on the irreverent and funky experimental reputation of the Grateful Dead and the band Phish with their Wavy Gravy and Phish Food ice cream lines. In both instances the sum was greater than the individual parts. By aligning themselves they have created an effect greater than what they could have created separately. One plus one equals three. These are examples where the alliance worked because the brands had overlapping but equally strong and positive identities. There are also examples where these branding alliances didn't work. During the craft brewing boom of the mid-1990s Jack Daniel's, the whiskey maker, decided to enter the market. They licensed their brand to a regional brewery that churned out an acceptable albeit generic version of a craft-brewed beer. However, the Jack Daniel's loyal consumer was generally not interested in craft-brewed beer so sales fizzled and outdated beer sat on the shelf. The alliance between Jack Daniel's and the craft beer segment failed because there was no real harmony between the two entities. One plus one equaled zero.

The same math applies to alliances between smaller companies as well. There is no company too small to take advantage of the potential power of aligning themselves with another small company. The alliance can be as simple as a sandwich shop that offers free delivery to other members of a downtown Chamber of Commerce or a dog-walking business that offers free Alpo bones with each excursion. The important variable for a successful alliance is that it offers an equitable and harmonious advantage for all parties involved.

In another attempt to increase sales in the slower winter months, I introduced myself to the owners of the other small businesses in town.

There were a handful that stayed open year-round catering to the locals. We needed to gain the loyalty of these businesses and their customers if we were to succeed as a year-round business. I made flyers advertising our off-season discounts with coupons that could be redeemed at the brewpub. To display the coupons, I built and painted wooden oversized holders that were hand-stamped with the Dogfish Head logo. I took these holders to the local businesses that I respected and felt shared an overlapping customer profile with Dogfish Head. These places included local clothing, music, book, and health food stores. I made sure I had appointments with the owners of each store and asked them face to face if they would be willing to display my coupons in their clunky holders on their checkout counters. I also made them each laminated cards entitling them to 20 percent off anything they ate, drank, or bought at Dogfish Head. They all agreed that it was an equitable proposition and used the display. The obvious benefit was the additional traffic and revenue that the coupons brought to the brewpub. The most significant benefit was less noticeable to our bottom line. I found that these business owners really did use their 20 percent cards often, and I worked with the staff to make sure they understood we were happy to have their business. They saw me busing tables and delivering food and they appreciated my hard work. I always tried to take time and ask them how their business was doing and we would trade helpful suggestions with each other for attracting business in the slower months. I respected their hard work and ingenuity as they respected mine, and I still look forward to having a pint together when they come by the brewpub.

DEVELOPING ALLIANCES TO FURTHER YOUR COMPANY'S UNIQUE IDENTITY

Many alliances can be formed locally as we all seek to support the community that supports our business. This local initiative is even more powerful if it has a direct correlation with the identity of your company. The identity of our brewpub is centered around three things: original beers, original food, original music. We make our own fresh beer locally and believe in doing things the same way in our kitchen. As we were formulating our menus before we opened we took extra time to locate and meet with local growers and food companies with whom we could do business. We knew that we would pay a premium to use locally grown products and that service might not be as regular as it would from a national food distribution company but we felt that this local, fresh connection was germane to our company identity. Not only did we gladly pay the premium for their wares but we set aside a large fraction of our menu space that we call Local Yocals. We use this section to list the different local mushroom growers, herb growers, dairy companies, and fish purveyors and tell a little something about their companies as well. There is obviously a great deal of harmony between Dogfish Head and these independent businesspeople, and I'm proud to say that many are customers as well as suppliers. I don't think there is a marketing tool that is more underutilized than this celebration of local connections between small businesses.

The equity and harmony of these alliances can be measured using different metrics. There are financial, marketing, efficiency, and environmental considerations that can be explored. The important thing is that you quantify the expectations of the alliance so that everyone is happy and understands the desired results. We are currently working with a local farmer on an alliance project that is as unorthodox as it is exciting. In the brewing process, the largest fraction of solid waste is the barley grain and husk left over from the mashing. While a lot of the natural sugars and flavor are extracted from the barley during brewing, the remaining material is actually very nutritious and high in protein. In fact it makes an ideal cow feed. So we give our grain away to a local farmer to feed to his cows. We went out to visit the cows with the farmer one summer evening to watch them literally run after the grain cart. You see, the juice left over with the grain undergoes a spontaneous fermentation as it sits in the summer sun and the cows seem to really enjoy the extra kick they get from their food during the warmer months. The farmer brought us some meat one day and it was excellent. By utilizing our spent grain the farmer could use a lower fraction of cheap fillers and cereals to make up the balance of the cows' diet, and the result was higher-quality meat. So we shifted our purchasing of hamburger and steak beef away from a giant slaughterhouse and toward this local farmer. In this process we have closed a unique agricultural circle. The beef that you eat at Dogfish Head was raised eating the grain that we brew with at Dogfish Head. Ergo, if you like our beer, you are bound to like our burgers. This particular alliance has all of the aspects of a home run. We save money by having the farmer use the spent grain instead of disposing of it ourselves. We are efficient because we are buying higher-quality beef that was raised on our barley. We can market the environmental benefits of this closed loop initiative. The only question that remains is, Do people really want to know what the cow they are eating ate? We shall see.

EXPANDING YOUR HORIZONS... AND YOUR BUSINESS

As Dogfish Head grows we are in a position to entertain alliance opportunities of a larger scope. We have been approached to open brewery or restaurant locations with partners in Chicago, Philadelphia, even Russia. We met with a few of these potential partners but never sensed that the harmony of our identities was aligned. We never felt comfortable that Dogfish Head's identity would be safe in anyone's hands but our own. That recently changed as we entered into a licensing deal with a restaurant group that owns the Baja Fresh and Cheesecake Factory franchises in the greater Washington, D.C., area. As our conversations evolved it was clear that they really believed in what Dogfish Head stood for. Freshness, quality, and professionalism were obviously priorities with them as we talked and toured each others' establishments. They saw that Dogfish Head beer had a strong and growing presence in their market and recognized that our casual restaurant theme and menu would work well in the upscale neighborhoods outside of the city. We saw a positive opportunity forming. They get the built-in recognition of our regionally strong brand name. They get the great products from our menu and our brewery. We get licensing royalties, and we extend the geographic reach of our brand and the opportunity to sell a lot of beer to a captive audience. We know that we make great beer and have a great restaurant and plan to open another one in our big brewery in Milton, Delaware. But we also know that we don't have the infrastructure or the seasoned key personnel to take us to multiple restaurant locations outside our immediate geographic area without overtaxing our company's limited resources. So as we've explored this opportunity, I've homeschooled myself in a course called Licensing 101.

I don't pretend to know everything about franchising and licensing, but I do know that they can be powerful ways to extend your brand equity and penetration. I have been working with lawyers, and accountants, and reading books to make sure that I set us up for success. The first step is to have something worth licensing. The next is to make sure you protect everything about your company that is worth licensing. For us this means brands, logos, menu items, design, even some of the phrases that we use in our marketing. There are books and web sites that can help with this process, but I've found it easier to work with professionals. In this area, why reinvent the wheel?

How we came to believe in our licensing project was through the terms of our contract. We start with one location and one location only. If the licensors cannot deliver the level of quality, professionalism, and service that we have nurtured, we are not obligated to open any other locations with them. Their willingness to take this risk for the one location while still making plans of opening many other locations shows me that they have great confidence in Dogfish Head, but, more important, it shows me that they have great confidence in themselves. I admire that. I look at this relationship with our restaurant licensors as another opportunity for a powerful alliance. I believe in them, and they believe in Dogfish Head. This has been an especially difficult project for me. I consider myself to be the father of the Dogfish Head brand and now I have a suitor for my daughter knocking on my door. She will always be my daughter so I need to be sure of the suitor's intentions. I think we have found a really strong prospect. That doesn't mean I won't cry on my way down the aisle into the first D.C. restaurant on opening night.

SUCCESSFUL PUBLICITY

Compared to a small company, the media presence of bigger competitors is usually not only oppressive but offensive in the true sense of the word. The big companies are on the offensive; they are pummeling your potential customers with advertising, marketing, and sheer presence in an effort to keep you out of the picture. They are predatory in their all consuming goals of growing market share, sale, profit, and shareholder value. Using this rationale it would seem the small businesses they compete with would have to be on the defensive: defending our rights to access the marketplace, and to offer consumers an alternative to the status quo. But when you construct your defense around the valuable components of your product itself, you can go on the offense. Bigger is bigger, no doubt about it, but bigger isn't necessarily better. If you make a better product or offer a better service than your bigger competitor, you need to be consumed with proactively proving to the world why and how you do what you do. The alternative is to reactively navigate your way around the monolithic presence of your competitor. You will never grow your company to its potential if this is your main objective. You need to stand *for* something, and not stand as an alternative to something if you are going to stand out. You cannot stand for the biggest, but you can stand for the most innovative, most interesting, or simply the best. Regardless of its size, your company is only as consequential or inconsequential as the products or services it offers. Make something of consequence, promote it on the basis of its consequence, and you will succeed. With the example of Randall you can see that there have been times at Dogfish Head when we didn't even understand the magnitude of the unique circumstances on which we were building our company.

The best opportunities for publicity can be found in the most unlikely places. Creativity plays a big role in developing a successful publicity event like it does in developing a successful product. That is why it makes sense to base your event around the trial of your product. Your event should be as creative and interesting as possible, but the projected, long-term outcome of that event, whatever else it may be, should always be increased sales. Increased sales starts with increased awareness. Small companies are at enough of a disadvantage in the marketplace already in terms of consumer awareness. When you create your own opportunity to present your product to potential customers, you are creating an advantage. Don't squander that advantage on stuff that doesn't matter; all the free T-shirts, balloons, and marching bands in the world will matter less to your potential customers than the opportunity to try what you are offering and make up their own minds if it is worth purchasing in the future.

chapter 8
STALKING THE KILLER APP
creating innovation

Killer app, the term born in the high-tech industry of the mid-1990s, is essentially the application of an innovative idea in a way that leads to a change in the marketplace. As overused as it is, the term is relatively new. The idea behind it, however, is not.

The most successful innovations are those that are integrated into products or services to such an extent that they become highly coveted, then ubiquitous, then canonized as synonymous with their defining innovation. Some historically significant examples of the integration of a ubiquitous product with a killer app include the Ford Model T and the assembly line, Intel and the computer chip, and the Colt Revolver and the repeating pistol. The main idea is as old as commerce itself: the novel and intrinsic distinction of one product compared to another. Small-business owners must constantly invest time and energy nurturing the birth of a killer app. Few things could accelerate the growth of your brand as much as coming up with something new that nobody realized they needed until you brought it to market.

Of course the introduction of something completely new has inherent risks. The same high-tech industry that introduced the term *killer app* into the business lexicon also brought the idea of *burn rate,* a term that refers to the time it takes a company to expend all of its cash as it tries to launch its killer app before going broke. Unfortunately many companies in the high-tech industry were created based on killer apps that turned out to be less than killer, and the high-tech bubble burst somewhere between their overexuberance and the public's indifference.

There are ways to minimize the risk of implementing a killer app. The most obvious is to make sure that it is indeed killer to enough people that it will be worth producing. Fortunately, 9 times out of 10, the smaller the company the smaller the overall risk.

PRIMING FOR INNOVATION

If you are in an industry that champions innovation, include innovative projects in your budgeting process—even if you aren't 100 percent settled on what those projects will be. If you formally plan on doing them, put them into a schedule and they are more likely to get done. This exercise will also prevent these special projects from blindsiding your coworkers, as they should be involved in the budgeting process. You can plug the project into your normal budgeting process with a rough time frame and cost structure so you will be able to anticipate its impact on your business; this way you do not reinvent the wheel every time you work on something new.

At our restaurant we alert the local fish and vegetable purveyors to give us first show at anything new and different that they are offering for sale. A space is reserved on the menu for a "Daily Catch" and a daily entree special allows us to add new dishes as soon as the hard-to-find ingredients are delivered—a food costing program that allows for the addition and subtraction of individual ingredients to accurately cost out any new menu items as the recipe is being generated. There are many people involved with the seemingly simple task of updating these daily specials. The chef first communicates with the supplier and develops the recipe. The recipe is shared with the kitchen staff for preparation. The recipe is then shared with management who updates our computer with cost and pricing for the new item. The kitchen prepares a sample of the dish that the waitstaff tastes so that they can give our guests an informed description of that night's special. On a daily basis we are a group of people coming together to do something that hasn't been done before.

BIGGER ISN'T ALWAYS BETTER

The big companies that small-business entrepreneurs are up against are at a distinct disadvantage in terms of devoting resources to innovation. Small-business competitors are typically giant public companies with significant market share who are preoccupied with maintaining the status quo. Historically, through the complicated inner workings of stock valuation and corporate taxation, companies have been rewarded for showing slow and steady profit growth, and penalized for unpredictable surges in revenue growth. Innovation usually triggers surges in revenue growth and the relatively expensive costs that come with developing and marketing something new.

The investment necessary to launch a new product, and its inherent risk, keep the large corporate players in a world of stasis. "If it ain't broke, don't fix it" seems to be the mantra. The entrepreneur should concentrate not on fixing what's broken but creating what isn't there.

As your company grows, it is bound to become more complicated. As your business interacts with more customers, you inevitably interact with more business maintenance professionals like lawyers, accountants, bureaucrats, and regulators. Some can be very helpful and guide you down the path you want to explore. Others seem to come out of the woods and latch on to you like ticks, draining the life out of your company while making themselves healthier. These specialists mostly live in a world of allocated or billable hours. Without the status quo there would be a lot fewer of them. The more time they spend on your project the smaller fraction of their workweek they have to worry about filling up with new business, so these specialists and their bureaucracy sustain the inertia of big business and big business sustains the necessity of these specialists. It's easy to be stalled and sidetracked by their involvement. This phenomenon wears down major corporations to the point of inertia. They end up managing their companies by prioritizing the maintenance of the status quo. This creates an environment that downplays innovation because it disrupts business as usual. Small companies can't afford to operate under the same model. In order to grow your brand, you need to continually create innovative solutions.

The challenge, of course, is finding and developing truly innovative solutions. They come in all shapes and sizes. There are great examples of innovative techniques and products within the beer industry. The craft brewing segment, like the world of high-end wine, has historically been style specific. Instead of chardonnay, syrah, and merlot, American craft brewers define our own interpretations of continental styles with names like pale ale, pilsner, bock, and stout. As with most established industries, innovations in the beer world can be hard to come by. The low-hanging fruit has been pretty well picked over. The biggest ideas that appeal to the broadest amount of people have mostly been thought of and acted upon.

The big three breweries in this country dominate the production of industrial grade, light, easy-drinking lager beer that is made loosely in the pilsner style, which has an extremely low taste profile and so it appeals to an immensely broad range of people.

As with most small companies, small breweries are forced to find a niche in which their innovative ideas will be appealing. This is actually beneficial to small businesses. The niche that small businesses work within will be below the radar of the bigger companies. If your innovation is truly novel and valuable, you will be able to grow this niche and be the lead player associated with it. Depending on how adventurous your industry is, an innovative idea might mean a conservative but important deviation from how the major players execute a specific task, or it might be an opposite approach to what is already being done. Examples of each approach have worked within my industry.

BROAD GAP APPS

Sierra Nevada Brewing Company, one of the oldest and most successful craft brewers in America, has been around since the mid-1980s, a time when most "serious" beer drinkers didn't even know that hops was an ingredient in beer much less that it was a key ingredient responsible for adding flavor. Measured on a technical scale of International Bittering Units, or IBUs, beers that had a ton of hop character—over 20 IBUs—had been beaten into extinction by the big breweries and their championing of light lagers. Not that there wasn't an earlier time when hoppy beers roamed the earth: Ballantine's, an East Coast regional brewery that had its heyday between the two World Wars, was known to make a pretty wicked India pale ale before the brewery was gobbled up by the big guys.

When the owners of Sierra Nevada opened their microbrewery in the mid-1980s they believed that real beer drinkers were ready for a truly hoppy beer. They created a pale ale recipe based around the flavoring virtues of a West Coast variety of hop named Cascade that has a pungent, grapefruity character. Sure enough, it was discovered by a few early adapter hop-heads who fell in love with this full-flavored beer's distinct, pronounced hop character. This niche continued to grow mostly by word of mouth.

The original ten-gallon
brewery delivered via
UPS to Dogfish Head
Brewings & Eats in
Rehoboth Beach one
month before opening
day. We could not have
started any smaller.

Sam and brewery friend, Doug
Griffith at Dogfish Head Brewings
& Eats during the installation of
the upgraded brewery. The five-
barrel brewery, cobbled together
from steel tanks bought at a cannery auction, is still in use today.

Sam with
then-governor
Tom Carper of
Delaware signing
legislation into law
that allowed for
Dogfish Head's
growth.

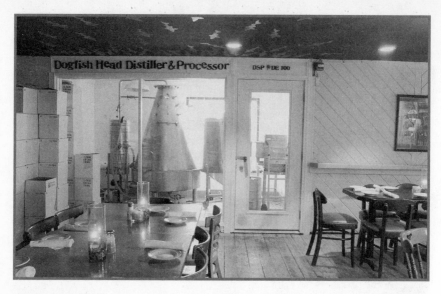

The homemade distiller and processor made from scrap yard metal. In 2000, after we changed state laws for the third time, Dogfish Head Brewings & Eats became America's first distillery/brewery/restaurant.

The main dining area of Dogfish Head Brewings & Eats in Rehoboth: the first brewpub in the first state.

Our newest and biggest brewing system, installed in the Dogfish Head Craft Brewery in Milton, Delaware in June of 2002. We are currently brewing around the clock: 20 batches per week.

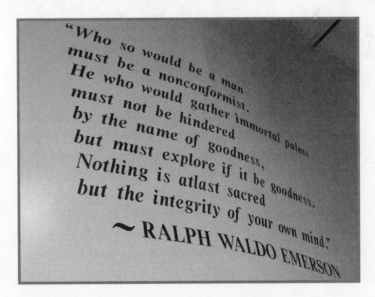

"Who so would be a man must be a nonconformist. He who would gather immortal palms must not be hindered by the name of goodness, but must explore if it be goodness. Nothing is atlast sacred but the integrity of your own mind."

~ RALPH WALDO EMERSON

The Dogfish Head mission statement printed 30 feet high on the wall of the new brewery in Milton, Delaware.

A shot of the fermentation tanks at the Milton brewery. Our original batch size was ten gallons. These tanks hold over 6,000 gallons of beer each.

The 100-barrel tanks. The labyrinth of brewing vessels, bottling tanks, pipes and hoses that make up the fermentation hall at the Milton brewery.

The 90 Minute Imperial I.P.A.—our fastest growing brand—coming off the line. The new bottling line runs at 600 cases per hour: a far cry from the first bottling line that bottled ten cases per hour.

A stack of kegs ready to go out for distribution. At Dogfish Head 75% of production is in bottles and 25% in draft.

Our best-selling brand, named "The most balanced IPA we've tried," —*The Wall Street Journal*. The marketing elements such as our logo and proprietary font contribute greatly to our unique brand image.

The first 18%+ alcohol by volume beer ever brewed. Since first brewing World Wide Stout in 1998, we have gone on to produce a number of extremely strong beers that age as well as wine.

An early example of a print ad we did incorporating an unso-licited endorsement from the British beer expert, Michael Jackson.

One of Sam's paintings used as print ad. As a David in a world of Goliaths, the legend of Paul Bunyan suits us well.

Unveiled at the 2004 inaugural Lupulin Slam, Randall the Enamel Animal, our invention for real-time hopping, Randall adds more hop flavor and aroma to beer. Over 150 of these are in use by hop-lovers across 4 continents.

Andy Tveekrem adding hops to "Sir Hops Alot." Another of our inventions, it allows us to continually hop our India Pale Ales. Version 2.0, as seen here, works much better than the original vibrating football game.

Lead brewer Bryan Selders and Sam as The Pain Relievaz, probably this generation's finest beer-geek hip-hop band…also probably the only beer-geek hip-hop band.

Sam and Mariah promoting Dogfish Head beer at a marketing event onboard the Kalmar Nyckel, Delaware's tall ship, located in Lewes, Delaware, the first town in the first state.

Sierra Nevada is now one of the biggest and most respected breweries in the country. In hindsight, theirs seems like a subtle and conservative innovation. It's not like they came up with a new ingredient for beer or a new way of adding that ingredient to the beer. All they did was add what seemed like an outrageous amount of a specific variety of hops to a really well made beer. But at that time, in the salad days of the craft beer renaissance, it was enough to differentiate them from all of the other beers on the shelf. There are hundreds of beers being made today with higher IBUs than Sierra Nevada Pale Ale but that beer will always be associated with, and celebrated for, its influence on expanding the beer-drinkers' palate. The route to innovation might be found in the ability to look at something that is a standard within the industry, or something used in the past, and approach it from a slightly different angle. As you consider possible innovative ideas for your business, you need to also consider the size of the potential audience. If it's huge and you don't have the resources to service it, you may be starting with the wrong innovation. If Sierra Nevada opened today in a market with dozens of examples of world-class pale ales, it would be difficult for them to stand out the way they did when they helped define the category in the late-1980s. While the niche for hoppy beers is now pretty wide, it wasn't when they opened their doors. How big is your niche? What innovation would best help you expand that niche?

An extreme example of innovation within the beer industry is the development of a beer from Alaskan Brewing Company located in Juneau. The brewery is in a beautiful, remote coastal city that is one of the most celebrated salmon fishing ports in the world. The brewery also happens to be located directly across the street from a small smoked-salmon factory. In one of those inspired, chocolate-in-the-peanut-butter moments, the brewers from Alaskan walked across the street and asked if they could smoke some of their barley grain over the peat fire smoldering in the salmon factory. They used the barley to make a batch of their dark porter beer, and Alaskan Smoked Porter was born. A beer that has an intense but balanced smoky character, it is revered for its complexity and distinction and has won numerous awards in the most respected beer competitions nationally and internationally. It is more of a regional success and illustrates the idea that, in most cases, the more unusual the killer app is, the smaller the niche it will appeal to.

As you would expect from the descriptions of the two beers, fewer people have tried, or would be interested in trying, Alaskan Smoked Porter than Sierra Nevada Pale Ale. Because Alaskan's innovative idea is more extreme, their niche is bound to be smaller. All beers are made with hops but not all beers are opaque and made with peat-smoked barley. This doesn't mean that this wasn't a killer app. Alaskan Brewery has not grown at the same rate as Sierra Nevada, but it maintains a strong and venerated presence in the Northwest beer scene. When you are stalking a killer app for your own company, the process should include a forecast of expected results. Your definition of success may be different from mine or the folks at Sierra Nevada. So defining success simultaneously with the design of your killer app will keep you focused on achieving the desired results.

At Dogfish Head we realize that our business model and the decision to focus on making off-centered ales for off-centered people means we will never have as wide an audience as some of the more mainstream breweries, and we are fine with that. We make some eccentric beers. Some are even more eccentric than others. A beer made with peat-smoked barley is an acquired taste, a peach ale intentionally inoculated with bacteria is an even more acquired taste. Our beer called Festina Lente is brewed with overly ripe local peaches and two types of bacteria. I know what you are thinking, it sounds delicious, and you are right, but not everyone would agree. While brewing beers with bacteria is a tradition that goes back centuries in Belgium, it is a relatively recent phenomenon in America. After we released this beer about one-quarter of what we sent to distributors was returned. It was just too extreme even for some of our biggest proponents' tastes. But times change, and the market evolves. As this beer gets older it gets better and we now get as many requests to bottle Festina as we do for some of the more immediately well received specialty beers that we have made in the past. We know what our strengths are and we stick with them. We were hopeful that this beer would be embraced by our core customers, whom we respect so much, and we were disappointed at first when there was a bit of a backlash. But Festina Lente now meets our expectations and those of our customers so everyone is happy. When we find a niche we don't just scratch it, we rub it until it is raw and red and sticks out like a sore thumb. While it is doubtful that Dogfish Head and probably Sierra Nevada and Alaskan Brewing will ever compete with Anheuser-Busch to be the biggest brewery in the world, there are some giant, global companies that got their start with a killer app.

AN INNOVATION'S SUCCESS IS BASED ON ITS CUSTOMER RESPONSE

The story of Ralph Lifschitz' rise to power is a quintessentially American rags-to-riches story based on the successful introduction of a killer app to the stodgy garment industry. Ralph was an itinerant clothing salesman who always dreamed of designing his own line. Inspired by European tailors he decided to come out with his own ties. In the 1970s, when he started, ties were thin, similar, and conservative. The Brooks Brothers business suit model was held up as the standard issue uniform and a tie was meant to complete the businessman's outfit, not to stand out. Ralph designed a tie that was nearly twice as wide as those of the Brooks Brothers business suits being worn at the time. He also used expensive and luxurious fabrics with eye-catching patterns and charged twice as much for them as those being sold by the established tie makers of the day. He sewed his new name into the back of the ties: Ralph Lauren. Within a decade or so his brand became a household name around the world and is still synonymous with preppy, well-made American clothes. His killer app—a wider, more exotic tie—evolved into one of the most respected affluent-lifestyle brands in history.

Another, more unorthodox, example of a killer app would be the launch of New Coke. Remember New Coke? Not everybody does. The world's most successful beverage company doesn't even market a soda under that name anymore. But it was a name that was on everybody's lips in 1985. That was the year that the company decided to stop making Coke and start making New Coke. Much speculation surrounds the reasons for their decision to take such a risk and move away from one of the most famous secret recipes in the history of business. It was thought to occur because foreign coca plantations were financially unstable, so the company wanted to focus on a recipe that didn't incorporate the coca plant as an ingredient. It is also a known fact that they were getting beat by Pepsi in the Nielsen ratings for volume sales in supermarkets—a critical segment of the soft drink wars. Whatever the reason, they launched New Coke with an impressive international advertising campaign only to have the introduction explode in their face. Their Atlanta headquarters was inundated with thousands of calls daily from consumers who were outraged with the change. Distributors sent back truckloads of the new soda, and it was soon a modern-day version of the Boston Tea Party. Their lifeblood loyal consumers were revolting in staggering numbers. Coca-Cola responded quickly and relaunched Classic Coke within a year. Less than two decades later there was no New Coke to be found anywhere.

Being the gigantic, hedge-betting company that they are, Coke did a ton of research and focus-group testing before they launched New Coke. It consistently beat the original recipe and Pepsi in blind taste tests. But at the end of the day none of that research mattered. People wanted their old Coke back. The company delivered. But through the public upheaval and subsequent corporate submission, Coke received millions of dollars in free publicity and proved that it listened to its customers. The whole debacle shifted the control of the marketing plan for the company out of their own hands and into the hands of their customers. It was a powerful moment in business history, which served to redouble the brand loyalty people felt toward Coke. Whether Coca-Cola intentionally orchestrated the failure of New Coke and the subsequent strengthening of Classic Coke will never be known. What we are left with is a pretty unique example of how a failed product launch can become a killer app for a company.

The example of New Coke shows how powerful the customer can be in moving a company forward or backward for its own good. The important thing is the movement itself. The world is always changing, and a company, whether it's as big as Coca-Cola or as small as Dogfish Head, can never guarantee the success of a new product launch. The only thing we can be sure of is that things change. What people desire today is very different from what they desired a century ago, which is very different from what they will desire a century from now. The central idea to remember as an emerging business leader is that you always need to be conscious of the impending changes and the opportunities to initiate change within your own industry. Charles Darwin built an everlasting philosophy upon the close examination of a world in constant change. He surmised and proved that if a world is always changing then the species that live on it must change as well in order to survive. Some species are able to make that change, and some are not. Those that do evolve and prosper. Those that don't become extinct. Every evolutionary change that has occurred on this planet to allow a species to continue to live and reproduce is as much a killer app as it is a natural miracle.

SMALL INNOVATION IS BETTER THAN NO INNOVATION

As a businessperson, every time you come up with an idea for improving what you do you should celebrate and promote that idea with everything you have. They don't have to be giant, billion-dollar ideas. If they move your company forward, even if only by inches or pennies, then they are worth doing. Dogfish Head has successfully incorporated a number of killer apps into our daily business practices, and we are a much stronger company for it. Neither of the following examples from our company cost that much to implement, but both led us to the strong competitive position we enjoy in our niche market today.

By 2000 our restaurant-brewery was already established and successful and our distributing craft brewery was moving in the right direction toward profitability. We had begun to establish a reputation for innovation and over-the-top, self-created beer styles. While most of our more successful brands like Chicory Stout and Raison D'Etre were aggressive in taste and alcohol content, they were not necessarily aggressively hopped. As I mentioned in the Sierra Nevada example, hoppy beers have become a booming style within the craft brewing niche. In addition to their trailblazing example of the style, by the late 1990s small breweries like Rogue, Russian River, and BridgePort were making really hoppy, aggressive India pale ales—a variation of a regular pale ale that contains more hops and a higher level of alcohol. The style evolved in Britain during the time that India was still part of the royal empire. Kegs of beer were shipped from England to India to slake the thirst of fellow countrymen stationed in that distant country. In early attempts, the beer arrived in poor shape. Through trial and error (or call it evolution) British brewers found that the more hops and alcohol they brewed their beers with, the better the odds that it would arrive in India in a drinkable state. They didn't have scientific proof back then but they figured out that hops and alcohol both act as preservatives in beer. Hence, the India pale ale style was born.

Back at Dogfish Head I was spending a lot of time thinking about the IPA style and how we could improve it. I knew from reading my trade magazines and roaming around beer stores and distributors that it was a style that was finding mass acceptance from the buyers who care about drinking full-flavored beers. I bought a bunch of American-made IPAs, tried them, and loved them. We had been brewing an apricot-laced version of this style called Aprihop that was both fruity and hoppy, but I wanted to make a more traditional interpretation of the style. I shared different examples with customers and coworkers whose palates I came to trust. I told them I wanted to make an over-the-top hoppy version of an IPA. While people loved the pungent hoppiness of these beers, some sample batches I made had such a pronounced bitterness that they seemed out of balance. I reviewed the technical aspects of brewing not just IPAs but beers in general and stumbled onto my killer app.

For as long as beer has been brewed with hops as an integral ingredient, the method of adding the hops to the beer has remained pretty much the same. Brewers make a few (usually two) additions of hops to the beer as it boils. They add one big dose of hops early in the boiling process to give the beer a bitter taste. They add another amount of hops at the end if they want the beer to have a hoppy or spicy aroma. It seemed to me that making these limited additions in ever larger doses was contributing to the lack of balance I experienced in my test batches. I decided to add smaller amounts of hops more frequently instead of larger doses less frequently, which was the traditional method of making hoppy beers. I know I wasn't the first brewer to stumble across this idea. I'm sure lots of small breweries were doing multiple-hop additions to add the subtle nuances they were looking for in their IPAs, and the companies I mentioned above, as well as dozens of others, were making great IPAs long before Dogfish Head. But I wanted to take this idea of smaller, more frequent additions to the extreme, so I created the concept of continual hopping. I would not add bittering hops early or aroma hops late. Instead I would feed the beer a continual thin stream of hop pellets the entire time it boiled. As I was exploring options for executing this idea in a brewery with an annual cap-ex budget that amounted to a few cases of duct tape and some used stainless steel pipe, I found my killer app.

One of the big toy companies used to make a vibrating, tabletop football game with plastic football players that was a popular toy in the 1970s. Do you remember this thing? There was always that one plastic player that just did endless 360s in the corner of the end zone. I found one in a Goodwill store and realized it would be the perfect tool for exploring my theory of continual hopping. I attached the vibrating game surface to a perforated 5-gallon bucket that I filled with hop pellets. I brewed a batch of IPA and as it came to a boil I angled this contraption over the brewing tank and pressed the on button for the football game. Sure enough, the vibration caused the hop pellets to shake out of the bucket and roll slowly down the game board surface into the boiling beer. By angling the game board, I controlled how fast the hops went into the beer. I angled it so that one pellet of hops dropped off the game board every second or so. Two weeks later the beer went on tap and I knew instantly that the idea of continual hopping was now a reality. The beer that was dosed with a slow, steady stream of hops was outrageously hoppy without being overly bitter. Our killer app was born from a $5 thrift store purchase. Of course the football game got wet during the brew and never worked again. Soon after the test batch I designed a more industrial version of this machine with the very technical name "Sir Hops Alot" that sits over our boil kettle and feeds a steady stream of hops into our IPAs.

I've spent a lot of time and energy explaining to the consumer and the beer press how our continual-hopping method works. People now understand that only our IPAs are hopped for the entire time that the beer boils. In fact our IPAs refer to the killer app right in the brand's name. We make a 60 Minute IPA as well as stronger versions named 90 and 120 Minute. The time referenced in the names refers to how long the beer boils and how long we continually hop the beer. It also alludes to the alcohol content and International Bittering Units in each beer as well. The fact that continually hopping truly works was further confirmed when *Esquire* wrote that our 90 Minute IPA is "probably the best IPA in America" and the *Wall Street Journal* recently called our 60 Minute IPA the most balanced they've tasted. I like to think they are both right. The real proof is evidenced in the sales trends we have seen since we began making these beers. The 60 Minute IPA is now our best-selling beer, and 90 Minute is our fastest-growing style. Having started brewing these beers in 10 gallon batches, I'm still awestruck when I walk out onto our production floor and see seven 6,000 gallon tanks filled with 60 Minute IPA, and yet we're still having a hard time keeping up with demand.

As you are considering potential killer apps for your own company you must be patient. Any innovation is a trial-and-error process and you usually only have one shot to introduce an innovative product the right way. Test. Improve. Test. Improve. The Wright brothers made so many trips between their launch site at Kitty Hawk and their workshop in Dayton to fine-tune their Flyer that I'm surprised they didn't invent Easy Pass before they successfully completed the first manned flight. I have seen a couple of breweries over the years come out with exciting-sounding beers only to be disappointed upon tasting them. As someone who believes firmly in the quality of beers being made by smaller breweries in this country, I often give an initially disappointing beer another shot and I'm frequently surprised to find that it tastes better than when it first comes out. But the average customer who has no connection to our industry will probably not be that forgiving. I'm confident that this situation describes the same reality in most other industries. Before bringing your innovative product or service to market, test it under an array of environments and with a selection of potential customers to make sure the bugs are worked out. Take the time to make sure you do it right the first time. The saying is: God is in the details. . . . The saying is not: God 2.0 is in the details.

PROMOTING INNOVATION WITHIN THE COMPANY

While I was fortunate to stumble upon the idea for "Sir Hops Alot," an invention that helped Dogfish Head quicken the pace of our growth, most of our success is due to the innovations that we champion at every level in our company. Invention is usually a solitary pursuit but innovation is a social pursuit. An innovative company is way more powerful than an inventive man. As a small-business owner you should incorporate a high level of attention to innovation throughout your company. It was your great ideas that got you into business in the first place, but it will be the great ideas of your coworkers (as much as your own) that will keep you growing into the future.

The best way to create an environment conducive to innovation within your company is to take the time to listen to the ideas that the people around you have. You will naturally be biased into thinking you know better than anyone what is good for your company. You'd be surprised what you could learn if you listen to the ideas of the committed coworkers around you. When you innovate and encourage innovation in others, you send a powerful message to everyone in the company about what is important. Implementing innovative ideas that are not your own demonstrates that your company rewards solutions to problems and not just the identification of problems. How many times have you spoken with a coworker who tells you about something that doesn't work at the company. You want to help figure out a solution. Sometimes you can and it makes you feel good but sometimes you are unable to and become exasperated. The best interaction comes when coworkers tell you of a problem at the company and then tell you how they fixed it.

Innovation need not be as complicated as developing a new style of beer, method of brewing, or invention to move the company forward. Innovation can be as simple as finding a way to store more of your products in a limited available space. Mike Eufemia, our warehouse manager, was running out of space for the ever increasing pallets of beer that were coming off our bottling line. They needed to be stored somewhere before being loaded onto trucks, and we just didn't have the space for our growing volume of beer. Mike's solution was to put 60 cases of beer onto each pallet instead of the usual 70. This might sound like a step in the wrong direction—less beer on each pallet means more pallets for the same amount of beer. But Mike also took the time to measure the height of our warehouse ceiling and the height of different pallet-case stack configurations. He figured out that we could get 3 pallets of 60 cases of beer stacked on top of each other instead of 2 pallets of 70 cases like we had done all along. That means we could store 180 cases of beer into the same space we used to put 140 cases. This additional 40 cases' worth of space made a huge difference in our warehousing logistics. Mike identified the problem, and Mike found an innovative way to fix it.

Every company large and small is confronted with problems. When employees show an ability to find solutions for their problems that benefit the whole company, then you have an innovative company. Everyone is capable of having good ideas. You want to encourage and promote the people in your company who are as capable of executing good ideas as they are at having them.

INNOVATION THAT STARTS OUTSIDE THE COMPANY

Another example of a Dogfish Head killer app is equally unorthodox as the New Coke–Classic Coke phenomenon in that its success was dictated as much by our customers as it was by ourselves. Since we opened our doors in 1995 we have worked hard to extend the Dogfish Head brand name into as many related and relevant products as possible. In addition to beer we make soda, rum, vodka, gin, even our own beer ice cream. All are made with the highest quality ingredients and their own nontraditional recipes. I'm constantly trying to orient my coworkers toward thinking of Dogfish Head not as a company that sells beer or food or whatever but as a company that sells a significant, valuable, and innovative experience. When our company was nothing more than a business plan and a logo, the idea of a Dogfish Head Experience sounded like delusions of grandeur. Today it is a growing, albeit still small, reality that is grounded on a continuing theme of innovation. The Dogfish Head Experience is now based on a body of work—our product line. The diversity of this product line, their off-centered bloodlines, and the high level of quality and value that each item shares, are the main defining elements of our brand. But sometimes it's difficult to figure out exactly where a new product fits within the Dogfish Head Experience.

In the late 1990s I was in the shampoo aisle of the grocery store when I had a solid gold 1980s flashback. A television commercial for a shampoo called Body on Tap came back to me in a wave of nostalgia. This was a shampoo that was supposedly made with beer. I did some research on the Internet when I got home that night and found that there was some validity to the idea of using beer in your hair. Beer is very rich in nutrients, especially protein—stuff that truly will make your hair more healthy and shiny. I began experimenting with a home soap-making kit. We would boil a reduction sauce of beer, and then add shea butter and olive oil to solidify the mixture into a manageable bar. First attempts worked, but upon using them you literally ended up smelling like a brewery. We figured out an appropriate amount of natural, essential oils like lavender and tea tree to add and came up with a workable recipe.

We worked with a local soap maker to produce bars of beer shampoo and beer soap in volume. The soap is made with our Chicory Stout and has chunks of grain in it for exfoliation. The shampoo is made from our pale ale and includes the tea tree oil. We launched the soaps in limited supplies on our web site, in our pubs, and with a local, forward-thinking chain of beauty salons called Bad Hair Day. The success was immediate if limited. *Jane,* the fashion magazine, did a small piece on the shampoo and orders rolled into our web site. Some people swore off other soaps and shampoos altogether upon trying ours, claiming an immediate improvement in the feel and manageability of their hair. But we found that sales reached a stagnant plateau of 50 bars or so per month. Then we received an intriguing phone call.

A woman called the brewery in a barely coherent fit of panic. She needed two bars of our shampoo, and she needed them by tomorrow morning. She told us that she had professional show dogs and that she had experimented with dozens of dog and animal shampoos but nothing worked as well as our stuff. She needed one bar for herself and one for her dogs. We told her we would send her one of the bars for free if she gave out another half dozen free bars to other top-ranked dog showers—or whatever they are called. She asked if it would be okay if she only gave them out after the next day's show and only to people who did not have dogs competing against her breed. A deal was struck. Sure enough her dog came in first in his category and second best in show. True to her word, she shared the samples with some of her friends after her show. Within weeks we received dozens of orders from dog groomers across the country. Our soaps and shampoos became a hit in the dog community because they are made with all-natural ingredients and actually work. Of course I'm sure the fact that our company is named Dogfish Head didn't hurt. My black lab, Phoebe, swears by the stuff and uses it after every evening dip in the harbor in front of our house.

Beer shampoo and soap sales at dogfish.com continue to climb. Of course it is kind of awkward to market a product to people and dogs. It seems to work, though. As you can see, the true success in finding the killer app for this product was tied to our ability to listen to our customers. Some killer apps evolve out of blood, sweat, and tears. Some, like our continual-hopping technique, arrive in moments of inspirations. Still others, such as our pooch-friendly beauty products or the successful failed launch of New Coke, are directed by the customer. Whatever the source, shape, or size of your killer app, it is important to bring it to market with every bit of attention and energy you can muster. It's easy to throw all of your passion and resourcefulness behind an innovative idea of your own creation, but make sure you bring an equal sense of purpose toward implementing the ideas of your coworkers that are sound enough to try. You will be sending a mixed message if you only half-heartedly embrace the ideas of those around you. But if coworkers witness the boss getting as excited about their idea as they do and then following through to make sure it gets a fair trial, then they and everyone around them will truly believe that they work at an innovative company. Not all innovative ideas will work—yours or your coworkers. If an innovative idea was meant to succeed it will, and if it wasn't it won't.

An innovative idea will only succeed if the customer can understand and quantify the difference between the experience your product delivers and their experience with the products that came before yours. You can't resist change, but rather than be swept along as unexpected changes happen to you, you can spearhead efforts to be innovative, create change, and determine your own direction.

Victor Hugo once said, "An invasion of armies can be resisted, but not an idea whose time has come." As a small businessperson enamored with the pursuit of the killer app, I believe these are words to live by.

OUR DUEL WITH DUALISM

When you take a risk, try something innovative, and it fails, you might be less likely to take a risk again. Hopefully you will realize that what you learn from your failures will inform your next success. As a result of our own misfires we have even stumbled upon an innovative way to innovate at Dogfish Head. Innovate in pairs. It takes a lot of guts to try something new, and experience has taught me that if you are going to try something new you might as well try two things new at the same time. Dualism is the theory that there are two primal principles: mind and body, female and male, yin and yang, country and western. The two principles are usually opposing but interrelated. Dogfish Head has used a dualistic approach in everything from product development to the ongoing analysis of the evolution of our brand.

The most important yin-yang factor for any small businessperson to recognize and direct is the relationship between how you want your product to be perceived by the marketplace and how (or maybe even if, at the outset) it truly is perceived by the marketplace. There will always be a gap between your perception of your company and that of the consumer. The goal is to always work to close this gap. Before Henry Ford came along, the automobile was considered a luxury item that was manufactured solely for the wealthy. Through his own efforts and vision in redefining the industry, the automobile became a commodity made by the people for the people. When Ford started, there was a tremendous gap between how the consumer viewed the automobile's relevance to everyday life and how Ford envisioned it.

There was a trade advertisement in *Rolling Stone* that I remember from many years ago. It showed the word *perception* above a bunch of hippies playing in the mud at Woodstock on the top half of the page. On the bottom half was the word *reality* and it showed a couple of yuppies enjoying themselves after work. The advertisement was directed at potential advertisers for the magazine. *Rolling Stone* was trying to say, "You have us all wrong, Mr. Procter and Mrs. Gamble; if you advertise in our magazine you will be reaching a coveted, wealthy demographic, not a bunch of burnt-out moochers." When I first saw the ad I thought how cool it would have been if, under the word *reality* they showed a bunch of hippies *and* a bunch of yuppies moshing together in the pit of a punk rock show. I think back on that ad now with my experience in business and recognize that *Rolling Stone* was illustrating a very common marketing dynamic. I've found that the obvious means to gauge your company's progress in the marketplace—like revenue or market share growth—only tell part of the story of how well you are closing the gap. If you are marketing a product, any product, perception is equally as important as reality. I believe that the best barometers for measuring how well you are closing the gap are located in the nuances of dualism.

Cyrus McCormick's father created one of the earliest versions of a reaper, but history remembers his son. The father had the technical genius to develop the product but lacked the marketing genius to sell it. There was a great gap between the father's vision for the reaper's usefulness, and the nineteenth-century farmer's vision of the best way to work his land. The Industrial Revolution would have stalled without the invention, promotion, and democratization of the reaper. Cyrus realized that the battle for belief in his product must be fought on two fronts—reality and perception. The reality side was tackled with tireless trials and demonstrations as he moved around the country to show farmers how the contraption worked and, more important, how much labor could be saved and ground could be covered with the use of the reaper. Seeing is believing. The perception side was covered by Cyrus' recognition of the value in unsolicited testimonials. After witnessing the reaper in action at a public demonstration, the *Virginia Spectator* newspaper printed a glowing review of the machine as a breakthrough tool for modern agriculture, culminating with the sentence, "It is certainly an admirable invention." Cyrus paid for advertising space in other newspapers around the country and ran a reprint of the *Spectator*'s review. The new perception gained from the outside review and the reality of witnessing actual demonstrations led to a boom in reaper sales and a giant step forward for the farming industry. International Harvester, Cyrus McCormick's company, is still recognized today as a leader and innovator in the production of agricultural machinery.

As I review the 10-year-history of accolades, affirmations, and awards that Dogfish Head has received, I can see the gap closing between what I wished the company would become and what it is becoming. I remember a review we received from a regional beer newspaper after we had attended a festival where we showed off our Boothbay Barley Wine. The year was 1996, our second year in business, and the recipe for this beer would eventually morph into the current recipe for Immort Ale, a strong ale aged on oak chips and brewed with peat-smoked barley procured from a whiskey distillery. Like Immort Ale, Boothbay Barley Wine was brewed with maple syrup from my father's farm in western Massachusetts, juniper berries, and vanilla beans. The newspaper did a best-of-show awards roundup for the festival and named Boothbay Barley Wine "weirdest beer." The review was neither positive nor negative; it just stated the ingredients and ended with a "what will they think of next" nod to our company. So that was the earliest unsolicited perception of Boothbay Barley Wine.

Flash-forward two years, our production brewery is now separated from our restaurant brewery and we are bottling three year-round beers: Shelter Pale Ale, Chicory Stout, and Immort Ale. An editor at *Wine Enthusiast,* a niche publication catering to the high-end wine lover, tried our Chicory Stout and Immort Ale and wrote an article in which he said, "These are beers of nuance and style." He particularly liked the Immort Ale for its depth of character and complexity. Over the course of 2 years and 2 articles, we saw the gap between our perception of this beer and that of the marketplace close significantly. We also saw the customer base for all of our beers grow to include wine lovers as well as beer lovers. In those 2 years, sales of Immort Ale quadrupled and there are now a number of beers that are aged on oak or use maple syrup as an ingredient on the market. We never thought what we were doing was weird—different or interesting definitely, but not weird. It took a couple of years before how we perceived Immort Ale aligned with how it was perceived by the consumer.

The history of the Midas Touch beer is a great example of the closing gap between the perception and reality of Dogfish Head. When we were first asked to make the beer we assumed we would brew it only one time, for the recreation of the King Midas Feast that was held at the University of Pennsylvania in Philadelphia. There is another business-dualism factor that plays into the story of Midas: love and money. They are usually interrelated and yet can be opposing factors in the face of hard business decisions. With Midas we knew it would be one of the most expensive beers ever brewed, but we also knew it was a project we would love to tackle. The molecular archaeologist, Patrick McGovern, had analyzed the residue on crockery found in a tomb in Turkey believed to hold the remains of King Midas, and found evidence of a beverage brewed with white grapes, thyme honey, and barley. Obviously this was a very special beer brewed as a focal point of the funereal feast for a very special king. When Dr. McGovern asked our little brewery to produce a version of this beer for the dinner, we knew he was approaching the project from a much more scientific angle than we did. He asked if we had a lab in which we could perform some studies on test batches. I assured him we did and we got the nod to proceed. Back then we didn't have the money for test batches much less sophisticated lab equipment. So we bit the bullet, bought all of the expensive ingredients, and brewed a single, full-scale batch of Midas Touch. Our lab test went off better than we even imagined it would; my black lab retriever, Phoebe, really enjoyed the beer. Mission accomplished.

With the testing phase behind us we drove a keg of Midas Touch to the dinner in Philadelphia. The room was filled with art lovers, archeologists, foodies, and wine enthusiasts. The beer was paired with a lamb stew that was also based on molecular evidence found in the tomb. Midas Touch was the hit of the dinner. A number of people came up to our table to congratulate us on the unique and remarkable beer-wine-mead we had made. Within weeks *Food & Wine* and *People* magazines did stories on Midas Touch. Our phone rang off the hook with calls from people who wanted to know where they could buy the beer. We went from thinking we would only make this very expensive beer once to realizing that the demand necessitated getting it into the bottle as soon as possible and selling it as a year-round brand.

While the media attention we received for Midas Touch was invaluable, sales grew steadily but at nowhere near the pace of our other beers. While it was unique and exotic and the beer paired beautifully with grilled fish and spicy food, it was hard to get the beer world as excited as the wine enthusiasts seemed to be. So sales plodded along. Midas Touch had its faithful followers but it was soon our lowest volume year-round beer and the interest level stagnated. This all changed in 2004 as the beer community suddenly took notice of Midas Touch. In April the beer won the silver medal in the Word Beer Cup: the largest international beer judging event with over 40 countries and 1,400 beers represented. In September Midas Touch won the gold medal at the Great American Beer Festival for the honey beer category; and it won gold again at the Mead Festival in Colorado in November.

It's great that we have won so many medals so suddenly for Midas Touch. The gold medal at the Great American Beer Festival is recognized as one of the highest honors in our industry. We had entered numerous other beers in this contest over the last few years but we've never won a medal before. We realized that it would be difficult for us to win any medals because none of our beers are brewed in accordance with any of the style guidelines. As much as any beer we make, Midas represents the best of what we do at Dogfish Head—creating a new and enjoyable interpretation of a traditional product. I was very proud of our brewers when we won those awards but I had to laugh at the irony, too. Legend had it that King Midas was buried in a tomb resplendent with gold when in fact all he was buried with was the remains of a heady funeral feast to sustain him on his journey to the afterworld. A couple of thousand years later Midas finally delivered on the legend and brought forth gold to our brewery. It's funnier still that our most highly awarded beer is the slowest selling one in our portfolio of year-round brands. The excitement has been rekindled but I know that sales of Midas Touch will never catch those of our 60 Minute IPA or our Raison D'Etre. That's okay with me because making this beer is more a labor of love than a means to wealth and riches. It's amazing to witness the closing of the gap between the perception of Midas Touch the first time that we brewed it and what it had grown into after winning so many highly coveted awards. Immort Ale started as a beer that was brewed for beer lovers and found a new niche with wine drinkers. Midas Touch started as a beer that was brewed for wine lovers and found a new level of appreciation from beer lovers and judges the world over. Along the way both beers helped to close the gap between what we wanted Dogfish Head to be and how the consumer perceived us. It's now much more accepted to brew beers with nontraditional ingredients than it was when we brewed our first beer with maple syrup 10 years ago. As I reread recent articles on Dogfish Head I see adjectives like *innovative* and *adventurous* are used more frequently than the *crazy* and *weird* labels we used to get. More than anything, from this closing of the gap I can tell we are headed in the right direction.

It's important to recognize and explore the most relevant dualisms that affect your business. I'm sure they are out there. The closing of the gap between your own perception and the public reality of your company is something all small businesspeople need to be engaged in. Making a better product is only half of the equation for success; the other half is marketing it better. Marketing, in its broadest definition, is the bridge between the reality and perception of what you do. A simple and revealing means of identifying the gap between the perception and reality of your company is initiating a program of customer feedback cards. These are great tools to gauge how well you are servicing your customer but they can also be great tools to identify the gaps between perception and reality. We use ours to get feedback on straightforward questions like, "How was your meal?" and "How was your service?" But we also ask gap-defining questions like, "What is your favorite Dogfish Head beer," "What other beer brands do you drink regularly," and "How did you hear about us?" From questions like these you begin to understand how the perception of your company differs from the reality. For instance, if the majority of answers are "Budweiser" to the question "What other beer brands do you drink regularly," it would show a frightfully huge gap between what I want Dogfish Head to be and what it actually is. Thankfully, I've only ever heard this response once and it turned out to be a brewer friend who was in town and just trying to get my attention. Cyrus McCormick, the founder of International Harvester, recognized two tools to help him build the bridge between perception and reality: product demonstrations and reprinting unsolicited testimonials. I recognized two different paths for beer and wine drinkers on the bridge between the reality and perception of our Immort Ale and Midas Touch beers. It's funny how great business ideas often come in pairs.

DUAL PRODUCT RELEASE

For any small business the cost of bringing a new product to market can be exorbitant. All of the energy expended in introducing something new can be defrayed if you bring out two products at the same time. When you work through each phase of product development—packaging, recipe formulation, costing, distribution—you learn that it does not take anywhere near twice the effort (read money) to introduce two products as it does for one.

Aside from the hard costs associated with a product rollout, there are countless timing considerations to be factored into the product launch. For instance, in the beer industry you need to get label approval before you can produce one beer. This process allows the federal government to make sure you don't put any false claims or profanity on your label. The government also has a more stringent definition of beer than we do at Dogfish Head. In other words, they like to see labels where the only ingredients are barley, yeast, hops, and water. Of course they make an exception for the big breweries who like to add a lot of rice and corn into their beers to keep costs down. When the paperwork for one of our beers comes across their desks I imagine flashing emergency lights and bells go off throughout the rows of cubicles. All of the nontraditional ingredients and methods that we like to add to our beers need a lot of explaining. In addition to the normal label approval process that we all must go through, we usually have to submit an additional statement of process that shows how and where and in what volumes we are adding the specialty ingredients. This process can take upwards of 3 months and involves more specialists and lawyers than I would care to list. I don't really blame them for paying so much attention. I would hate to be the federal labeling specialist who approved "Tear Yer Arse Lager (brewed with three different kinds of turpentine)" by accident. But we have found that when we send in more than one label at a time it often takes less time than when we send in just one. There is strength in numbers, and once they realize that we are trying to make great, unique beers that rarely involve turpentine I think they actually get a kick out of reading about the different ingredients and methods we use.

Once we knew there was enough interest in our Midas Touch beer for us to bottle it, the next challenge was charging a price that would make it worth our while to produce. Thyme honey, white muscat grapes, and saffron don't exactly grow on trees. Well, I guess a couple of them do actually grow on trees and vines, but the point is these ingredients are extremely expensive compared to those used in traditional beers. I decided that since this beer had so much of the character and ingredients of wine it should be packaged and marketed like a wine—in a cork-finished champagne bottle. Of course our bottling equipment was only set up to accommodate traditional 12 ounce beer bottles. So we had to search all over Napa Valley to find used wine bottling equipment that would serve our needs and meet our budget. In order to package it the way we wanted, we had to get a rinser, a corker, a wire hooder, and a labeler. The stuff we found barely worked and wasn't as cheap as we'd hoped. To defray the cost of the new used equipment I decided we would launch a sister product in the same packaging. So now the inventory of corks, case boxes, bottles, and hoods could be shared by two products. Along with Midas Touch, we launched 90 Minute Imperial IPA in the corked wine bottles as well.

We had been brewing our 60 Minute IPA with our proprietary continual-hopping method for a couple of years as a draft-only product and sales were escalating. The 90 Minute would be a bigger, bolder version, with even more hops and more alcohol. I knew the Midas Touch would be sweet and light on the palate and would appeal primarily to wine drinkers so I wanted to make a yin to its yang: 90 Minute Imperial IPA was more bitter and intensely flavored to appeal to true beer geeks like us. Midas Touch had a fancy label with a golden thumbprint and a lot of verbiage that told its interesting historical story. For the 90 Minute I found this really cool picture of a circus freak in some old book that I thought would perfectly summarize the experience of drinking the beer. It showed this old guy with a leather bomber hat, jamming a big nail up his nose with a hammer. His neck and arm muscles are bulging from the effort. I thought, this is exactly how it feels to take the first sip of a beer this intense. I figured this old photograph in my pile of old photographs was one that I got from The Library of Congress along with the others we used in our advertising. The photographers whose pictures are in those files are long gone and their work is in public domain so it can be used without copyright.

We released Midas Touch and 90 Minute Imperial IPA simultaneously. Our distributors were happy to get two beers in the same, big bottle format. Our retailers brought both in at once with 90 Minute sneaking in on the coattails of the much hyped Midas. By having two similarly packaged beers on the shelf next to one another we created a billboard effect and increased the visual profile of Dogfish Head substantially. Of course Midas Touch initially outsold 90 Minute by a long shot, but within a year 90 Minute was outselling Midas as hop-heads (freaks like our brewers and me who have never met a beer that was hoppy enough) made 90 Minute a cult favorite in the beer enthusiast circles.

Our decision to launch two brands at once worked perfectly, sort of. Both beers received national attention and helped to close the gap between our perception of Dogfish Head Brewery and the reality of the market-place. Midas retailed for $10 per bottle. A price point that was almost unheard of in the beer industry when it was released in 1999. Of course there were a couple of hiccups along the way. It seems that the theory of dualism works for the bad as well as the good. The equipment we were using for corking couldn't keep up with demand.

I also realized that the photograph of the circus freak was not in public domain when the artist who shot it called me. He wasn't all that dead, and he turned out to be really cool. His name is Joel Peter Witkin and he's an amazing and successful fine arts photographer. Someone told him about a story on our beer in *Esquire* that featured his photograph on the label. He was less moved that the publication called the beer that his artwork graced "probably the best I.P.A. in America" and more moved by the fact that I had never asked his approval to use the photograph. I explained that I thought he was dead, which only made the conversation more awkward. He was finally very gracious and said that if I sent him a couple of cases of the beer for his private collection and an impending gallery show, and promised not to use it again, he would let it go. As I do now, I had more beer than lawyer money so I was glad to accommodate. Like Midas, 90 Minute is now available in 12 ounce bottles. We still do some special limited-release beers in cork-finished wine bottles like Pangaea and Fort, but we are brewing nearly 2,000 cases a week of 90 Minute. If we had to cork all of that by hand I'm pretty sure my whole staff would have mutinied by now. Midas sales have really increased since we won all of those awards but 90 Minute sales are off the charts. It is now our second-best-selling beer out of 20 styles. Number one is 60 Minute IPA. Number two is 90 Minute IPA. I'd like to point out that the fact that our two best-selling beers are two different IPAs is another example of the dualistic reality of the business universe. I'd like to but I can't. We make a third IPA, 120 Minute that is the strongest IPA in the world and also sells really well for us at $150 per case. I guess I better get cracking on exploring the theory of tri-ism.

Think of your own products and everything it takes to bring them to market with the limited budget you have. Conception, packaging, advertis-ing, distribution—if all of the costs associated with a launch can be shared between two brands instead of shouldered by a single product, the launch itself can be more affordable and the products more sustainable. Call it the Noah's Ark theory of product launch.

By introducing two brands at once you also greatly reduce the possibility of failure. If one product underperforms and the other exceeds expectations your risk has been substantially reduced. If you just have one product that comes out and sucks wind, you look like you don't know what you are doing. That's not good. If you release two at once and one succeeds you can quietly bury the failure while celebrating the success.

As the owner of a small company, innovation should be a thread that is woven through all aspects of your business: product development, marketing, logistics, advertising, and so on. You may not think of yourself as an inventor but you are once you've invented your own company. The need for inventiveness is secondary to the need for innovation if your company consists of more than one person. As I've said you can invent alone, but innovation is a social process that involves you, your coworkers, and your customers. Be open to any and all inspirations toward innovation, as the best ones often come from the most unlikely of sources. The testing and improving stages that come before launching an innovative idea are critical. However, the most important thing is to remember that the successful small businessperson must embrace the risk that goes hand-in-hand with innovation in order to construct a company that truly stands out from the competition.

chapter 9

SELLING DISTINCTION, SPECIALIZATION, AND VARIETY

In hindsight it is clear that we opened our production brewery at the worst possible moment in the short history of microbreweries.

After 5 straight years of 40 percent or more annual growth, the microbrewery sector lapsed into a zero-growth industry pretty much overnight. The romantic story of small breweries and the successful public offerings from Sam Adams and Redhook had infused the once-boutique industry with an exciting sheen within the business world. Suddenly everyone and their brother were opening breweries. Not to make beer but to make money. In time their lack of passion for brewing became self-evident.

By 1997, many small breweries were struggling to stay open. There was only a finite amount of shelf space, and all of these small breweries were fighting for it. Dogfish Head had an additional barrier to success that the other small breweries did not: our focus on unusual beers at an ultra-premium price. Our first three bottled products were Shelter Pale Ale, Chicory Stout (brewed with chicory, coffee, and licorice), and Immort Ale (brewed with maple syrup, vanilla beans, and juniper berries). Some of these beers retailed for twice the price of the average six-pack of micro-brewed beer and nearly four times as much as generic canned beer. This pricing was pretty much unheard of back in 1997.

Many consumers did not understand that paying more for a six-pack of really good, all-grain, handmade beer might be worth the difference in price. They had not realized that the diversity of styles of beer that we brewed could accompany different foods perfectly and have as much depth and character as the finest wines in the world. However, as recently as the

1970s many people didn't understand how one bottle of chardonnay could cost twice as much as the bottle next to it on the very same shelf. The American wine industry has done a great job of educating the general public about their product. Since then, dozens of small, artisanal wineries within the United States have worked hard to bring the quality of their wines up to world-class standards. They have differentiated themselves further from their old-world counterparts by focusing on special varieties of grapes or advanced production methods that create wines unique from, yet equally as good as, those being made abroad. They educated their customers as to why making small batches of high-quality and distinct wine costs more so that their customers understand why they are charged more for their wines.

For whatever reason people began to understand that a great bottle of chardonnay could justifiably command twice the price of a mediocre bottle, yet many of those same people did not yet see how one beer could be worth four times the price of another. I had my work cut out for me. Not only did I have to sell our beer in the most competitive environment in the history of our industry but I had to educate people on why our beer was worth the extra money.

While it wasn't easy I was encouraged to find a small but passionate faction of beer enthusiasts who were starting to acknowledge our efforts. It was still years before we reached profitability, but even then I knew we had the right idea.

SUCCESS IN SELLING

The best way to create a successful business is to provide a product or service that nobody even knows they need until you come along to sell it. Bringing a technological breakthrough to market is very different from a line extension or a new size package of an existing product. The more often you can create an entirely new product category (as opposed to slight variations on existing competing products), the better your odds for success.

The benefit in this approach is that when you have defined a new product category you can set the price and the standard. If yours is a small business, odds are you can't compete on price and, unless you are independently wealthy, you can't spend your way to create an identity through advertising and marketing. So your best option for creating success is to create a product or service so distinct and so relevant that your customers will fight through the mass media and marketing to find you. The less outside influence incorporated into your brand the more distinct your own identity will be. You will find a way to get your message out if you believe in it enough.

We have had a number of successes using this approach at both the brewery and the pub, and our core customers' continued interest in these groundbreaking products reinforces our desire to continue to innovate. Things are a lot clearer for us now than they were when we were still trying to figure out who we were and who we were marketing ourselves to. At Dogfish Head we produce almost three times as many year-round beers as the other small breweries that are in our marketplace. We established long ago that we would center our value proposition on our notion of providing "Off-centered ales for off-centered people." But in order to effectively sell our beer we have to break it down even further and figure out which of our off-centered beers appeal to which people and why. We would never be able to do this if we didn't take the time to understand our customers. Since we do not sell our beers directly to the end user, our list of customers includes not only the end consumer who buys our beer, but the retailer who sells it to them and the distributor who sells it to the retailer. We understand that each faction of our audience has different needs, and the selling points for Dogfish Head beer are customized not only for each entity we sell to but we break it down to specific selling points for specific beer styles for specific customers. For instance, our distributors like to sell our World Wide Stout because, as an extremely expensive beer, it brings them a much higher dollar contribution for profit. Our retailer likes to sell this beer because it is a specialized, seasonal variety that gives them something unique to promote within their store. Our consumer likes to buy this beer because, being stronger than your average wine, it will age extremely well and they will buy a few bottles and put some in their wine cellars to experience how each vintage changes as it ages. We take the time to dissect, delineate, and promote every facet of the experience of our beers. Through promotional materials and the knowledge of our sales force, any customer at any level can know not only what the beer tastes like, but what glassware it should be served in, how well it ages, what wines it would replace with a meal, and what foods it would accompany well.

TEACHING THE VALUE OF YOUR BUSINESS

Back in 1997, the community of people who appreciated better beer was still in its nascent form. At first there were not enough of these like-minded beer drinkers to pay the bills, but their numbers were growing.

Back then I *was* the sales department. I would drive our little delivery truck from one city to another, unload the three pallets of beers at the distributor's warehouse, head out on the road to sample our beers to potential customers, and finish the day with a beer dinner at a bar or restaurant. I remember driving 7 hours from Delaware to Pittsburgh for such a day. Exactly nine people showed up for the beer dinner that evening. I was pretty dejected at the outset of the dinner but I got to talk about our beers with people that were excited to try them, and by the end of the dinner all nine of them were singing the praises of Dogfish Head beer. I drove back to Delaware convinced we were onto something despite the fact that I had to pull over every 3 hours and sell T-shirts at rest stops for the toll and gas money needed to make it home.

As a small company it is especially important to err on the side of sharing too much information. Today's consumer is more cautious because he is more knowledgeable. The more knowledge you can share, the more you will break through that caution and into a position of trust. I believe you should offer as many choices as you can competently produce and clearly delineate. You will know if your product line is too complicated because your consumer will voice confusion. Communication is critical, as you need to be clear on what you are offering, what it will deliver in terms of buyer satisfaction, and how frequently your buyer will realistically repeat the purchase.

If what you sell is truly valuable, then the initial sale will always be the hardest. Once the customer understands and appreciates your product's value, subsequent purchases will need less involvement from your sales force. If your key customers are happy with their experience with your products, they will tell other people whose philosophy and standards are similar to their own and they will be a more effective sales force than anyone on your payroll.

We see this every time we introduce a new seasonal product at Dogfish Head. The first year that we launch the beer is always the hardest. Not many people really embrace change. We make sure that the first time we release something, there is not enough of it to satisfy demand. This sounds crazy, and we certainly are missing some sales opportunities every time we do this. But ours is not a commodity market and by not satisfying demand initially we create more demand for the future.

KNOW YOUR CUSTOMER

As you work to stretch the edges of a niche industry you must always do so with your core constituent in mind. At Dogfish Head, this constituent is made up of ourselves first, meaning all of the people who work for our company, and our key customers second. Recognizing a key customer is easy at our brewpub. These are the people who walk through the door to sit at the bar or a table to have something to eat and drink.

The definition of a key customer is a little broader at our brewery. The vast majority of the beer made is sold to distributors who in turn sell it to retailers who sell it to consumers. The people who work for our company are our employees, and beyond them, the distributors and retailers, as well.

Part of our success is that we've recognized that these key customers, the early adapters, exist in every step of this threefold process. First we must make a unique and interesting beer. Then we must convince the distributor why this beer is worth selling. Next we work with the distributor to convince the retailer. We then work with the distributor and the retailer to convince the consumer why the beer is worth buying. All of this convincing boils down to two simple things: education and experience. We must educate each and every one of these key customers on the value of our products, and we must get them to try the products for themselves so that they believe in the value and can help us spread the word.

Beyond those audiences I really don't focus on what and if the rest of the world thinks of us. That said, there's nothing I care more about than keeping these two core audiences excited and faithful to Dogfish Head. Don't get me wrong, I am all for expanding the pool of key customers. But I don't have the time or interest in trying to impress, pander, or lie to the people who don't understand the full-flavored beer, full-flavored food, or five-sense experience when they enter our brewery or one of our pubs, because that's what Dogfish Head is all about.

We will never be a mass-marketed brand; we are not generic enough. That doesn't mean we are great or destined to succeed; it only means that our ideals are not always aligned with those of Wal-Mart's key customer. Dogfish Head will never appeal to everyone. Relative to how many beer drinkers there are in the world, not many people know about our beer, but those who do really like it, appreciate it, and tell their friends about it, too. This is why I place less faith in the institution of advertising than I do in public relations.

Dogfish Head's targeted key customers don't pay attention to mass-market advertising. They care more about enriching their lives with people, products, and places of the highest quality and distinction. They recognize that, because they expect high quality, they do not even need to wade through the hundreds of advertising messages they are confronted with each day. They don't want to be told why a product is great so much as they want to experience why a product is great for themselves. These are the early adapters that Dogfish Head has always catered to and recognized as key customers. They look for an experience outside the norm, and if that something is better than the norm they are willing to pay more for it.

NAME YOUR PRICE

Whatever your business, you are most likely working in an industry dominated by giants, and charging a premium for your product. At least I hope you are because if you're not I don't see how you can survive. I'm no financial guru, but it's highly unlikely that you have the economies of scale enjoyed by your big competitors. Let them fight among themselves using discounting and price wars; it's a battle you can't win. But that is a good thing. When you can't win on quantity you are forced to win on quality. This means you must charge more in order to provide the quality that differentiates you from the crowd. This means that the consumer with the lowest expectations is not in your targeted demographic (he's behind a dumpster shotgunning a 16 ounce can of generic light beer). This also means that your ideal consumer probably wouldn't believe your advertising even if you could afford to get it in front of her. She's too smart.

COMPETITION: SETTING YOURSELF UP TO HAVE NONE

From industry to industry examples abound on how to successfully find a niche in an industry dominated by giant competitors. The big music labels think in terms of millions of listeners; the independent artist thinks in terms of one listener—the actual artist. The superstore thinks in terms of millions of consumers; the mom-and-pop shop, in terms of the individual customer. If your message-product-service-art is true to yourself and pertinent to other people, you have to do everything within your power to sustain it. Think of the independent musician who writes and records her own music on her own equipment, then books her own shows, tours in her own van, and designs and sells her own T-shirts. Think of the sense of accomplishment that this musician must feel when she creates a following. Think of how much more real, organic, and solid her success will be considering the grassroots nature of its arrival. She wasn't foisted upon the public. She foisted her bad self. She is an exact reflection of the product she is selling.

A recent example of this reality in the music world involves the band Wilco. Formed from the ashes of the seminal alternative-country band, Uncle Tupelo, and led by the excellent, if idiosyncratic, songwriter Jeff Tweedy, Wilco released a number of tepidly received albums in the 1990s on Warner Bros. Records. They were always the critics' darling whose album sales underwhelmed the powers that be at the label because, while they showed the potential to create a melodic, Top 40 radio hit, they lacked the desire to do so. Preferring to make challenging but beautiful music that satisfied themselves and a devoted but marginal (in numbers) fan base. The money Wilco earned through record sales and touring was not nearly as crucial to them as the opportunity for artistic expression. In 2002 after turning in yet another unorthodox album, *Yankee Hotel Foxtrot,* their label dropped them and let them take the album they made for free. Wilco took a grassroots approach and got the songs on the album directly to their fans via concerts and their web site. This created a buzz in the music industry, which resulted in a bidding war between labels to sign Wilco. The label that finally signed the band and released the album *Reprise* was actually a subsidiary of Warner Bros. So essentially Warner Bros. paid for the record twice. The album was released to critical acclaim due in part to the media attention on the David versus Goliath nature of their record label negotiations. If Wilco just released the album through the unenthused Warner Bros., it would not have been marketed well and would not have sold as well regardless of how brilliant an album it is.

The music industry and beer industry are strikingly similar. In the beer industry, this is precisely the same battle that small brewers face every day.

Three major breweries sell over 80 percent of the beer being consumed in this country. Five major record companies sell over 70 percent of the records being made in this country. The consolidation and culling-out of stylistic diversity within both industries occurred at the same time.

Not only do the three dominating conglomerates sell over 80 percent of the beer in this country, they exercise significant control over the distribution of beer on both the wholesale and the retail level. At Dogfish Head our beer has to be pushed through distribution because not too many people know about our beers. We are part of the alternative commerce world.

DEVELOPING A SALES BUDGET

When you are a small but fast-growing company, sales budgets can be strange and nebulous things. Our industry is only about 20 years young, so there isn't a wealth of information about trends. Our industry has gone from 40 percent annual growth, to completely flat, to the 5 percent growth we have experienced most recently. So, as small breweries we're all kind of doing slightly different variations of throwing beers at the refrigerator wall and seeing which ones stick. To compound the challenges in putting a budget together for such a volatile market, our own brewery has had the misfortune of never being able to make enough beer to satisfy orders. In 2004 we estimate that we filled roughly 80 percent of the orders that our distributors placed. But all that tells us is what the distributor would have taken at the times that they placed the orders. It doesn't tell us how much beer the distributors would have taken if we delivered all of the beer they ordered and were actually pushing them to sell more instead of saying sorry for being able to sell them less. You can imagine how much our inability to maintain inventory affected the confidence of the distributor's sales force in our brand. But we honestly didn't think there would be so much demand for our beer and neither did our distributors when we asked for their input on our sales budget. The good news is that our sales force and that of our distributors have seen the heightened consumer interest in our beer and the fact that we have run out so often means our beer is always fresh. We all recognize the potential for continued growth and this year we finally have enough capacity to deliver all of the beer that our distributors can order.

When you are constructing your sales budget, make sure that your sales force is given a lot of responsibility for and input to the budget itself. Our sales managers sit down with each distributor every year and create a budget for the next year based on the previous year's sales volume, brand mix, and mutually agreed upon goals for the coming year. We then construct a company-wide budget around this input and fill out the areas where we don't have direct representation. Since the sales force has a say in creating and signing off on the budget, they understand that their commission is directly related to their ability to meet this budget. You want to make your budget expectations fair, but you want an incentive for your sales force to go above and beyond the line of duty. If they can hit the ball out of the park, they should be rewarded for doing so. We adjust these budgets and commission levels annually with the goal of always offering the best package for our industry in the hope that it will allow us to keep the best people at our company. In addition to two full-time sales managers, we work with a few brokers throughout the country who represent other brands in addition to our own. Brokers exist in many different industries, and using a broker might be an affordable way to have another level of sales representation in the marketplace for a small company. Like our in-house relationships, we make sure that these part-time salespeople know everything about our company and share our values. So far it has worked well, and I couldn't be happier with the performance of our sales team.

There are certain personality traits that all of our salespeople share. A genuine passion for beer and people is where it all starts, but beyond that we have found that different personalities and strengths can work well in different markets. There are lots of different kinds of bad salespeople, but there are really only two kinds of good salespeople. Let's call the types hunters and gatherers. Hunters are the people who are good at getting new business. They need to be both aggressive and empathetic, but they are more aggressive than empathetic. Gatherers are the personality types that are better at herding the accounts that have already been established. They maintain the existing accounts' relationships with the company more effectively than they create new relationships. They usually are a touch more empathetic than they are aggressive. It's when the aggressive-to-empathetic ratio is way out of whack in one direction or the other that the salesperson is ineffective. There are companies out there that will test a potential hire for sales aptitude to help you make your decision. We have used a company called Caliper that does a great job of fleshing out a potential hire's weaknesses and strengths. These tests have proven to be very helpful for our company.

If you are in a small business, then you are in sales. Whether it is just you doing the selling for your company or you are managing a sales team, you will need to champion a sales-centric mentality for everyone in the company, regardless of what area they work in. The personality trait that best summarizes a sales-centric mentality is compassion. You need to be compassionate and empathetic to sell. As advertising and marketing methods become more transparent to the better-informed consumer of today, being genuine in your compassion is critical to effective salesmanship. If your objective is to sell someone something they don't need, in the long run you will fail. However, if you take the time to find out what a consumer truly desires and you are able to deliver it, you will succeed.

FINDING SUPPORT WITHIN YOUR INDUSTRY

I am proud to be 1 of 13 people on the board of directors for the Brewers Association. We represent over 800 American breweries on issues as diverse as marketing, legislature, distribution, and licensing. I serve alongside some of my professional heroes on this board. Some own breweries that are much larger than Dogfish Head like Kim Jordan who, along with husband Jeff Lebesch, owns New Belgium Brewery in Ft. Collins. Some own breweries that are smaller than ours like Brock Wagner who owns St. Arnold's Brewery in Houston. When we sit down to work out the issues confronting us, we come together for a common good and recognize that our individual trials and successes are what we bring to assist one another. We understand that in helping each other, the entire small-business community stands to benefit.

Brock Wagner left the field of investment banking with a partner to open his brewery in 1995. Not only did he face the challenge of selling a niche product, but his local market, Texas, was dominated by the big three breweries to an extent unmatched in nearly any other state. To make things more challenging his partner viewed the brewery venture more as a cash-generating investment than a labor of love and was disappointed by the brewery's sluggish start. Instead of giving up on his dream Brock used his life's savings to buy out his partner, and he redoubled his efforts to make a go of it. Brock personally leads public tours through his brewery every single Saturday and educates potential customers on the virtues of fresh local beer. His hard work is paying off. St. Arnold has achieved double-digit growth in each of the last 3 years, and Brock continues to apply his will and passion to his daily professional life.

Kim Jordan started New Belgium with her husband in 1988 after returning from a beer and bicycle tour of Belgium. They fell in love with Belgian beers that were unavailable here in the states. They literally built a brewery in their garage. Jeff would brew the beer, and Kim would deliver it to local accounts. Their Fat Tire Ale took off, and they capitalized on the bicycling connection by sponsoring Tour De Fat road races and rewarding long-term employees with profit sharing and bikes likes those depicted on the Fat Tire label. New Belgium is now one of the largest craft breweries in the country, and they are also one of the largest private buyers of wind energy, paying a 20 percent premium to purchase energy from a windmill farm due to their stewardship philosophy for the environment. Each board member comes from a different perspective, and we may have different titles like CEO, president, and brewmaster. But we are each essentially salespeople. In this official capacity, we are selling the agenda of the entire craft brewing industry.

PROPHETS, PROPONENTS, AND PATRONS: YOUR SALES FORCE

The worst report I ever received about one of our salespeople was that as he was working at our booth at beer festivals giving out samples of Dogfish Head beer he was taking covert sips from a can of cheap domestic lager he kept hidden beneath the booth. One of the best reports I received was when a liquor store in Delaware called to thank me for employing a salesperson who talked them out of carrying our beer. The worst report example is obvious: If our beer isn't good enough for our own salesperson to drink, why should anyone else bother to try it? The better report example is a little more complicated but becomes clearer when you accept that sales is more about people than money.

This particular liquor store was in an emerging neighborhood; there was a bunch of upscale condos going up near the highway a couple of miles from their store. But the local clientele was fairly blue-collar, and they did a brisk business in jug wines and 30 packs of domestic canned beer. They had a couple of imports and no local micros and had called our brewery after reading a story about us in the local newspaper. The story was about our Raison D'Etre, a beer we make with raisins and beet sugar that was named the American Beer of the Year by *Malt Advocate* magazine. The liquor store owner said it sounded great and asked to get some samples of that and all of our other bottled beers. Upon arriving, the liquor store owner informed our salesperson that she had already ordered three cases each of our three year-round styles of beer. The salesperson dropped off the samples of that beer along with samples of our Shelter Pale Ale, a much more traditional English style beer that was lighter in alcohol and a bit less expensive. After speaking with the liquor store owner, checking the stock of other beers, and watching what the customers who were coming through were buying, the salesperson asked the owner to please reconsider her order. He felt strongly that the Raison D'Etre and Chicory Stout were too aggressive and different for the store's clientele. He asked instead if he could leave an extra case of our pale ale to give out to her best customers during in-store wine and beer tastings. The liquor store owner agreed and sent all of the beer back to the distributor except for the pale ale.

A week later the sales manager of our Delaware distributor called to talk to me about what happened at the account. His salesperson was furious because although the customer had ordered all our different varieties of beer, upon the Dogfish Head salesperson's interference two-thirds of the beer ordered was sent back. This sales manager asked if I was aware of the situation. I informed him that not only was I aware but I was in fact the salesperson who pulled our beer out of the account. At first he was even more upset once he had this knowledge—how was he supposed to sell our beer with confidence if the brewery's own president was running around the state discouraging accounts from buying the beer? The sales manager calmed down enough to listen to my reasoning and eventually came to understand my decision.

Sales is what business is all about. If you don't sell, you go out of business. The selling process seemingly would be the simple proposition of provoking a buyer to open her wallet and actually pay you. But to sell something effectively you must have a broader point of view. The relationship between the seller and the buyer is not the means to an end. The end goal is not the actual sales transaction itself. The sales transaction is simply a means of furthering the relationship between the seller and the buyer. Sales is business, and as I've said before, I believe business is more about people than it is about money.

I could have left all of the beer in that liquor store. But I knew after visiting it, the store owner's excitement for Dogfish Head would wane if our beer just sat on her shelf collecting dust. I knew that our pale ale was our only beer accessible enough to be interesting to her clientele. I made sure she had a nice sign in her window that said "Delaware-made beer available here" because I knew her customers would be more interested in buying a locally made beer than because of the quality of ingredients. I didn't know all of this before I went to her store. I learned through talking to her and talking to her customers.

Genuine empathy comes from genuine knowledge of the buyer's needs. How can you expect the buyer to listen to you try to educate her about your product if, as the seller, you are unwilling to take the time to be educated on what that buyer wants and truly needs? It's easy to view sales from your own perspective—that of the seller; it's easy, but it's not very helpful. You know what your value proposition is because it's just that: yours. It's easy to take it for granted that your passion for what you sell will be infectious and the value of what you sell will be self-evident after the buyer witnesses your own conviction. But that's not how it works. You must always consider your value proposition from the perspective of the customer first. Of course you need to know your customer very well in order for you to do this. That can only happen once you are less obsessed with figuring out what it takes for you to sell something and more obsessed with figuring out what it takes for someone to buy your product.

As the marketplace becomes more complex and fractured, so does the process of selling and buying. Whether you think you are selling a product or a service, you are really selling your promise of satisfaction. Today's consumer is confronted with seemingly limitless choices. How do you convince a customer that your offering is going to provide them with the most satisfying solution? You do this by finding out what it is in your sales pitch that allowed them to convince themselves. Once you have figured out what motivates the buyer to choose your offering, you should expand all of your sales activity around that reality.

YOUR SALES ARE ONLY AS GOOD
AS YOUR SALESPEOPLE

The first year we made our World Wide Stout we made only 100 cases. At the time it was released, it was the strongest beer in the world. We only held that title for a few weeks before Sam Adams made a beer even stronger. But we held it for long enough and the beer tasted so good that we got a lot of regional and national press coverage. This media attention resulted in 100 cases being sold in a matter of weeks. Our distributors went from freak-out mode for having to pay $100 per case to freak-out mode for not being able to buy more than their initial 10 case allotment in the same amount of weeks. The next year we made 300 cases, and the year after that we made 1,000. Our goal is to always produce just a little bit less than we could sell. If the beer wasn't worth the price we would have a harder time selling it each year even if we did get great initial press coverage. But I'm proud to say this has never been the case with our beers. It sends a powerful message to our retailers, distributors, and customers when we can say we have never introduced a beer that has shrunk in sales from one year to the next. We've never discontinued a beer, either. The fact that we make so many styles wreaks havoc on our production schedule, inventory control, tank utilization, and brewers' peace of mind. But if we say we are all about off-centered ales for off-centered people we need to put our money where the pint glass is.

If good salesmanship starts with genuine empathy for the customer, then it ends with genuine empathy for the company. Whether you have three employees or 300, you need to recognize that everybody in your company, regardless of title, is a salesperson. Our brewers go to beer tastings to teach customers about our beers. Our bottling line workers conduct public tours of our facility to educate customers on our production methods. The hostesses at our brewpub spend time in the brewery learning the process so that they can speak intelligently about our off-centered ales as restaurant patrons are waiting to be seated. In my heart even I am a salesperson before I am a businessman or an entrepreneur.

Every time there is a situation in which someone in your company contacts someone who is capable of buying your product, they are in a selling position. This doesn't mean our janitor carries samples of cold beer in his backpack, but it does mean if someone asks him who owns the company or if we make ales or lagers he knows the answers and shares the information professionally and compassionately.

Once your company is of a size that requires you to hire and train employees specifically as salespeople, you must also start from a point of empathy. This begins with making sure they have a genuine belief in the company, which goes back to the corporate values discussed in Chapter 1. If the way you want your company and products to be perceived is in line with how your salesperson wants to be perceived personally, then you have found a good match. Passion, honesty, strong work ethic, innovative spirit, belief in the power of education—these are components of our corporate values at Dogfish Head. We try to make sure that our salespeople share these values before we consider them for the job. Once we are confident that we have found a good match, we make sure we set our salespeople up for success by arming them with as much knowledge about the company as we can. They come to the brewery for a few days, wake up early, put on a pair of jeans and rubber boots, and make the beer with our brewers. They spend time on our bottling line helping to package the beer. They spend time with me in the marketplace, watching how I sell our beer and interact with customers. All of these training components inform their individual selling style. If they are going to form genuine relationships with the people they sell our beers to, then they need to be genuinely themselves. We are not an IBM-type company with required dress codes and hard sell tactics. I expect our salespeople to dress like they believe their customers would expect them to dress, and act the way their customers would expect them to act, but most important, to always be themselves. If they aren't comfortable selling our beer then our customers won't be comfortable buying it.

Once you have identified an appropriate salesperson, you need to figure out a way to compensate her that is fair to the company and to the salesperson. The only worthwhile business transaction is one that is good for the company, good for the salesperson, and good for the buyer. We don't have a large sales force. The plan for 2005 was for our brewery to generate $10 million in sales with only two full-time, regional salespeople, a sales service manager, and myself dedicated to supporting this level of sales. Our part-time sales affiliates' financial compensation varies, but the system we use with our full-time employees has developed into an effective compensation package. If we have the best beer out there, I want the best salespeople selling it. That's why we construct a compensation package comprised of a base salary plus commission that allows them to be paid as well as any craft beer salesman if they make their budget. And even more if they beat their budget.

A base salary says, "We know it might take you a while to get your feet under you and earn the trust of your customers." It says, "We know that the brewery could run into production problems and not be able to deliver you all of the beer you ordered." Providing health benefits also tells your salespeople that the company they work for cares about them. I make sure I attend a certain number of events each year in each of our sales manager's territories. I can tell more about how well they are doing in those visits than I can by watching their sales volume, by witnessing how much respect they have earned from their distribution and retail customers. I can tell by how many genuine relationships they have established in their marketplace. But I cannot fully compensate them on such subjective feedback. So I think of the salary fraction of their compensation as relative to these subjective aspects of their performance, and the commission fraction as more relative to the quantifiable aspects of their jobs.

chapter 10

CASH IS KING
(WELL, SORT OF)

As the four other board members and I sat around a conference table at the Dogfish Head board of directors meeting in the spring of 1998, I was surprised by the looks of confusion and despair being directed at me. I was giving my state of the union address in which I informed my fellow board members that our company was headed in the right direction. We each had balance sheets and income statements for both the brewpub and the microbrewery before us. My wife, Mariah, and our accountant helped draft them while I concentrated on selling beer. Back then, I couldn't be bothered spending my valuable time looking at sheets of paper covered with numbers. During my speech I informed everyone that we should celebrate the fact that the brewpub was well into its second year of profitability and revenues continued to grow. I then reviewed the microbrewery's condition.

I noted that while we were not yet profitable at the end of our first year, had underestimated our start-up cost by over 50 percent, and were using the cash flow from the brewpub to pay monthly bills at the microbrewery, revenues were increasing and the future looked really bright. My father-in-law and fellow board member Tom Draper sat on the far side of the conference table across from me. He let me speak, but I noticed he kept looking down at the financials as I said my piece. I could tell he had something to say. I finished and looked up to him for some words of encouragement and direction. He said, "Cash is king." I nodded, pretending to understand these words until he drove his point home: ". . . cash is king, Sam, and you have no cash."

While I have never been particularly knowledgeable about financial analysis, I was smart enough to recognize my weakness in this area from the outset. I formed a board of directors before we even opened our doors. By 1998 this board consisted of the following five people: Tom Draper, one of the most successful entrepreneurs in the state of Delaware who owns a couple of television stations, a telecommunications company, and a real estate company as well; Lawton Johnson, Mariah's uncle who had an impressive career on Wall Street as a partner at a firm specializing in mergers and acquisitions; my father, Sam Calagione Jr., the founding and managing partner of Connecticut Valley Oral Surgery; Mariah; and myself.

Between Tom and my father I had the experience of two successful self-made entrepreneurs who had grown their companies into multimillion dollar entities. In Lawton I had a financial adviser who could read a balance sheet with the ease and comprehension that I only experience when flipping through *People* magazine. In Mariah I had my most honest critic, strongest supporter, and a person who seems to have genetically inherited her father's financial prowess. Each of them had skills that complemented and augmented my own.

As is the case with most small-business owners, I did not have the financial training or inclination to manage the details of the financial picture of my company. Most business owners go into business because they possess a passion for the product or service they sell, but rarely do they possess the financial background necessary to successfully manage their finances to the full extent. Most business owners open their companies to devote time and energy toward creating and providing the service or product they are passionate about, not to toil over balance sheets and cash flow statements. This is in part why most small businesses fail.

TOOLS OF THE FINANCIAL TRADE

The lifeblood of every business is its cash. Businesses that fail to manage their cash flow also fail to survive. Having a positive cash flow is essential to keeping all of the elements of a business running. The years of negative cash flow at our microbrewery were the most trying years of my life. The calls from vendors demanding their money and the half-truths that I had to tell just to keep the ingredients and package materials flowing so that we could make the beer, sell it, and use the money to buy more packaging and more ingredients became a vicious cycle. When faced with the decision of potential bankruptcy or telling a white lie about the status of an overdue bill, I made the choice I had to. There were month-long stretches when I could have just changed the outgoing message on my voice mail to, "Hello, this is Sam, please rest assured that your check is in the mail." Sometimes the checks were really in the mail; sometimes they weren't. I never shorted a vendor payment for work that they did. But I made a lot of them wait for payment beyond what is reasonable. At my most desperate, I resorted to telling random accounts-receivable henchmen that my computer had caught fire the very moment I was speaking to them and I needed to hang up immediately or risk third-degree burns. But usually I reasoned with the vendors, invited them down to let them witness the company we were trying to create, and tried to appeal to their respect for business in general to extend us terms or forgive a late charge. Most of the people that worked with us are still our vendors today. The ones who never gave us a chance or threatened us with collection agencies I haven't forgotten and I won't do business with to this day.

You can only be behind on paying your bills for so long, though, before the situation goes from bad to worse. Although the brewery's finances remained at a level where there were no finances to speak of for a couple of years, offsetting the losses at the brewery with the profits from the brewpub kept the situation from getting worse. Regardless of the nature of your business, cash flow is necessary to pay vendors and cover the cost of payroll, even if you are your only employee, and to finance growth and expansion. If any of these elements do not have financial coverage, the business will fall apart.

One of the most valuable and easiest ways to manage your financial status is through the use of a financial system. Whether you use Quickbooks, Peachtree, or any of the programs available, having a financial system in place when you open your doors is critical to managing cash flow. Prefab accounting software packages like Peachtree and Quicken can be amazingly efficient tools for helping you wrap your arms around the ebb and flow of money in your company, but they are usually outgrown by a business at a certain point. We used Peachtree from day one and were happy with the result until we grew to about $5 million in sales between the brewpub and the microbrewery. The point at which you graduate to a more robust, industry-specific software package varies from business to business.

CALL IN THE EXPERTS

While the logic behind cash flow is simple—maintain a positive cash flow by taking in more dollars than you spend—creating this position is a constant balancing act. Because the majority of small-business owners do not have the time or inclination to learn financial analysis, the aid of an accountant or financial analyst is perhaps the most important step to ensuring the success of your business. Whether you involve one individual who sits down with your books once a month, or a group of people who meet each fiscal quarter, having an expert help you through the financial aspects of running a business is key.

I recommend that any budding entrepreneur form a board of directors to bring an element of experience to your venture. Earlier, I suggested the idea of sharing your business plan with respected local businesspeople from different backgrounds to receive some initial feedback and advice. This group of people could also represent candidates for a board of directors. Ideally you would sit down with this board and review performance on a quarterly basis.

With large public companies it is usually the board of directors that sets the course for the company and elects its operational leader, usually a person with the title of president or chief executive officer. Of course this is a very different dynamic from the leadership structure of most small, private companies. You may own 100 percent of your company and therefore have complete unchecked control to run it any way you see fit. In other words, a board of directors cannot vote you out of your own company if it is underwhelmed with your performance. That doesn't mean the resources offered by a board of directors would not be useful to your company. While not powerful enough to vote you out of your own company, a board of directors can be instrumental in giving direction to the company and bring a new perspective to your endeavors. At the very least, forming a board that includes respected area businesspeople would give you a small but important customer base and cheerleading section to introduce your new venture to the community.

A board of directors may have an equity stake in the company or they may just be a group of businesspeople interested in mentoring a fellow businessperson. There are lots of different models for constructing a board of directors. In my situation the people on my board invested in and held minority equity positions in our company. All business is risk. As the business founder and majority owner you obviously have the greatest risk, but when members of your board hold equity stakes in your company the risk is disbursed and to some degree shared. This can be comforting and effective because when this board is advising you and they are invested in your company monetarily as well as emotionally they have further incentive to see your company succeed. If they are savvy businesspeople they will recognize that their risk deserves reward if the company succeeds. If it fails they may lose whatever money they invested and will realize that, as well. Our equity investors have seen the value of their stock rise substantially in the last few years, and they are happy to stay involved with our company for both personal and financial reasons. Regardless of how close you are with your investors, be they friends, family, or simply business associates, it is critical that you take the time to run the board as officially and legally as possible. This means regular meetings, voting on changes to the corporate bylaws, and compiling and dispersing monthly financial data. Taking the time to do this right keeps things formal and clear enough that situations where misunderstanding, poor communication, and frustration can be minimized. A well-rounded board can force you to make major decisions that you may not have made without their strong opinion. This is the situation I found myself in during the spring of 1998.

Each member of my board of directors looked at our current predicament through different eyes but with the same perspective. As Tom said, cash is king and we were out of cash. If I cared enough and had enough time to understand our balance sheet, I would have understood that better. My board was telling me it was time to get real. They believed in me personally as a leader and they believed in Dogfish Head as a company, but they recognized that without a sound financial infrastructure our company was going to struggle. They impressed upon me the necessity of not only understanding our numbers but respecting them and relying on them as well.

For the first 3 years we were in business I don't think I could have told you the difference between an income statement and a balance sheet. I soon learned that the solution to our predicament lay within the columns of these two critical financial documents.

THE BALANCE SHEET AND INCOME STATEMENT

Although you can delegate much of the responsibility of interpreting and translating your P&L, balance sheets, and cash flow statements, you must still review these documents and have a basic understanding of what these numbers tell you.

Simply put, your income statement is an ongoing report set up on a monthly basis that tracks revenues, expenses, and income. A balance sheet is a quick snapshot of the overall financial health of your company. It represents a simple mathematic equation: What you own (assets) minus what you owe (liabilities) equals the worth of your company (equity). An income statement is revenue-centric; it is centered around the sales of your goods. From that you subtract your direct costs and your operating expenses. What is left over is your profit. The balance sheet is also known as a P&L statement. At the end of the year the sum of all profits (revenue minus expenses) are added into one line item on your balance sheet. The balance sheet is dynamic and updated month to month; the income statement is static and updated every year.

At the time of our greatest challenge these two reports told a troubling story. Our income statement told us that we had a cost structure at the microbrewery that would allow us to move toward profitability but that we weren't close yet. Our balance sheet showed that as we continued to take profits from the brewpub to subsidize the losses at the microbrewery we would jeopardize the survival of both.

I believed that we had done a good job of pricing our beers and they provided an adequate profit margin for us to grow strong, but we had very bad cost controls and lacked any true economy of scale. Before you open your doors the exercise of creating a pro forma financial plan including presumed build-out costs and operating capital requirements is very important. But it's equally important to update and adjust your financial plan after you are up and running. Very rarely does an entrepreneur nail her cost structure, budgets, and build-out costs. Rarer still is the entrepreneur whose business initially exceeds expectations in terms of profitability, cash flow, and controlled costs. When you put together a business pro forma always assume costs are going to be higher, and sales lower, than you think. This will give you a worst-case scenario that will show whether your business model is truly viable even if it doesn't meet your optimum expectations. When we opened our microbrewery separate from our pub in 1997, we underestimated the cost of building our physical plant and overestimated the production efficiencies of our equipment. Our worst inefficiencies came from our bottling line.

The bottling line we originally installed was a 1969 East German soda filler that was very used by the time it was up and running in our brewery.

I'm pretty sure it was sent to the United States as part of some sort of Communist, Cold World initiative meant to wreak havoc on unsuspecting small American beverage companies. Sometimes it would fill the bottles with 12 ounces of beer, and sometimes it would put in only 6 ounces. We could not figure out how to make the system act more predictably, so at the end of an 8-hour bottling run we would have 300 cases of sellable 12-ounce-filled bottles and 50 cases of unsellable 6-ounce-filled bottles. Essentially 17 percent of the beer we were packaging was unfit to sell, and our entire profit margin was being eaten up by this tremendous rate of loss. We needed to replace our bottling line fast if we were going to lower our operating costs and save our company.

I found a good 5-year-old bottling line in Florida that a brewery had outgrown, but we didn't have the money to buy it. We were stuck looking at a balance sheet that showed us having more liabilities than assets at the microbrewery. Looking at the income statement for both the brewpub and the microbrewery, it was obvious that the cash flow of the brewpub could not support the purchase of the bottling line for the microbrewery. I needed to raise some money to buy the Floridian bottling line.

Most manufacturing businesses' largest expenses are their equipment. In our case, aside from the expense of the brewery system, the bottling line was our second largest investment. The purchase of such large equipment can cause an unnecessary drain on a business's cash flow and be detrimental to the survival of a company. Rather than tie up thousands of dollars in equipment that will continuously depreciate in value, you may wish to explore options of financing or leasing equipment. This can be an expensive decision. You need to always be aware of your cost of capital. Most leasing companies recognize that small businesses are usually starving for cash. They are willing to help you purchase equipment, but their terms are usually much less reasonable than those you would find with a traditional bank loan. Every single equipment lease I've signed I've ended up regretting. That's usually because our financial health improved after the decision of whether to lease had been made. Hindsight is 20/20 and sometimes you have no choice but to lease when you don't have the cash flow, bank position, or equity to sell that would allow you to make the decision based on the best cost of money. With our plan to replace our pathetic bottling line came the decision about how best to finance the upgrade. I knew I didn't want to lease it but I also knew our balance sheet wasn't strong enough to allow for additional borrowing from the bank.

WHERE THE MONEY'S AT

All of our experienced board members agreed that, in its current condition, Dogfish Head was not a good candidate for a bank loan. At the time Mariah and I owned 100 percent of the brewpub and 85 percent of the brewery. The remaining 15 percent was owned by Lawton and Tom, and my father owned preferred stock. All three agreed to up their financial investment if I would be willing to combine the two companies. They rightfully wanted a stake in the more successful company if they were going to make a risky investment in the microbrewery.

Jay Stevens, our accountant, helped us draft the paperwork, and the brewpub became a corporation that was wholly owned by the microbrewery. This deal diluted Mariah's and my equity stake to 73 percent, where it still stands today. By combining the companies, we could blend the strong balance sheet of the brewpub with the weak balance sheet of the microbrewery. Our combined assets were equal to our liabilities, and we could write off the losses at our microbrewery against the profits at our pub.

With the reorganization that my board of directors not only helped me put into place but also reached into their own pockets to help see through, our financial health looked more promising. The amount of money that Tom, Lawton, and my father put into Dogfish Head at the time was less than the revenue that the brewery now generates in a week. But in 1998 that amount represented a very significant contribution to our floundering company.

I have used a lot of different combinations of bank and private financing to grow Dogfish Head. A fraction of our start-up money came from personal loans from my father, my father-in-law, my Uncle Arnie, and a friend of the family. Another fraction came from a bank loan that my father kindly cosigned. The banks also mandated that Mariah and I put up all of our personal assets as collateral as well, which, at that time, consisted of two used cars and a dog.

The first round of money that I raised to open our brewpub totaled $255,000. It doesn't seem like an insanely large sum as I write it now but, as a 25-year-old inexperienced kid making his rounds from bank to bank, it felt like the gross national product.

Once we were on our feet we fueled growth mostly out of cash flow and bank loans. Last year alone we bought seven new brewing tanks directly out of cash flow for an installed total cost of $320,000. Now, of course, the banks are very willing to work with us and we have found a great partner in Citizens Bank. We have also taken advantage of some great federal and state programs for low-interest loans offered by the Small Business Administration and the Delaware Economic Development Organization. I would recommend that any entrepreneur look into the SBA for possible assistance in financing a business; it's an excellent resource.

There are really only a few choices for financing your small business beyond the investment of your personal assets: bank loans and private investors. Banks seem to only want to lend you money when you don't need it. In other words, they don't want to loan money to a company to help it grow strong, they want to lend money only when the company is already strong. This is inevitable; like any business the bank is trying to minimize risk. As a small, unproven entrepreneur, you reek of risk. You might be able to start your business with just your own money or the investment of family and friends. But you may soon have to find true outside professional investors as well. They will want a return on their investment that is greater than traditional bank interest. It makes sense that if they are willing to assume greater risk they are due a greater reward when the company succeeds.

As you explore options for financing, you will learn there are many different approaches that could work for you. Expect to be asked to collateralize your personal assets against the sum of money you borrow from a bank. Private investments can be made as some form of a loan, or you can sell some fraction of actual equity in exchange for the investment. Regardless of how big you envision becoming, it's important to recognize just how valuable and critical every single percent of ownership is. Your decisions regarding who you let invest in your company matter greatly, so make sure the investor is someone you trust, respect, and can reason with. I'm very lucky that the investors in my company also comprise my board of directors and are members of my family. It would make for some pretty tense holiday dinners if our potential success was still as tenuous as it was when we combined the companies in 1998. When my investors decided to put in more money and help us buy a better bottling line, they believed our lack of positive cash flow was only part of the microbrewery's problem. They also didn't have complete faith in our business model and marketing plan. While they recognized my potential to sell beer, they were now asking me to quantify the methods to my madness. I would have to use the numbers to gain their respect.

MAXIMIZING SHORT-TERM PROFITS VERSUS LONG-TERM FINANCIAL HEALTH

To reduce the hemorrhage of cash at Dogfish Head, I needed to take a few immediate steps. The financial model showed me the way and speaks to a business reality that every entrepreneur needs to acknowledge. For every business in every industry, there exists opportunities for maximizing profits and long-term financial health. It's most important to recognize that these two ideals do not always mean the same thing and that there can be significant repercussions for prioritizing one over the other. Public companies face this issue with the same varying degrees of success as small businesses. We face it every day at Dogfish Head, but we face it today with a much clearer perspective than we did in 1998.

While Tom Draper's assessment of our cash-poor predicament was accurate and his advice on restructuring our company toward financial health was sage, his business plan for improving our financial future was very different from my own. To his credit he believed in me enough to let me see my plan out but I had to earn this belief by showing that I could use the numbers to prove myself. He forced me to educate myself in the world of small-business finance.

Even with the new bottling line in place to cut production costs at the brewery, more changes needed to be made before the company could move closer to profitability. The short-term issue was the lack of profits at the brewery and the cash crunch it created. The new bottling line was in place and pumping out beer more efficiently, but we still had the challenge of growing revenues at a rate that would get us to break even within a year. Tom recommended that I stop making strong, esoteric, expensive beers and stop trying to sell beer up and down the eastern seaboard. He was right that we needed to concentrate more on our backyard, and we hired a full-time regional sales manager within 2 months. But I saw the way our industry was growing and that the interest level in our more expensive and unique beers was growing as well. I knew that there were too few people that cared about these sorts of beer at the time to fully support us, but the trend was encouraging and our growing reputation for innovation and pushing the envelope would serve us well in the long run.

I wanted to stay the course and continue selling less beer in more markets for more money rather than more beer for less money in fewer markets. It was a decision to have a wide and shallow marketing impact versus a local and deep one. We could have focused all of our energies locally, but I don't think our company had a strong enough identity or the right styles of beer to make this work. Within a year of close income statement monitoring, I had the facts that showed that making more expensive beers but charging more for them was indeed moving us steadily toward profitability.

Of course other decisions could have been made to impact our financial position. I could have easily increased my short-term profits at the brewery by forgoing maintenance and upgrades to equipment, freezing salaries, reducing our workforce, or substituting cheaper ingredients for our beers. In the short term, these efforts would have had a positive effect on the bottom line but within months our equipment would have broken down, our undercompensated coworkers would have left, and our underwhelmed customers would have moved on to a superior-quality beer.

Every company is confronted with some version of deciding whether to maximize short-term profits or focus on long-term growth. There are so many opportunities to cut corners in a small business that may not seem important when taken individually, but they can have a barely perceivable, incremental effect on future success. Of course there are also opportunities to prevent the expenditure of cash flow that is vital to sustaining a business. Extreme actions lead to obvious results. It's easy to view the expense area of your income statement and see the effect of only keeping one lightbulb on or by setting your thermostat at 50° in the winter and 80° in the summer. You can watch your utility costs go down but you'll notice nobody wants to patronize your place of business because it's too dark and too cold. Some aspects of long-term versus short-term prioritizing are common sense. But there are other options.

The ideal business model maximizes short-term profits without compromising long-term growth and financial returns. Various avenues of short-term cost management must be explored while you continue to reinvest and expand your company. For the small-business owner, seemingly insignificant efforts, including finding waste and cutting back, can mean the difference between operating at a loss and being profitable. This can mean anything from buying supplies in bulk, to regularly auditing vendors, to counting paperclips. A second overlooked method of maintaining a positive cash flow is to negotiate terms of payment with banks and vendors. Developing strong relationships and maintaining constant communication with the people with whom you do business can translate to flexibility in terms of payment should you need it. This could mean the difference between paying for goods in one lump sum or having a flexible payment schedule, and defaulting on a loan or being permitted to skip a month's payment. Being vigilant about such details while focusing on innovation or expanding your customer base will help ensure a stable financial picture in the short term while you invest in the long-term success of your business. As with the example of banks that would rather lend to a strong, proven company than a fragile start-up, your vendors will be flexible and creative with your payment terms once you have proven that yours is a viable business. We never sign contracts for more than 1 year with any of our vendors. Actually, I can say that now, after having spent years paying a ridiculous premium for propane as a result of not reading the fine print of a contract, never make critical deals on a handshake. A contract protects every party involved and keeps things from getting messy when you are trying to dissolve a relationship that is counterproductive to your company. With vendors as with banks, you want to negotiate from a position of strength. As you grow, audit your biggest-volume vendors annually and get quotes from their closest competitors to make sure you are always getting the best deal.

For the last 9 years our brewpub has been open 12 months a year. This year we can see that our brewpub is budgeted to lose money in the months of January and February. Taking a short-term view of this situation would immediately lead us to the decision of closing for those months. We do business in a seasonal town, but, as locals, we recognize the value of maintaining the loyalty of our community throughout the year. If we shut down, our costs would be reduced dramatically but our loyal local customers would find somewhere else to go for pints and wood-grilled pizza, and our loyal staff would have to look elsewhere for employment. The long-term view on financial health leads us to make the right decision. These examples of deferring maximum profitability in the name of long-term health are straightforward, but it's important to recognize the risks that come with taking this long-term view. If you are in a seasonal or cyclical industry, you may want to include a line of credit in your bank package. You can draw against this line in your soft months and pay it down in your strong months. The problem is that a line of credit can be habit forming. You begin to think of that money as your own when in fact it is the bank's.

THE CHICKEN OF RISK AND THE EGG OF RETURN ON INVESTMENT

"Cash is king" is an idea that needs further consideration. I've given examples of how prioritizing short-term cash gains can hurt your company in the long run. It is important, however, to consider the true value of the dollar and the nature and magnitude of the risks that you take as you make these short-term concessions. Every time you decide to reinvest a dollar of income into your company, you need to recognize the truth to the adage, "a bird in hand is worth two in the bush." You can be sure of the value of the dollar that you put into your cash register today. You can walk it directly over to the bank and insert it into your savings account or you may choose instead to invest that dollar back into the growth of your company. You can't predict inflation or what your dollar will be worth tomorrow. If you don't put that dollar in the bank, you won't collect interest on it. Even if you invest that dollar in your growth, there's no guarantee that a competitor won't open next door to you and drive you into bankruptcy, thereby reducing the value of that dollar to nothing. You need to realize all of these things, and you need to still willfully, gleefully invest that dollar in your own company. If you believe in the worthwhile business proposition that you have created, then you should believe that you can get a better return on investing your money in your own company than you can in putting money in the bank and collecting interest. This is a big part of what being an entrepreneur is all about. That being said, just as there will be daily considerations on prioritizing short- versus long-term profitability, you will frequently be challenged to make decisions based on the risk of an endeavor, and gauging the value of its return on investment.

Once you do have a positive cash flow, it's important to establish some sort of war chest that can get you through hard times. The definition of hard times can change as your company continues to grow. While we are a strong and profitable company now, we still get tight on money some months when we are forced to buy equipment out of cash flow. When you are spending money that you didn't anticipate in your budgeting process it all comes immediately out of your bottom line. The budgeting process is a form of business clairvoyance; you are challenged to see the future. You can make sound estimations based on sound financial and marketing data, but you can't predict everything. This is why you need some sort of reserve to fall back on. The marketplace is unpredictable, and you need some insurance against the possibility that the future you assume in your budget planning turns out to be different in the reality of an ever-changing marketplace.

If Dogfish Head were a public company, it's very unlikely we would brew a beer like World Wide Stout. Each year this beer clocks in around 20 percent alcohol by volume, which is nearly five times as strong as the average beer sold in America. It retails for roughly $150 per case, which means you won't often find it in the "impulse buy" stack located conveniently by the checkout counter. Each batch of this beer takes approximately 4 months to brew, which means it bears an extremely high opportunity cost as we could fill the very same fermenting tank with 12 batches of our Shelter Pale Ale in the time it takes us to ferment one batch of World Wide Stout. We didn't even start making this beer profitably until the third year we were producing it. Our old tanks were too small and our lack of efficiency too taxing. But it is a project that we believe in, and we recognize that World Wide Stout is a critical component to the perception of our company as it embodies our risk-taking, over-the-top-product-making status.

A cash-draining investment can seem foolhardy in the short term but prove fruitful in the long term. As entrepreneurs we need to recognize that oftentimes the greater the risks we take the greater the opportunity for a return on investment. You can invest a buck in the lottery and maybe win $10 million. Or you can invest a buck in your own company, work your ass off, and see that you made that dollar worth $3 in a few years. The difference between the lottery and your own company is that, with your own company, you control the level of risk that you take, and your planning, skill, and hard work reduces the magnitude of that risk. With the lottery, it's, "Hey, you never know." With your own company, it's, "You control your destiny."

CALLING FOR BACKUP

In spring 2002 we had finally reached a level of sustainable profitability at the microbrewery but our costs were fluctuating wildly from month to month. My younger sister Christa was finishing her first year in the MBA program at Carnegie Mellon. A huge supporter of Dogfish Head, she decided to use the brewery as a model company for a marketing project. She and four other students analyzed Dogfish Head in the context of what our market position and opportunities were in their local market of Pittsburgh. One of the students doing this project with her was Nick Benz.

Nick was a process engineer in a chemical manufacturing plant before returning to graduate school, so he had an evolved understanding of manufacturing and production. More than this, his wife, Fran, was born in Belgium, home to many world-class breweries, and both of them loved great beers long before I met them. I worked with Nick on the marketing project and was impressed with his analytic and quantifying skills as well as his ability to shake off the pocket protector and have a few beers. I knew our company needed stronger financial management, and it wasn't long after meeting Nick that I was able to lure him down to Delaware to be our chief financial officer. He has brought our company forward more quickly than I would have imagined.

He immediately set to work straightening out the cost side of our business. We made an $80,000 investment in Great Plains Manufacturing software, which brought us light-years forward from the glorified home-accounting Peachtree software we previously used. Nick does financial modeling, which we incorporate into multiyear pro formas, but they are based on empirical analytic data grounded in the here and now. The biggest assumption that he has to make is that sales will go where we are forecasting them to go. That's because the sales growth is mostly up to me (as the sales and marketing side of the company) and our production crew continuing their highest level of quality control.

I always did a half-assed job of overseeing the financial health of our company because I don't have the right brain for it. Nick does, and his efforts have allowed me to concentrate on the right-brained activities that I am good at. Essentially Nick is the boss of costs and I am the boss of revenues. Mariah can live in both worlds, so she acts as the bullshit meter between us. I concentrate on growing the business, and he concentrates on the health of the business as it grows. Tom's mantra of "Cash is king" applies equally to Nick's area of control and my own. I have to generate the sales, and Nick has to make sure that a fair fraction of our income makes it into the profit line of the income statement. The more profitable we are the stronger our balance sheet. The stronger our balance sheet is the stronger we are as a company and the less I have to fret over our financial hurdles.

THE ANALYTIC AND THE CREATIVE

In business you must use both sides of your brain. The right side of your business brain is the creative side, and the left side of your business brain is the analytical side. Both need to function in top form if you are going to make headway in a competitive marketplace. Some businesspeople have brains in which the two sides are equally evolved: Bill Gates, Jack Welch, and my father-in-law come quickly to mind. If you are one of these lucky people, congratulations; the majority of us lean significantly in one direction or the other. I know this left/right brain analogy has been used in business books before, but I think you can take it a step further.

Research has shown that people who have better-developed analytical and quantitative skills (left brain) have longer attention spans and better focusing ability than people with strong theoretical and qualitative skills (right brain). *Focus* means the left-brained person can concentrate better on what is happening at any given moment and will remember more details of that moment later. The right-brained person is probably thinking of something beyond the moment; something in the future, the past, or some strange parallel universe that only exists in his head (I see thirsty people). I'm pretty sure I'm an undiagnosed ADD-sufferer but I revel in my suffering. In some weird way I enjoy chaos and thrusting myself toward the unknown. I make impetuous, radical, emotional decisions that I know have taxed the patience of some of the left-brained people in our company. I recognize these tendencies as a weakness in some areas and strength in others for my company. My wife could write her own book about dealing with me on this level. We used to laugh about it when we got home from the brewery at night. She would say, "What do you mean you just kegged a beer made with oysters for a seafood festival without costing it out or doing a test batch to see how it would taste?" And I would lovingly reply, "I don't remember the last sentence that came out of your mouth, but do you want to go play tennis?" As our company grew rapidly the quantitative details became overbearing for her and our office manager to stay on top of. It wasn't as funny as it used to be. To grow strong we needed more focus.

For most small-business owners a day will come when the decision must be made to concentrate either on the left-brained or right-brained business activities. It is a very rare leader who will be able to oversee everything and not stymie either the growth or the health of the company. You have to be honest with yourself and recognize where you are strong and where you are weak. I am good at growing Dogfish Head, but I am not good at maintaining the health of Dogfish Head as it grows. The health of a company involves the development of its financial and organizational infrastructure. Before Nick joined our company, I relied more heavily on guidance from my board on financial matters. I now have the confidence that we can analyze all of the decisions facing us, be they creative or analytical in nature. Even now that we've reached this point, having an active board of directors is an asset to our company. Instead of helping us figure out how to pay our bills next month, they guide us through considering and formulating the shape of our business for years down the line. While our creative direction as a company may change, our focus on financial health will never waver. I have lots of great people around me now, helping me make sense of our company's future.

THE BEST DECISION YOU'LL EVER MAKE: FINDING SOMEONE ELSE TO DO THE JOB

As a bootstrapping entrepreneur, it might not be initially clear whether you are stronger with the left or right business brain. That's because, as a start-up, you won't have the time, resources, or personnel depth to only pick and choose doing the jobs that you are good at or those you enjoy. You will need to do it all. This will be frustrating in the short run because there will be jobs you have to do and decisions you have to make where you know darn well you don't have the traditional skills in place to make them efficiently. But if you care enough about your ideas to open your own business around them, trust your gut and your heart, most of your decisions will work out for the better. In the long term, having been forced to make decisions outside of your comfort zone will make you a better, more well-rounded businessperson than farming out those decisions prematurely. But it can be surprising to learn how quickly bringing in a skilled, complementary-brained coworker can pay off. It starts with throwing up the white flag, surrendering to the knowledge that you can't do it all. If you intend to grow your company quickly and profitably, the long-term financial health of your company depends on this decision.

chapter 11
LEADERSHIP
in theory and in practice

A lot of entrepreneurs look at trailblazing companies as sources for inspiration. The renegade spirit of Nike, Starbucks, or Apple are often cited as standard-bearers for the idealized entrepreneurial model. In a lot of ways I have tried to model Dogfish Head upon the ideal of Black Mountain College, a school that very few have heard of that went broke after being open for less than three decades. I can see where it would seem like a pretty inauspicious source of inspiration. This school, located in the mountains of North Carolina, opened in 1933 and closed in 1957, but left an indelible mark on the creative world.

The community of Black Mountain College created and actively embraced experimentation and eschewed homogenization in the course of education. Luminaries such as John Cage, Merce Cunningham, and Buckminster Fuller helped to create this community. The school's unofficial motto was "We shall see what we shall see."

The school's organizers were successful in creating a community but they were failures at sustaining it; they ran out of money. Owned and operated by the faculty that taught there, the leadership model utilized by this school emulated the basic tenets of good leadership. All small businesses are exploring commerce from a "we shall see what we shall see" basis. If what you hope to achieve with your own business were already available, then there would hardly be a reason for you to move forward with opening yours. I also like this phrase because it suggests the excitement of the unknown that is the future. You are more than just a businessperson—you are an explorer, and the exploration that comes with establishing a new business is an exploration of yourself. You are valiantly looking forward to the challenge of putting your own fingerprint on the world. The plural pronoun in the phrase also recognizes the fact that there is more than one person involved on this exploratory journey. As your company grows, the challenge will shift from motivating yourself to create something unique and worthwhile to motivating a team (2, 20, 200 people) toward mutual creation.

Like small business, Black Mountain College was an alternative learning environment that was unrestrained by conventional boundaries and structures. In essence they built a sound community in theory and went forward to develop and grow this community with the best intentions, but they were not able to clear the practical hurdles of running it. There was a lack of harmony between the leaders' day-to-day interactions regarding how best to run the school, typical of any environment in which a group of motivated individuals are involved. But they shared an idealistic vision of where they wanted to go; the challenge was getting there together.

In order to move your company from the theory of what you hope to achieve to the actual achievement itself requires strong leadership. There are followers and there are leaders at all levels within a position—even on a board of directors. Just as a bottling-line worker can be a leader, in essence a CEO can be a follower in terms of his skills and experience in certain areas compared to others around him. This leadership must be present in both the theoretical and practical challenges that come with organizing and motivating a community. There are three central principles to successful leadership that must each be exercised as you grow your company. First you must establish an inspiring, worthwhile business proposition. Next you have to effectively communicate this worthwhile business proposition. Last, you must continually track, recognize, and reward the efforts and achievements of the people who work with you toward proving that yours is a worthwhile business proposition to your potential customers. All three principles are interrelated, and they apply to your target consumer as much as they apply to your coworkers. I have found that if you are able to successfully execute these three principles with your coworkers, it will lead directly toward success in the marketplace.

CREATE AN INSPIRING AND WORTHWHILE BUSINESS PROPOSITION

The Black Mountain College motto, "We shall see what we shall see" is an ideal rallying cry for any entrepreneurial business. It implies that a group of people are on a journey together to discover if their belief in their product or service is valid. It also implies that these people are not going to rely on or adhere to the status quo, but they intend to define this world for themselves.

the ever-evolving and expanding "we"

The plural *we* in this statement is critical. Regardless of how many people you work with, you are not on this journey alone. The unified group can be as small as a consultant and a client or as grand as the management team of a public corporation. The important fact is that this group of people recognizes that they must come together as a cohesive unit in order to achieve their goals.

Nearly every example I have given about lessons learned at Dogfish Head have been written using the pronoun *we* instead of *I,* except in instances where I would seem crazy for choosing this pronoun (where it would seem as though "we" had multiple personalities or something). Seriously, my decision to use *we* in relaying all that we've accomplished and all that we've failed at over the 10-year history of Dogfish Head is a recognition that I've accomplished nothing myself since we opened our doors. There have been lots of ideas that have come from my own head since we have opened, and there are many that have come from other people who work at our company. Unless you are a one-person operation, taking any idea and making it a reality involves everyone in your organization.

In a lot of ways I still struggle with the notion that I'm working in a capitalist society. Yes, I get to create something I'm proud of, but I have to sell it in order to sustain my livelihood. If you look at a company in the context of a community, it becomes easier to have hope. The *we* of Dogfish Head reflects our belief that everyone we work with is capable of greatness and in a position to contribute in a monumental way toward the growth of our company. I love it when I'm out with one of our sales managers and they tell an account about "our" Chicory Stout or I'm at our pub and hear a waitperson say "our" pizza is made with prefermented wort in the dough. It reminds me that we are working toward something together and the only way we will succeed is if the people I work with have a sense of ownership for everything we do and sell.

I admit there is a buy-in period. It usually takes about a year before we start thinking of a newer coworker as part of the royal "we." It takes about a year for a new hire to understand enough about Dogfish Head to mean it when they say *we*. As we are putting together the space for our second brewpub to be opened at the same place as our microbrewery in Milton, we decided to use a giant room with full-size bocce courts for public use. We built the bocce courts long before the restaurant opened because we love to play bocce. My love of bocce stems partially from the fact that it's a sport you can play with a pint glass in your hand and partly from the fact that it's a game that requires teamwork. It takes a lot of skill, strategy, and working together to win at bocce. You can't win alone.

Next to our bocce courts I've installed a 100 CD solar-powered jukebox with a serious Bose surround-sound speaker system. Every coworker that has been at Dogfish Head for over a year has been given the opportunity to name their favorite album for inclusion in the jukebox. The company went out and bought every album that was requested. So we stand around, listen to music, drink beer, and play bocce together. We think of bocce as bocce and not as some team-building exercise because we already think of ourselves as a team.

We don't have any draconian mandate that our coworkers speak with this sense of ownership. We don't have shock collars set to go off every time a bartender says *I* recommend this or that. I do occasionally remind and encourage a coworker to say *we* or *us* but if I'm doing that after they've been with us a year or so it means that they are not really fitting into our company culture. I'm not trying to build an army of mindless androids. I want an army of individuals rallying around a shared goal: working together to continue growing Dogfish Head. Usually the people who think of themselves as separate from the company, the people that can never bring themselves to say *our* beer don't work with us for that long. I can't prove any correlation but these people also usually suck at bocce.

expecting the unexpected

An aspect of the unknown is contained in the motto—what will be seen is not clearly in focus yet but the group is committed to discovering their goals together. In the mercurial world of small business, the only thing that is certain is the uncertainty of the future. Managing a small company has its own set of challenges specific to small business. Small-business owners who hope to succeed in the erratic, unpredictable environment of the market-place cannot assume the slow and steady attitude employed by larger cor-porations. Your management style must take this into consideration.

As you captain your ship through uncharted waters the crew needs to be as nimble as you to navigate your company through the marketplace. You need to communicate to them when you are planning to change course so that they can help you do so. Being alert and flexible is necessary when you are the little guy. This is an essential element of the entrepre-neurial approach.

In the 1970s and 1980s it seemed IBM could do no wrong and would continue to dominate the world of business computing. But they grew into a rigid, monotonous, bureaucratic invalid. Innovative, nimble, small com-panies like Compaq, Apple, and Sun Microsystems discovered chinks in Big Blue's armor and toppled the giant. They didn't do so by mirroring IBM's business plan; they executed business plans all their own.

At Dogfish Head we are constantly using our small size to our advan-tage. It's a lot easier to turn a small boat around than it is for an ocean liner to pull a 180. We do a seasonal, draft-only imperial pilsner called Prescription Pils. It is a strong lager and needs to be fermented with a German pilsner yeast. After the beer was brewed we accidentally added the Belgian yeast that we use to ferment our Raison D'Etre beer. This yeast gives a lot of spicey, clovey notes to the beer—not at all in keeping with the flavor profile of a pilsner. It didn't taste like it was supposed to, but it still tasted good. Over the course of a day we decided how to turn this problem into an advantage. The brewers, salespeople, and finance person all sat down at a table and created a new concept for the release of a new beer. We added aged, Belgian hops to the beer and rechristened it Hummel Beer (*hummel* is Flemish for hoppy). Within 2 weeks of pulling all 80 kegs of this beer out of the tank, it was sold out. Had this happened at a large corporation, the variation would have probably been looked upon as an error rather than a new opportunity for success. Rather than consider the possibility that this brew might be an improvement, it would have been immediately discarded because it was different from what was expected or planned for. However, we instead communicated our way through the challenge and came together as a team to create a solution, and a new style of beer.

Having clear leadership and communication at both the brewery and the brewpub allows for the successful and seamless integration of local and timely beers into the product line. Between product design and R&D, most large breweries take 9 months to a year from the time they decide to go forward with a new product and the date on which the product hits the shelves. Dogfish Head Craft Brewery is known for experimentation, so a "Product X" and a "Product Y" are built into the budget every year. Rough numbers for the cost of producing that beer and very real numbers for the packaging and labor that will go into the finished cases are plugged into our budget. This policy allows flexibility for the introduction of new products. Despite all the federal and state red tape that must be navigated before selling a new label, we can move from concept to product delivery within 3 months. This is roughly a third of the time that a big brewery would need to complete such a project.

Of course there is a lot of communication and cooperation between coworkers that must take place for a business to work smoothly and efficiently. There are always glitches, but it usually works well if everyone truly believes that the decision to introduce these products is a worthwhile business proposition. That employees will buy-in to a goal and work with you to achieve it can be ensured by including them in the numerous steps from idea to implementation.

good leaders have good plans

The single, glorious revelation that led you to open your business is the essence of your worthwhile business proposition—your big idea. We are all struck in different ways, but the idea that strikes you is the weapon that opens the chink in the marketplace's armor. You need to define this business proposition first for yourself and then for those around you. The format for this definition is a full-blown business plan. Regardless of the size or type of business you engage in, it makes a lot of sense to write a business plan. Traditionally a business plan is the tool peddled to banks and investors that describes why your business idea is a worthwhile investment. The marketing section of the plan describes your big idea and why it will work. The financial section outlines how this idea will lead to profitability. At the very least you should write a business plan to prove to yourself that your idea is well thought out and worth pursuing. At most it will be the bible of your company. It will be the road map that you and your coworkers use to lead you toward executing your business proposition. A new business is a living, legal, tax-paying entity. Therefore, it has its own personality. As your company's personality outgrows your own, your leadership skills become extremely important.

At first, if you are a sole proprietor, the personality of your company may be indistinguishable from your own personality but as you grow to have other people working next to you it is your responsibility to introduce these new people to the personality of your company. They have to understand why your company is a good company and why their time spent working there is worthwhile.

COMMUNICATING YOUR WORTHWHILE BUSINESS PROPOSAL

sharing the plan with the people

Once you have a sound and worthwhile business proposition that is well defined and documented, it is time to preach your own gospel. The mission and message of your business and goals must be continually conveyed to employees and customers. You can't lead unless people trust you. People won't trust you until they understand you. Your business plan in hard form and your business practices in everyday work situations will provide your coworkers with the information they need to decide if they should trust you and buy into your big idea.

As the leader of Dogfish Head it is my job to show key managers how a project will work and how to accomplish it. It is up to the key managers to do the same job for the people who are working on the project in their specific areas. I am successful if I can translate the company ideology to new coworkers in a way that allows them to truly believe in what they are doing for themselves. As leaders and managers we need to learn to delegate to coworkers only after we are sure that they understand the kind of company we are trying to build. As a leader, it's useless to say, "We are doing it this way because I said so."

Before Dogfish Head opened I spent a lot of time trying to convince bankers and potential investors that my idea was a sound one. These people hold their positions of power mainly because they have great bullshit detectors. They see a lot of business plans; they get pitched on lots of "can't lose" ideas. The first and seemingly biggest question you are asking these people is "Will you lend me money?" The equally important question that you need to ask them after they have responded yes or no to your question is, "Why?" Their answers will help you formulate the language and methods with which you educate future coworkers on the validity of your idea. In a way, "Will you lend me money" is a loose translation of the question, "Do you believe in my business proposition?" Even if you do not need any outside money to start your company, you should give your business plan to a few different people from different walks of business life (entrepreneurs, bankers, accountants, lawyers, etc.) for their opinions. Their comments on whether they *think* it is a good idea are only as important as *why* they think it's a good idea. These answers will tell you if your sound business proposition is as clear to the outsider looking in as it is to the insider, you, who created it.

balancing act

In a leadership position, there must be a balance between fiscal responsibility and creative inspiration in everything you do. The financial component to your business plan must be grounded in accessible, empirical data whenever possible. The marketing section is where you can let your creativity sing. I have learned that adhering to a marketing plan and a budget can actually enhance creativity. Once these guidelines are in place, the people you've entrusted to help you reach these goals can more effectively bring their personal skills (including creativity) into play in order to help you achieve them. You can best help others succeed by providing clear management and direction. Leadership in the world of a growing company is inherently creative and intuitive—you are taking a company and people somewhere that didn't previously exist. We shall see what we shall see. As Dogfish Head began to grow I learned that it takes different skills to lead than it does to manage. I learned that, in order to properly lead people, everybody involved needs to understand where you are leading them to. The leader of a company is the manifestation of the corporate vision. The ongoing communication of the leader's vision, if it is a sound one, is the essential tool necessary to motivate others. This was probably the hardest lesson I've learned thus far.

where the rubber meets the road

Once we decided on a location for the brewpub my best friend, John, began working with me to open the restaurant. It was decided months earlier that he would be the general manager, and I would be the brewer and president. He would run the day-to-day activities, and I would brew the beer and develop the business.

John and I had been college roommates for 3 years. Our friendship started when we sat down with the dean our freshman year to talk about rooming together and the dean responded, "Why should I let problem number one of this dormitory live with problem number two?" We scowled as he reminded us how much we had in common when he recounted instances in which one of us set a door on fire and the other had been reprimanded for decorating his neighbor's door with baloney and superglue. So we had that going for us. Similar dislikes—doors that were in our way, being told what to do, deans, etc.—and similar likes—sociability, lunchmeats, fire, etc. As we lived together over the years we began to recognize that our personalities and skills complemented one another more than they overlapped. He was more organized, analytical, and pragmatic; I was more creative, imaginative, and emotional. I would think of something to do (climb an abandoned water tower), and he would help me figure out how to do it (use the ladder). I knew he had the skills for running the brewpub, while I had the skills to figure out what the brewpub would be and how it would evolve. It was apparent that I would assume all of the financial risk since it was my concept and my business plan and he would earn a sweat equity position over a number of years.

Things started off well enough. My hunch was right and our concept was viable—mostly because it was based on a sound business proposition for a restaurant that was very different from those around it. In the first year we discussed John's sweat equity situation a few times but were both focused on just making the business profitable. We said we would get to it. I had a mattress in the cellar and slept there the first summer as often as I slept at home. We would both fall asleep sitting upright counting money in the office at 2 AM, only to awake in the morning to begin working again. In short, we worked our asses off.

In our second year in business, when we separated our brewpub from our new production facility, I remember having all of two real meetings to discuss how our evolving company would be run. With two locations it was informally decided that I would run the production brewery and John would run the restaurant. The reputation of the food, beer, and music gave the brewpub great momentum, and, by the time we opened the microbrewery, the brewpub was already profitable. To his credit, John did a good job of managing the brewpub but my frequent absence was soon resented.

OVERCOMING MEETING-AVOIDANCE

In those first months running the brewpub was hard work, but it was easy to convey my vision for the company to my coworkers because I was always there. They saw the menu I created put into use. They saw me brew the beers, put them on tap, and discuss them with our customers. They saw my passion, and they understood my goals, and I didn't have to explain them because we were reaching them together, day-by-day. However, in a growing company you cannot expect to motivate everyone directly forever. The point at which you are removed from day-to-day interactions with anyone in your company is when your organization needs scheduled meetings. I was not having regular meetings with key coworkers as early as I should have. I used to shudder at the thought of organizing a meeting. I felt like I was pretending to be something I wasn't—some big-shot CEO instead of a rubber boots and flannel-shirt clad brewer. I was so caught up in the romance of *creating* a business that I forgot to pay attention to the details of running a business. I was young and naïve and recognized the value of meetings too late to salvage some substantial relationships within my company.

In order to maintain communication, small-business owners should schedule management meetings at least once a month. This should be done whether there is only one person managing a facet of your business other than yourself or seven managers overseeing distinct parts of your company. As you grow, more people will occupy management positions.

Organized, scheduled meetings are the only appropriate forums in which to officially communicate business propositions. While they must be run professionally, they don't have to be dry and boring. We have meetings with pizza and beer. We've had meetings with "educational" movies like *Dogtown and Z-Boys* (a study in creativity and teamwork disguised as a skateboard flick) and *The Godfather* (a study in hard-nosed business practices disguised as a gangster film). The important thing is that there are regularly scheduled meetings with an agenda, that important business is discussed, and a follow-up process occurs at the next meeting to check the status of what was agreed upon previously. Sometimes meetings last all afternoon, and sometimes they last 15 minutes. I have weekly meetings with brewery production, brewery management, brewery sales, restaurant, kitchen, and distillery management. The entire company then sits down as one big group midway through each month to see how we performed versus budget in the previous month. Sometimes we don't get everything we want to do done. Sometimes the same questions are asked week after week until we finally reach an answer. Sometimes I walk into a meeting planning to discuss a certain minuscule detail but get blown away by a huge new business idea a coworker brings to the table. On the highest level, the particular details of the meetings are less significant than the symbolic achievement of sitting down as coworkers and saying, "Let's communicate."

A meeting is where you review your company's progress in achieving your worthwhile business propositions. Meetings should be held in the middle of the month. This will give you and your bookkeeper (accountant, CFO, etc.) time to put together a review of the previous month's financial performance. You can share information about how the company met sales, labor, profitability, and other goals with the people who are directly overseeing those areas. You can discuss with specific managers how they are meeting goals and how they are not. More important, you can ask them how they plan to meet them in the future. They will see that their areas of concern are important enough to you and the company that you are willing to spend the time each month monitoring their progress. From this process everyone will see that the worthwhile business propositions you have chosen to center your business around will only come to fruition if the tangible steps taken to make them a reality are reviewed, monitored, and updated each month. Those managers that are succeeding at their assigned tasks are capable of doing the task and buying into the corporate philosophy embodied by the worthwhile business propositions. Those that fail are either incapable of doing their job or don't buy into the corporate philosophy.

As the leader you have the ability and the obligation to hold these people accountable and help them to succeed. If the wrong people are in the wrong positions or are failing because they don't buy into the corporate philosophy, you are equally responsible for redirecting them toward the company's goals and philosophies. You should create written outlines reviewing what was discussed in important meetings and who will be responsible for doing what in the future. When either good patterns or bad ones are established, the managers in question should be recognized and rewarded, or reprimanded and possibly even terminated. You have an obligation to the people who are competent, motivated, and believe in the company, to not let it be dragged down by those who are not equally attuned to the company's needs. I hate losing a coworker with great potential or belief in the company who just couldn't be guided toward success because of a lack of effort or ability by me or other coworkers. If you don't have regular meetings and review your progress toward your goals in an organized fashion, it will be difficult to hold anybody accountable and you will miss the opportunity to redirect a potentially crucial coworker when they go off-track. Sometimes a difference in philosophies will lead to separation and that's okay, but the company will only move through this separation unscathed if each party understands where the other was coming from and both believe that the separation occurred in a manner that was fair and reasonable; this is where I got myself into trouble. Communication and leadership are most effectively implemented through a management philosophy that incorporates a schedule of regular meetings.

In casual conversations on Saturday nights over a few beers at the pub, I would tell John about the challenges we were experiencing at the brewery. While the brewpub was paying its bills, the brewery was not. As the president of the company I was hopeful this scenario could be turned around if I continued to work hard at educating people about the uniqueness of our beers. And, for my company, this meant I was on the road more often than not. In hindsight I realize that this was when John became disillusioned with Dogfish Head because he became disillusioned with me as a leader. I was not doing a very good job of communicating my vision for the company to the key employees who worked there. I wish that John had as much faith in what I was doing as I had in myself. Although that was once the case, it was no longer true. This moment marked a shift in our relationship due to a then unperceived shift in our desired positions and interpretations of the corporate philosophy.

LACK OF COMMUNICATION

A company becomes unilaterally opposed when a follower ceases to believe in the vision of the leader. Remember, if you have hired well, you have a bunch of smart, perceptive coworkers. They can sense when the unity of faith and philosophy erodes between a leader and a follower. Whether that follower is the only other coworker you have, your chief operating officer, or your general manager, strong leaders are dependent on strong followers. Your followers will only be strong if they believe that their leader is worth following. If they don't, your company is in trouble. This lack of faith can be the result of a few different occurrences: the follower is in the wrong position, the follower is incompetent, the leader is incompetent, or the leader poorly conveys a sound vision. The last scenario is the one experienced in the early years of Dogfish Head.

A budget was established for both the brewery and the brewpub, but the planning process was anemic and simplistic. At the restaurant the budget plan was basically: "What did we do for revenue last year? Let's shoot for 20 percent over that." At the brewery we just stopped looking at projections since we were so far from the initial goals it was cringe-inducing. In order to meet bank payments, profits from the brewpub were used to pay down the growing debt of the brewery. From his perspective, John was working hard at the profitable location while I was off chasing windmills for the money-losing part of the company. When I would call the restaurant to check in on a Saturday night, I could hear the resentment in his voice. I was doing a beer dinner in Philadelphia while he was cleaning vomit off a bathroom wall. I would tell him that things would get better, but only on the phone or over a few pints when I would come work with him at the pub over the weekends.

develop good communication skills

At one rare meeting I told John that I had to cross-collateralize another loan between the pub and the brewery. Instead of *telling* him that we had to do it, I should have spent a lot more time and effort explaining *why* we needed to do it. Granted it was my name on all of the loans and I was 100 percent financially responsible for the company, but I wasn't the only person putting time, energy, and faith into the company. I am always an optimist and I think, as an entrepreneur, you have to be. In a lot of ways the deck is stacked against the average entrepreneur's success, so your optimism becomes a kind of shield that you heft to protect you from the harsh realities of the marketplace. I believed in the brewery and I assumed that John would trust my belief. My belief in Dogfish Head's worthwhile business propositions had served us well up to this point. I hoped John would recognize that I would bring the same passion, creativity, and conviction to the brewery as I had brought to the brewpub. He did not. Instead he proposed that I close the brewery and declare bankruptcy for that fraction of the business. I wouldn't even consider that option for a moment.

Within weeks of this meeting John resigned. He asked to be paid for stock that was never issued from a combined company that, at the time, had a negative net worth. I did offer him a five-figure check as an impromptu severance package (I wasn't sure if we could even afford to pay him that). He refused it. Instead he opened an Irish restaurant a couple of blocks from our front door. He's still there, and I sincerely wish him success. We haven't spoken more than a couple of sentences to each other since the day he walked out almost 6 years ago.

As I've grown older I believe that parting ways may have been inevitable. But we should have been able to do this amicably. After John left I felt frustrated and abandoned. He had believed in me enough to come and manage the restaurant. He believed in and supported my idea to start bottling beer. He believed in and supported my idea to open a separate production brewery. When this entity didn't quickly prove profitable, he lost his belief in, and support for, the company.

His disillusionment was infectious and soon most of the restaurant staff seemed to be taking sides. Many of the people I worked with were now unsure whether they were part of something special and I was remiss for not pointing out the potential for our company that I saw on the horizon. I always recognized the unique and worthwhile business objective of Dogfish Head very clearly, but I did not always communicate it well when we hit hard times.

THE PRICE OF NOT COMMUNICATING

I'll never know if holding regular management meetings, and compiling the financial data monthly to inform us where we stood compared to our goals, would have been enough to salvage John's relationship with the company. I do know that every key coworker was affected by his resignation and that I could have done a better job of keeping them excited and motivated about Dogfish Head if we had the number and nature of meetings that we do now.

After John left, Dogfish Head limped along for a few months on the backs of some well-intentioned, if undermanaged, true believers and a few bad eggs. I began having more regular meetings and tried hard to convey my vision, our brand identity, and the Dogfish Head culture to the people I worked with. This wasn't easy as I was being torn between my drive to educate people about the brand and expand the customer base, my need to manage operations at the brewpub, and my efforts to right the financial ship at the brewery.

As key people lost faith, they, in turn, did not communicate their disappointment to me. We held a few meetings in those days, but obviously there weren't enough meetings for me to properly explain where we were going to the people it affected the most.

My explanation should have started with John. Because of our history, I took it for granted that I didn't have to explain things to him. While I could usually see the forest real well, he was mired in the trees, and I did very little to help him step back and gain perspective. Despite our significant growth in revenue, customer base, and staff, life is less complicated, stressful, and confusing at Dogfish Head now than it was on the day that my best friend walked out. The reasons for this are simple: I became a better leader and I found people who were as enthusiastic as I was in helping to grow the company.

LEARNING FROM MISTAKES

There are still times at our company when interstaff problems and prejudices arise. What keeps them from derailing our momentum to the degree they did in the old days is that everyone knows they have a voice and, in the meetings, they will be given the chance to express themselves. As the leader, your voice must be the most consistent, fair, and compassionate of anyone you work with.

We now have a conference table that seats eight people. I like to think that no matter what size Dogfish Head becomes, this table will accommodate all of our management meeting needs. That's because one person can only effectively manage a finite number of other people. As our company has grown, meetings have developed from including everyone that worked at the company, to just the managers and assistant managers in each area, to just the managers of departments within our company. Meetings are about community and accountability. I cannot personally communicate with and hold all 70 of my coworkers accountable. As you grow, you will need to develop different layers of management so that everyone is accountable to someone and that someone might be accountable to someone else.

I became a better leader mostly by prioritizing the communication of my business objectives for both what the brand of Dogfish Head is on any given day and what I envision it becoming someday in the future. In the early days I never actively planned for the evolution of Dogfish Head so much as I just pursued what was fun, and then adapted to the natural evolution of our company. Sure I had beliefs: Original beer. Original food. Original music. Off-centered ales for off-centered people. But I wasn't spending much time teaching my coworkers exactly what these things meant, or how they were ideals that we needed to embrace every day.

M.C. Richards, a faculty member of my beloved Black Mountain College, once wrote of his school:

> I liked the strong personalities and vivid talents, the residual community taking its meals and recreation together. It was a place for growth and tempering. When my life and the college fell apart, I took it very hard . . . I felt we should be wiser than we were, more able to keep our college together through thick and thin. I was critical of the gap between our ideals and our performance, our creativity so far from human perfection.

I interpret this "gap" as a lack of balance. The balance between the theoretical and the practical. The balance between reality and ideals. It is nothing more than communication that bridges these gaps and keeps an organization in balance. There was a time in the early history of Dogfish Head when the *reality* of our performance was not meeting our *ideal* expectations. I was taking the company in a direction in which the two would balance some day, but many of the people around me didn't realize this.

They ceased to believe in my vision as a result of my poor leadership skills, and this dislocation between capable leaders and capable followers temporarily impacted the company. I was leading the company from the perspective of "I shall see what I shall see" and that just doesn't cut it. A similar lack of balance cost Mr. Richards his cherished community. This almost happened to me once. I work hard every day to make sure it could never happen again.

TRACKING, RECOGNIZING, AND REWARDING THE SUCCESSFUL EXECUTION OF A WORTHWHILE BUSINESS OBJECTIVE

One of the most important lessons to small-business owners is that, in order to grow your company, you need to build a community. While a community has many participants, and each is as important to the community as the other, it can only have one leader. You need to build this community around the common goal of reaching a shared vision or objective. Your coworkers only become part of your community when they share this vision, which can only be sustained if the community is financially viable and the worthwhile business propositions you have chosen to prioritize are realistic and sustainable. As the leader of a company you have a responsibility to outline and nurture a vision for your company built around these propositions. You only truly act as a leader when you take the time to reward and recognize the people who help the community grow for the better, and redirect or let go of the people who are incapable or unwilling to help the community grow. This is never an easy job. You will never be able to do it perfectly all the time. But the more frequently you address the inevitable challenges and recognize the successes faced by those struggling with them, the more regularly you will succeed.

chapter 12
EFFECTIVELY MANAGING EMPLOYEES

Too often in business we think of labor as an expense. There it is every month on our income statements. The most successful companies are those that recognize labor not only as an asset but as the most important asset a company has. Of all the mistakes I've made running my company, I have never made the mistake of not caring enough about the important details in life and business. It makes it easier when you believe that what's important in both life and business is exactly the same thing: people. If you don't like people, then I guess that's fine, too, but don't open a company.

When you are starting out and just beginning to hire employees, you probably can't offer the same salary and benefits that a giant public corporation can. Many of the principles that motivated you to open your own business are the same principles that lead people to work for a small company: more autonomy, more excitement, more variety, more say. They might not run the company, but they work with the person who does, and she's not some mythical suit cracking a whip from a skyscraper five states away.

Above a high salary or business perks, the main motivation for employees is a feeling that they are contributing to the success of the company. Numerous case studies have documented that people are more motivated by recognition than they are by money. I know this to be true for myself but I also know I have an obligation to my coworkers to make this company as strong and as efficient as I possibly can so that we can continue to do the creative things we enjoy. If a company proves that it genuinely believes in and trusts its coworkers, then those coworkers will believe in and trust the company. Encouraging the participation of coworkers leads to the implementation of innovative ideas and products. When employees feel they have contributed to a new product, service, or way of doing business, they develop a strong sense of loyalty to the company.

I'm convinced that we can attribute Dogfish Head's explosive growth to our success in finding and nurturing highly educated and motivated coworkers more than any other factor. Our recipes and marketing are unique, but they would mean nothing without the input and hard work of the people who bring them to reality every day. By highly educated I don't mean they all have PhDs or colossal IQs. I mean that we continue to spend time teaching them what our company is all about and they actively learn more about why and how we do what we do. The more employees feel like they are listened to, the more they feel like they matter in the grand scheme of your company. The more they feel like they matter to the company, the more they care for it. They begin to believe that the future of the company is truly their future as well.

In order to grow a company you need organization, hierarchy, and a balance between the creative and the orderly. It has taken me a long time to recognize that bureaucracy, if established fairly and creatively, is not entirely bad. As the leader of your company you are the conduit for evolution. In order to lead you must inspire the right people to follow. By "right" I mean a group that has the necessary blend of skill sets to keep the company moving forward and the personal belief that the company is pursuing worthwhile objectives.

The entire Dogfish Head brand image is built upon striving to provide innovative and dynamic product offerings that are not for everyone. It would be hypocritical of me to not champion individuality within our company when, as a niche producer, we champion the individuality of our customers. And yet, if everyone that worked at Dogfish Head prioritized their individuality it would be chaos and there would be no sense of community.

TREATING COWORKERS LIKE FAMILY

In the same way a successful entrepreneur must keep a small business nimble, and wear a lot of different hats, she must also assume multiple family roles. Different circumstances that arise within a company call for different techniques to find resolution. The techniques used within a small business vary from those used at larger corporations because the relationships between the coworkers at small businesses are much more personal. At different times a business owner may act as a father or mother, a sibling, or even a child to the different people you are trying to manage. One of the biggest reasons people choose to work for a smaller company is they want their work to matter. They want to see tangible results of their efforts and be recognized for their hard work and accomplishments. I don't think it's too sentimental to call this a desire to be cared about and cared for. The only difference is that with a true family love is unconditional and knows no bounds; even when you screw up everything in your life you expect family to be there for you. If you screw things up completely at work, a company cannot always stand by you. That's because there are other people involved who count on the company to provide for them. If people expect to be paid, as the business owner you have an obligation to run a profitable company. At Dogfish Head, I try to develop a standard of care for my coworkers that is one degree removed from unconditional love. It's love with very clearly defined performance expectations. You can only successfully incorporate a family dynamic into your company if the coworkers who care about the company are repaid by the company caring for them.

It was particularly hard to assume these different familial roles in the early days when I was trying to run the brewery and brewpub as an inexperienced businessperson. It is easier to point out instances when a manager must use the traditional disciplinary tactics associated with a father's role or the nurturing tactics associated with a mother's role. I once found myself in the role of a frustrated sibling with a coworker who had the knowledge of how to do a job but had lost the belief that it was a job worth doing. Bryan Selders is the lead brewer at Dogfish Head Craft Brewery. Over the years his passionate attitude and professional ability have been key factors in our explosive growth. He went to art school and shares my artistic sensibilities toward brewing. He is a self-taught brewer and a relentless perfectionist. A couple of years ago I noticed he was agitated at work. He would lose his temper and act like he didn't care when things didn't go smoothly at the brewery. This attitude was completely out of character. I invited him into the conference room and asked what the problem was. He curtly informed me that there was no problem, and coldly said that he would come to work on time, he would brew the beer, he would do what he was told to do, and leave the building as soon as he could. I felt like I was speaking with a complete stranger. None of the passion and drive that I associate with Bryan was evident that afternoon. I told him that it disappointed me to hear him talk that way and that it sounded like he had simply fallen out of love with his job and the company.

He broke down a little bit and told me that there was a deeper reason for his changed attitude. He became disenchanted with the company because he saw that a person in a position of authority over him was not working as hard as he was and was not working for the company as much as he was working for himself. The manager in question would say he cared about the company to my face and then ridicule the work we were doing to Bryan and his other subordinates after I had left the room. In short the company was caring for a coworker who didn't care for the company. Bryan was appalled that, as the leader, I was allowing this to happen. In essence we sat at that table as siblings. I was the brother that tarnished our family name by not protecting what it stood for. Bryan was saying that he could go through the motions of being in the Dogfish Head family, but unless I cared as much as he did about this particular situation his heart couldn't be in it. Bryan was right. I promised him that I would make sure the situation improved. I assured him that I had an obligation to him and the company to make sure that it improved, and it soon did. Bryan saw how seriously I viewed his request, he saw me actively working to correct the problem, and he was soon back on track to being a fully committed member of our family.

This whole idea of creating a community or family can seem trite when it is used in the context of business. You cannot fake a true family environment but when it is genuine it's the most effective motivator because it is self-sustaining and contagious. The success or failure of your community depends on the establishment of a management hierarchy that acknowledges the realms of responsibility for both followers and leaders, but is a flat hierarchy in terms of transcendent respect.

DEVELOPING STRONG MANAGEMENT SKILLS

I recognize that I am becoming a better manager every time we reach a critical management decision together and believe in the decision equally. In this sense, I haven't always been a good leader. I used to employ a personnel-management technique loosely based on the Amish practice of shunning. When a member of an Amish community acts against Amish rules (premarital sex in a custom-modified, turbo-charged buggy, for instance), the rest of the community just ignores, or shuns, the offensive person until the offender either leaves or pleads for forgiveness. I used to pretend that it was enough to just lead by example. I would work 12 hour days and do everything I could to move the company forward and indoctrinate the world to the Dogfish Head way. Sometimes a coworker would do something inappropriate and harmful to the image of our company, like being rude to a customer, showing up late for work, or just sucking at their job, and I knew the problem couldn't be ignored. So instead of ignoring the problem I ignored them. I let the coworker continue to wallow in his mediocrity. I would promote other people around him. I would socialize and extend preferential treatment to the coworkers I felt worked most closely in the spirit of Dogfish Head and ignore the offenders until they pleaded for forgiveness or quit. This is not a humane or effective way to manage people.

HIRING AND KEEPING STRONG PEOPLE

From the time I first met Fred Mazzeo at a beer festival I saw in him someone I suspected was capable of caring as deeply as I did for the company. He was the general manager for the Wilmington location of a national brewery restaurant chain. He saw me arriving late (as usual, after getting lost) to the festival and rushing to set up. He came over and offered to help. I tapped a keg without checking to make sure that the beer line had a gasket, and we were both sprayed with streams of stout. Instead of freaking out Fred commented that it tasted better than the beer his brewery had brought as he patted his ruined shirt. We both laughed and introduced ourselves. I was immediately struck by the feeling that I had met a kindred spirit. Within a few minutes of conversation he intimated that he felt stifled by the micro-management he received from his corporate office. He said that while his company offered great pay and benefits, to them he was just another cog in the machine. I felt stifled by the daunting task of managing a brewery and brewpub at the same time. Within weeks I invited him to come and work with me as the general manager at the brewpub.

I was determined to make Fred feel like a part of the Dogfish Head family. I knew that our methods and products were idiosyncratic and abnormal. I also knew that these differences were intrinsic to our identity. I realized that, in order for Fred to succeed, he would need to not just accept these differences but embrace and foster them as well. I also knew that he needed to understand the importance of nurturing the fraction of the Dogfish Head community he managed. On his first day with us, he stepped out of his car in our parking lot holding a briefcase, which I immediately asked him to put back in his car. I handed him a mullet wig, a set of brown fake teeth, a flannel shirt, and one of those dual-cup-holder hard hats that enables you to drink two beers from a straw at the same time—essentially the Dogfish equivalent of an HR new-hire packet. We drove off in my pickup truck (each wearing similar, ridiculous outfits) to a cow pasture to shoot a print ad for our beer that revolved around the theme of pasteurization. As we drove I talked seriously about my vision for what Dogfish Head was and what I imagined it could be. I talked openly with him about my faith that he could help me grow this company in a way that embraced our unorthodox alt-com ethos. I talked openly about building a serious company that didn't take itself too seriously. I talked openly and Fred listened and talked, and I listened and talked, and we both ended the day on the same page.

This openness is what helps cultivate a sense of community within a company, and trust is the result of this openness. Fred believes in the Dogfish Head community and has contributed to its growth at every level. You don't have to mix hops and barley in a boil kettle to contribute creatively. The creative aspect of management is the creation of the community. Food-runners, busboys, and dishwashers all participate in the creative act of sustaining the Dogfish Head community. Fred has continued to lead our restaurant through consecutive years of double-digit growth, and he has built a team of skilled individuals that have helped him reach these goals. He believes in our company, our management, and our leadership so much that he recently invested his own money in our continued growth.

Ideal coworkers look at their jobs as something to do well because that is the right thing to do and not just because they've been told to do it. The true definition of a job well done is one that enhances the community of the company, from a personal desire to do something well. The most successful people at Dogfish Head are those who recognize that life and work are not mutually exclusive. If you are truly passionate about something, your passion doesn't punch out at 5 P.M. I'm not saying a person has to work 70 hours a week to be successful. What I am saying is that I love to work with people who love their work because they love themselves. Buried within this elliptical thought pattern is the very essence of the Dogfish Head brand and ideology: There is a spiritually nourishing element to creative work. God is the creator. Man was created in God's image. Therefore, man is closest to God when he creates. I'm not referring to God in an organized religion kind of way but as the essence and impetus of creation: the Walt Whitman, "God is the eldest brother of my own," definition of God. And I'm not relegating *creative work* just to the construction of beer or a product to sell. I'm saying that man is at his best when he is creating. And the best thing he can create is a community. In business this community may be as small as a kid at a lemonade stand and his customer, or it may be as big as a multinational corporation. The ongoing creation of a community that relishes passion and creativity is what we are in the business of at Dogfish Head. We're not in the business to make money. That is a by-product of what we do. Money doesn't help you feel better—connecting to other people does.

Defining who the "right" people are for your company is subjective. Once you understand what your company's goals and values are then you are capable of sharing them with coworkers. Through the normal course of day-to-day interactions with coworkers, you will know who is right for your company and who is not. Reward and nurture those whose care for the company mirrors your own. If there are people who work at your company who aren't upholding the values you prioritize, your first objective should be realigning that person to the company. As you spend time in the marketplace, you will meet other qualified and capable people who you could picture working well in your company. Don't be afraid to tell them about what you do and ask them candidly if they have any interest in joining you on your quest. That's what I did with Fred, and I don't feel at all bad that I ripped him away from his previous employer. That employer was capable of making an enticing counteroffer if it cared enough to have him stay. The work environment and coworkers' responsibilities at your company are probably very different from those at our brewery and brewpub. Therefore, my definition of the "right" person might be very different from your own. That's to be expected. But what isn't different from one business to another is the objective of surrounding yourself with people who share your passion, knowledge, and drive for the industry in which you work. The "right" people are those who are as capable as you are at caring for the company.

The community that we create at Dogfish Head revolves around beer and a sense of dislocation. A lot of people feel shell-shocked by the bombardment of advertising done by the big breweries. More than that, they are genuinely disappointed when they drink their beer. It tastes bland, and it's all the same. Corporate beer was not made in the image of these people—they are not bland or homogeneous. They are individuals with discerning tastes who know what they like. They have formed a community of individuals who feel the same way. They don't want to be told what to buy. They want to be given the choice to decide for themselves what to buy. They want to know that the people making and selling the beer they buy feel the same way. They want a human transaction. Big-commerce tries to tell people we are all the same. Alt-commerce celebrates the fact that people are different. The challenge for Dogfish Head will be to continue nurturing this human scale as our company grows.

When you are just starting out, the benefits you can offer key employees may be limited to a paycheck that doesn't bounce and a creative, safe, respectful work environment. As your company grows in position and profitability, you can start offering additional benefits that show how much you care. Within a few years of opening, we created a bonus structure that was based on net profits for key managers. This keeps the decision makers in your company focused on the bottom line and lets them share in the fruits of their labor. We now offer health benefits, sick and vacation time for full-time, salaried employees. To find out what benefits are most important to your coworkers, ask. We sent out a questionnaire to all employees asking them to list in order of importance the benefits that they would care most to receive. Health care was far and away the most common first priority for everyone. As a result of this questionnaire, we are implementing a more robust health care plan that allows us to extend coverage to full-time, tipped employees (waitstaff, bartenders) and full-time, hourly employees as well as our salaried managers. Doing this won't be cheap for a company of over 70 people, but it shows that we view labor as an asset and not as a liability. Whatever level of benefits you can afford to offer, start there. As your business evolves ask for the input of all your coworkers about what is most important to them. This will lead you to make investments in them that show your company is willing and able to care for the people who care for the company.

The successful entrepreneur not only has unlimited faith in the quality and potential of what she is selling, but she must have as much faith in the quality and potential of her target consumer and (especially) her coworkers. Typically a company's employees become the face of a company. They determine the first impression a customer has about a company. Odds are your coworkers will more often be those who convey your company's identity to the world than you will. If they don't understand that identity, then you, as the leader of the company, haven't done your job. Once you have a vision for your company you need to transfer this vision to everyone in the company. You need to create an environment of empowerment where employees perceive the company as something belonging to them as much as it belongs to you.

SETTING DEFINED EXPECTATIONS

To manage employees effectively you need to clarify not just the grand long-term goals of the company but your expectations of everyone who works with you. You will succeed if you can translate the company ideology to new coworkers in a way that allows them to truly believe in what they are doing. As leaders and managers we must learn to delegate to coworkers only after we are sure that they understand the kind of company we are trying to build. As a leader, it's useless to say "We are doing it this way because I said so."

I learned the hard way in my work with John that there is a need for clear and exact job descriptions. People should be rewarded and reprimanded with regularity for their ability to complete their defined job. For me the most important question upon which to consider hiring or promoting someone is, Does this person fully understand and embrace the mission of our company? The second most important question is, Can this person perform the job we are asking her to do? The knowledge of how to do a job is secondary to the belief that it is a job worth doing.

REWARDING EMPLOYEES

While a company's management team is responsible for creating and maintaining a sense of community, it also has a responsibility to compensate coworkers fairly for their contributions toward building this community. You can't do this unless your business is strong and profitable, and your business can never be strong and profitable without the help of good people. Again, you need balance. It's difficult to achieve this balance as a young company unless you are building your brand or reputation and your community simultaneously from day one and working with people who believe in what you are building.

Our HR director is charged with making sure no bodily harm comes to our workers, that all of the safety procedures and emergency equipment is in place. But, as the leader, I am responsible for making sure that no spiritual harm comes to my coworkers. This starts with providing personally rewarding jobs. We have worked hard to set clear definitions of job descriptions, a comprehensive organizational chart so that everybody sees who is responsible for what, and better than average compensation in line with our expectations for better than average work. We are not perfect and never will be. Sometimes it doesn't work between a coworker and our company, and that coworker needs to find personal reward somewhere else. Our corporate culture is unique and not all-inclusive. Some people need more structure than we are willing or able to provide. But other people really blossom with the freedom we try to provide. I now have a group of managers that believe in the vision of Dogfish Head as much as I do.

We believe strongly in sharing the success of the company with the people most responsible for helping us achieve it. We have an aggressive bonus program for key managers based on net operating profit. I strongly recommend this program to any small businessperson. People start thinking about the bottom line and recognizing that controlling costs is every bit as important as growing business. Everything remaining after bonuses and fair salaries goes right back into the company. We expect significant capital expense budgets from every area of the company each year. We want to put the money back into the company because in order to sustain strong growth you must continually reinvest in the organization. That means new tanks, new bottling lines, new ovens, new awnings, new paint jobs. When your coworkers see the company money being reinvested instead of fueling off-season Florida golf junkets for the owners, it sends an important message about leadership priorities. Plus, the more you upgrade the facility, the better your work environment, the happier your workforce.

Our bonus program and aggressive capital expense investments show a

high level of responsibility and respect to our key managers. Bonus packages are important compensation tools. We've worked hard to establish an
aggressive profit-sharing program with key employees at both our restaurant and our brewery. We set goals that are fair and within a person's control, and they are rewarded when they meet them.

There is a rigorous annual budgeting period each fall when we expect
a lot of input from our key managers. Great responsibilities come with these
decisions, and Mariah and I entrust six-figure budgets to certain managers
every year. We have to believe in these people and trust that they know
their jobs better than we do. If a budget is your road map for the coming
year, then it makes sense to involve the people who care about the company's success in that budget. If you don't do that, how can you expect
them to care when the company falls short of budgeted goals? How will
they understand what is expected of them in the shared goal of reaching
this budget? When Dogfish Head was a smaller, less-enlightened company,
the budgeting process was less inclusive. Mariah and I would share the budgets with the key managers only after they were completed. This system
didn't work well nor did it show much respect for the people with whom
we worked and counted on to help us hit our goals. In the same way that
you will be rewarded if you ask your coworkers what sort of benefits matter most to them, you will be rewarded if you involve them in the budgeting process.

It used to be that I was the most ambitious person in our company; I
would set absurdly high revenue goals and work my hardest to hit them.
When I didn't reach them, I took it very personally. Now we set our budgeting goals together. Sometimes my expectations are higher, other times
they are lower than the budget drafts put together by the managers in each
faction of our business. I learn a lot about our company when I ask why
their expectations are different from my own. If their reasons are sound, then
I am willing to adjust the budget accordingly. This process allows everyone
to participate in the process and prove how much they care about the company. Now if we fall short of a budgeted goal I don't take it personally, and
if we exceed a shared budgeted goal I am more ecstatic than I would have
been if it were only me who dictated what that goal would be. Once the
community shares responsibility for the company's goals, the joy that comes
with reaching those goals increases to the size of that community.

I don't know much about bees. I'm not a very scientific person, and

I'm allergic to pollen. But I always liked the idea of bees as a business metaphor. When you start a company, it's usually just yourself and maybe a handful of coworkers. The customers are your flowers, and you buzz around them—you know, busy as a bee. In the early days your coworkers are buzzing around beside you so your enthusiasm and belief in the importance of the task at hand is both infectious and immediately apparent. But, as your company gets bigger, more and more flowers need attention. Some of the other worker bees may not be in the area where you are buzzing. It's important to make sure bees are near every cluster of flowers and that they understand what the mission is and believe in that mission for themselves. These are the bees that will guide the other newer bees through the methods and machinations of their tasks. They are all part of a shared community, and the whole of this community is greater than the sum of its parts. There's a lot of pollinating going on in building a business, and you can't do that all by yourself. As I write in this moment in a quiet farmhouse, Mariah and Fred and Bryan and other bees are out there doing the hard and critical work of bringing the word of Dogfish Head to the customer and motivating a whole bunch of other bees to do the same.

chapter 13

WORKING TOWARD IRRELEVANCE

Around the time that the brewpub opened, I read an interview in a newspaper about a big brewery that was opening in a city north of us. The interview was with the founder who had an impressive business pedigree, particularly compared to my own, so I was hopeful that I would learn a thing or two by reading it. The founder had all of the facts down pat: the size of the overall beer industry, the growth rate of the microbrewing segment, an understanding of which geographic and demographic markets he would explore, and the potential for a future stock offering. It all seemed to make sense until the interviewer asked a final question, "Which of the beers that you make is your favorite?" The businessman responded that he actually didn't like beer and preferred to drink Juicy Juice. I remember reading it twice to make sure I was reading it correctly. I was still quite naïve about business and wasn't 100 percent sure that Dogfish Head was a brewery that would be around for a long time, but I was sure of one thing: This guy was screwed.

The owner obviously loved money more than he loved beer. He had no passion for his job. He was just making a widget with the hope that it would lead to an IPO. I heard from other brewers that this brewery owner spent his days sitting in a fancy office suite high above the production floor reading the *Wall Street Journal* and calling his distributors to yell at them for not buying more beer. He had zero connection to the people who worked for him or the people he was selling beer to. I remember being seriously offended that he would do such a disservice to his customers as never even drinking the product he expected them to buy. If you don't like beer, fine, but don't open a brewery.

Of course it did not take this brewing company very long to go out of business. As a business leader, there's a productive way to work toward irrelevance and a destructive way. The story of this particular guy illustrates the destructive way. The owner had been working his way toward irrelevance since the day he gave that interview, and probably long before that.

DELEGATING YOUR WAY TO OBSOLESCENCE

Of all the challenges I've faced in running this company, each pales in comparison to the one before me now—working my way toward irrelevance. It's not what you think; I haven't just wasted your time and money by taking you through the trials and tribulations of a small company on the brink of going out of business. Dogfish Head is stronger than ever in every sense of the word. The company is now well out of the start-up phase but nowhere near the static, mature phase of business as usual. I hope it never gets there. There are still so many new kinds of beer to brew, so many other business opportunities to explore. So many off-centered people we have yet to turn on to our off-centered ales.

I spend a lot of time in meetings with the key managers of my company, but the amount of hours I spend in those meetings seems very small compared to the amount of time I spend away from the brewery in the greater community of beer and beer enthusiasts. I'm lucky I have the strong support of my management team to allow me to spend the time I do outside of the brewery. I know what my strengths and weaknesses are as a businessperson, and while I have improved in all areas over the last 10 years, I'm still a much better salesperson than I am a manager. I'm on the road at least a couple of days of each week attending beer festivals, meeting with distributors, talking with other brewers, riding with salespeople, meeting retailers, and conducting beer dinners. I am happiest when I am creating—riding my bike or driving along and being struck with an idea for a new beer style or a themed beer dinner. The opportunity to turn little daydreams into bigger realities is probably the most rewarding aspect of my job. These moments of inspiration usually come as a result of some interaction I have with a customer, retailer, or distributor. I really enjoy interacting with our customers and spending time in the marketplace. I learn more about the gap between what I want Dogfish Head to be and what it actually means to the customers every time I'm out there. It's been inspiring to watch that gap close as we continue to do a better and better job. My responsibility is to share what I learn about Dogfish Head with the people I work with. We recognize the good things and take pride in those achievements, and we take responsibility for addressing the areas for improvement.

Gathering feedback from the marketplace and interpreting it with my coworkers is a big part of my job these days; so is managing managers. I like being on the road, but I also enjoy working at the brewery. I am slowly learning that the more day-to-day responsibility I can give to capable managers, the more I can focus on the long-term challenges we face. It has taken me a decade before I stopped fearing irrelevance. As a business owner it can be very painful to willfully dislocate yourself from the minutiae of day-to-day decisions connecting the short-term course of your company. It's natural to fear becoming obsolete. You might ask, How can I run a company that doesn't seem to need me? I have learned the opposite is true—you know you are running a company well when it doesn't need you to make the sound day-to-day decisions any longer. This means your managers are well trained, well educated, and well acclimated. They have been indoctrinated so completely in your company's philosophies and identity that they can make decisions in harmony with those you would make, and their decisions are made for the good of the company and the brand. You need to accept that while similar, the decisions they make will not always be exactly the same as the ones you would make. You must acknowledge that this is okay, for both you and your managers, at the same time that you coach them on the long-term decisions that require your input. You need to trust that their take on what your company is all about has been informed by the education you've given them and the example you have shown during the time you have worked with them. Until I found the right people and began to trust the decisions that were being made by them, I had a hard time leaving the brewery and feeling confident that things would go smoothly and efficiently when I wasn't around.

It used to be a lot more difficult to go on the road than it is now. I would come back to one disaster after another at the brewery and the restaurant. Equipment would break down; coworkers would quit; and managers would be frustrated. I was spending too much time trying to get to know our customers and what they wanted from Dogfish Head, and not enough time getting to know my coworkers and making sure I had the right people in the right positions. If you have the wrong people in positions of management, you have too much managing and not enough leadership. If you have the right people in position, you spend a lot of time giving them the resources and knowledge they need to successfully carry out their responsibilities and the vision of the company. This proved to be challenging when we were moving from my involvement with every day-to-day decision, to relying on others to make those decisions in the best interest of the company. The problem was that I didn't always do a good job providing direction or instilling a clear understanding of my vision for the company in the people I counted on to help me see it to fruition.

PASSING THE TORCH

Most small companies are run more by intuition than by design. The leader delegates direction to the workers whose tasks and focus change on a day-to-day basis. This is the way it has to be as a start-up. The owner needs to roll up her sleeves and immerse herself in every seemingly minute decision until it becomes clear what the values and the direction of the company will be. This will only be clear once a true and tested relationship between the customer and the company is established. Once this relationship is set and the components that describe it are clear to the founder, the hard work of transferring the responsibility for that relationship from the owner to others within the company begins. The relationship will never grow into something meaningful if you hide in an executive suite reading the *Wall Street Journal*.

As your company grows beyond yourself, you are charged with sustaining a vision for your coworkers that blends the pursuit of profit and financial strength with a commitment to social awareness and community. To foster a community you must know that community. We have learned that the more time and energy we spend in selecting the right people for key positions the better off the company will be. Finding the right people with leadership potential is only half the battle. The other half is to make sure you give the new hires enough time and tools to learn their jobs well, and enough authority to make the occasional mistake as they learn to think for themselves about what are the best decisions they can make for the company.

There are really only two types of workers: doers and thinkers. When you are growing your company and it is growing beyond your control, it is time to find people to help you grow the company back into control. As the leader you will be tempted to hire people who seem most willing and able to take direction and follow your orders exactly. At Dogfish Head we call these people doers. They are capable of doing exactly what you tell them to do. At first that would seem like the perfect hire, but if you are a small company that intends to grow, everybody in your organization needs to realize that growth is synonymous with change. Every reaction to change in a growing company cannot be filtered through a single leader. So a doer that can do exactly what you need him to do today is not going to help your company as much as a thinker that can do what you tell her to do today, anticipate what is on the horizon for tomorrow, and react to it with confidence that her reaction is formulated on the best interest of the company. We have all worked with people who are fantastic at completing assigned tasks but, upon finishing that task, need to be told what to do next. A thinker will do the assigned task equally well but will be thinking of ways that it might be done better in the future. The more thinkers you can promote into key positions, the more smoothly your company will grow.

As your company matures from just a few people working under one boss to a bunch of people working under a bunch of bosses, the clarity and consistency of your vision becomes critically important for two reasons: opportunities for advancement and continued growth.

I look for certain qualities in potential leaders. I want to be surrounded by people who think big. I want individuals with high desire for personal achievement. I want to find and nurture people who are focused on realizing a different vision of the world than the one they currently live in. People who can think as well as they can do. People who see that their role in the company offers them the opportunity to effect a change on the world. For our production manager and lead brewer, that means making the best and most interesting beers that are commercially available. For our restaurant general manager, that means creating and sustaining a unique, comfortable, memorable dining experience. Each key person has a different role but in essence the same goal—continually moving the shared vision of Dogfish Head toward reality. I want to hire managers who are more capable and ambitious than I am in their areas of expertise. In terms of expertise, I look forward to being upstaged in every realm of responsibility that I have ever had at Dogfish Head. This is what I mean by working toward irrelevance in a positive way. As the company has grown, I have been able to find the key people who share my vision and motivate them toward making it happen. I am still concerned with issues such as our cost of goods sold, payroll, insurance, maintenance, and production efficiency. I'm concerned but not worried. I know that there are people at Dogfish Head who are better skilled than I at managing these details. At each monthly meeting when the previous month's numbers are reviewed, I observe who is performing well and who is underperforming. This is an opportunity to help the underperformers improve and the chance to thank the people who are meeting their objectives. At the end of the day I know that I have given each manager the tools needed to either succeed or fail. I have learned that the people who expect the most from Dogfish Head are those who expect the most from themselves.

The best of us work primarily for personal satisfaction and secondarily toward satisfying a role within the company. Work can be as rewarding or spirit-breaking as you make it. Similar to how the closer you align your products to the core values of your company the better the odds are that they will find an audience, the closer your coworkers' values are to those of your company the better the odds are that they will find happiness in their work. The vision of Dogfish Head is to continually create a company that delivers an off-centered experience to off-centered people. This vision is based on a set of values. As in a family, in which the greatest gift parents can give their children is a clear set of values, we are obligated to provide the same gift to our coworkers. The primary value is respect. Respect for people, for helping them to work and consume in an environment rich with ethics, honesty, and compassion. Respect for customers, coworkers, and everything we produce. We continually try to increase this respect through our work. Other values are central to our philosophy such as an ongoing commitment to innovation, and to a continued exploration of all things off-centered, but the final key value is happiness. If something is not fun, it's not worth doing. We make beer, not nuclear armaments. We don't take ourselves too seriously, but we take our jobs very seriously. We wear flip-flops to work, swear at each other like sailors, and play practical jokes on one another any time we see a chance. This wouldn't work if we didn't have the utmost faith and respect in one another's ability regarding our jobs. We do. To work in this kind of environment is wholly rewarding.

DETERMINING YOUR OWN FATE

I would never try to prescribe a specific set of values or a vision that would work for every small company. There is no guaranteed set of guidelines for success applicable for everyone. Especially since it's the uniqueness of your company and what you do that will make you stand out in a crowded marketplace. Regardless of what sort of vision you set for your company, as it evolves and matures you will need to create increased opportunity for the people who help you move it forward. As the leader of the company, part of your job is to continually champion and expand your vision, and recognize and reward the people who share that vision by making sure they find their work and their place in the company wholly rewarding.

SHARING YOUR SHARES

I am proud to say that I am well on the road to working myself into irrelevance. There are still a few things that I feel I am best suited to do in the company: new product development, strategic planning, partnership and licensing projects, certain marketing initiatives and promotional events. They are not exactly minor issues. It will take a while before I will be comfortable handing these responsibilities over. But the vast majority of work at Dogfish Head is now being done better by somebody other than myself. Mariah is better at evaluating advertising opportunities. Mike, our distiller, is better at making rum. Nick is better at controlling costs. Our chef, Jeff, is better at ordering food. The vision and values of this company are recognized and internalized in many of the people that I work with. As the company grows stronger, I need to make sure that their financial reward is in balance with their spiritual reward.

Material riches and the accumulation of wealth have never been a motivating factor in my life. As a businessperson I have also recognized the responsibility of putting the financial health of the company before my own comfort. There were some tight times in the early years of the company, when I had to skip cashing my own paycheck, but the business is now healthy enough to pay me a fair salary in line with the other key managers in the company.

As I continue to work toward irrelevance I am exploring a level of compensation beyond pay increases and bonuses for certain key managers: the opportunity to buy equity. Mariah and I have identified five key positions that we are working to fill with dedicated, responsible people. Once the people in these positions have proven that they are up to the challenges that come with their responsibility, Mariah and I might be willing to dilute our own equity in the company and give them the opportunity to buy in.

Fred Mazzeo, our restaurant general manager, was the first person to be given this opportunity. After helping us grow the business we extended him the offer to buy shares in our company at a reduced rate. He still has to pay for it, but, in acknowledgment of his hard work, we discount the value. As Fred puts it, he decided to invest his life savings into the company because he believes in Dogfish Head and he believes that he can help us continue to grow, which will directly affect the value of his investment. That to me is the ultimate win–win scenario.

I am implementing methods that allow key people to buy into the future of Dogfish Head for a couple of reasons. The first is so that Mariah and I have people that care as much about Dogfish Head on every level as we do. Some coworkers have continually gone above and beyond the call of duty for this company. In some ways a bonus acknowledges the past, while an equity stake acknowledges the future. Recognizing a high level of accomplishment with a bonus works well as an annual reward—it shows that you appreciate the hard work that the person put in over the last year. Recognizing that commitment with an opportunity for an equity stake is one way to show that you believe the person's hard work will add value to the company in the future.

I count my blessings every day that our company is healthy and growing. If we weren't growing the way we are, I wouldn't be confronted with these decisions. As you contemplate the potential size of your own business, you should be considering the number and nature of key management positions that you will need to develop to get you where you want to go. While you may only be in the early stages of your long-term plan, considering future key personnel positions now will help you prepare for and identify the best potential hires. Most sole proprietors or mom-and-pop-run small businesses might not have to consider profit sharing, management bonus programs, or the potential sale of stock or equity. But, if your company grows to include multiple locations or multiple layers of management, one, some, or all of these compensation options might be appropriate.

It takes years of working with a key manager or executive before it becomes apparent that he or she is a candidate for an equity position. Much of the analysis for that decision goes back to the corporate vision. It should not be a question of whether they are willing and capable of carrying out your vision but whether they recognize that vision as their own. Of course another consideration will be whether they are in a financial position to make such an investment.

The other reason we are considering certain key positions and people for potential equity stakes is that I may not want to work at Dogfish Head for the rest of my life. Just writing that sentence makes me anxious, which means I know I'm not there yet. But that doesn't mean I don't want to be there some day. As I previously mentioned, there are crucial jobs within the company that I believe I'm the best person to handle—product development, long-term planning, and marketing are the three I am most passionate about. I know it will be years before I would even consider handing these responsibilities to someone else. I also know that my coworkers recognize I am still the best person for this job. That makes me feel pretty good about what I do. Starting this company, running this company, and growing this company have allowed me to live out one of my biggest dreams, and I'm indebted to a lot of people for helping me make it happen.

KNOWING YOUR OPTIONS

As Dogfish Head continues to grow and receive more media attention, we have approached the outer reaches of the business radar. We are not a giant ping in the beer and restaurant world, but we are an ever more audible blip. We have received calls from business brokers who have clients interested in acquiring our company. We have gotten calls from venture capitalists inquiring about our desire to take the company public. I always take the calls personally to thank them for their interest in Dogfish Head, but I quickly explain that we enjoy running the company ourselves and seem to be getting better and better at it. If we weren't, then I doubt these people would be calling us at all. It's kind of surreal to think about how Mariah and I might separate ourselves from a company that we have spent all of our energies growing from its birth. I don't know if our business ages in people-years or dog-years or if it is immortal and will live with us forever. Right now it seems to be aging in people-years. It's 10 years old. It doesn't need us to hold its hand when it crosses the road anymore. But it still needs us to tuck it in before it goes to sleep each night. I still feel like I am the best person to guide the company—on some levels Dogfish Head still needs me and on a lot of levels I still need Dogfish Head. But I don't want Dogfish Head to overstay its welcome in our lives. Right now it doesn't feel like it ever could, but I don't know what the future holds. I don't want it to become the 30-year-old slacker-child that finishes off the basement and lives off of Mariah and me until we are old and gray.

No matter what kind of company you want to have, or have now, or hope to have in the future, you need to think about if and when the day will come when you are no longer the best person to run the company. I've heard it described as an exit strategy but for me it makes more sense to have a bunch of different exit strategies. As I have said so many times and in so many ways in this book, the only thing you can count on in business is change. I don't think you can guide your company toward the single best exit strategy, but it makes sense to think about how your company could best grow beyond your involvement.

Ideally most business owners who enjoy their work would like to stay the course, continue to run the company, and empower key coworkers to help run the company. Once you have reached a certain level of success, options for selling your company are bound to present themselves. Remember, if the potential buyer is a shrewd businessperson, she is interested because she thinks she can create more value in your company than you have been able to create on your own. Using this logic, it makes the most sense to consider selling your company only after you have exhausted all of the possibilities you have considered for growing the value of the business. I'm not there yet. I still have a lot of projects that I want to do at Dogfish Head. The main reason I want to do the projects we are currently working on is because I think they will be fun and complement everything we've done this far in establishing our brand. One of the results of these projects, if we execute them properly, will be an increased value in our company.

Other than running out of ideas for how to increase the value of your company, the other sound reason for selling might be that you've built up an immunity to the thrill of risk. Risk is adrenalin pure and simple, and risk is a sort of opiate to the entrepreneur. You may build up an immunity to risk, or your appetite might be insatiable and continue to expand as you expand your company. Different people have different tolerance levels to risk. If the feeling you get from taking a risk—that "Oh my god, what am I doing" positive feeling of exhilaration—mutates over time to a feeling of "Oh my god, why am I doing what I'm doing," it might be time for you to consider doing something else.

I don't know if it will be 5, 10, or 20 years in the future, but I imagine the time will come when I will want to do something either instead of or in addition to Dogfish Head. Mariah and I have talked about this day, and we may choose to sell the company or some fraction of the company when it comes. I couldn't imagine ever selling Dogfish Head to one of the giant domestic breweries I assure you, but to a like-minded company who sees the opportunity to grow Dogfish Head beyond our own capacities.

Aside from Mariah and our children, Dogfish Head has brought me more joy than anything else in my life. I wake up, jump out of bed, and can't wait to get to work. At the end of the day I jump in my car and rush home because I can't wait to be with my family. My life is hectic but joyful. The only other professional aspiration I've ever had was to someday return to Northfield Mt. Hermon, the high school I was expelled from, to teach English. I would only do this if I could also afford to keep my house and friends here in beautiful, coastal Delaware. But I always figured it would be nice to spend the first half of my life learning and the last half teaching. I don't think I would have much knowledge to share with students without the experiences I have had at Dogfish Head. My goal was to somehow, some way be able to move back to New England, near where I grew up, and return to the campus where I learned about what kind of person I would like to be. Maybe I could use everything I've learned since then to help young people figure out exactly what kind of person they want to become.

I would love to teach a course rich in the tradition of American ingenuity—to incorporate the writings of people like Walt Whitman, Ralph Waldo Emerson, de Tocqueville, and Henry David Thoreau into a curriculum celebrating the goodness and potential of the motivated individual. To tell the stories of historic innovators like Sam Colt, Henry Ford, Walt Disney, and other great Americans who have shaped our country and the world. To convince kids that they should recognize and develop the innovative and inventive capacities within them regardless of what career they choose. To show them that they are each capable of greatness and that the journey down the road to success starts with self-respect and self-reliance. To show how the American entrepreneurial spirit provides good lessons for anyone willing to look for them and anyone willing to work hard to create something that is a reflection of themselves. This is what I've tried to accomplish at Dogfish Head, and this is what anyone who goes into business for themselves is trying to achieve.

I suppose we may choose to take Dogfish Head public (I'm biting my tongue), although I realize that decision obligates me to a full day of treading beer inside one of the tanks in the brewery. Or possibly we could sell either a majority or a minority equity stake in the company to a team of our own managers and investors if that's what makes sense. I can't say for sure what will be best for us as a family and what will be best for Dogfish Head as a company in the long run. Right now I know that the majority of my focus needs to be centered around the continued growth of Dogfish Head.

THE FUTURE IS UNCERTAIN

I don't know exactly what the future holds for Dogfish Head. There are as many options for leaving a business as there are for starting one. It may seem especially strange to be considering an exit strategy for a company you are only now thinking of starting but it's a great exercise to help you construct a long-term vision for where you want that company to take you. If your goal is to make money, and you genuinely care about the business you are in, then you can reach that goal and sell your business for a profit. If your goal is to create a business that will sustain your family for generations, then that could happen, too. My father-in-law is in the process of transferring ownership of his company into the hands of his children and he has done an admirable job of tending to the details and relationships that make this transformation a possibility. My son and daughter, Sammy and Grier, are 5 and 3 years old, so it will be a while before I know if they truly care to continue in the family business. Sammy brought in a drawing from school the other day depicting what he wanted to do when he grew up. The picture showed some bottles moving through a machine, and he wrote that he wanted to be an archeologist and a beer maker. I imagine I was more proud of this revelation than his teacher was. Our company is definitely a part of our family, though. I spend a lot of time telling our children what their mother and I do and what Dogfish Head is all about. We tell bedtime stories that involve Peter Pan hopping in the truck with us to deliver a load of beer to Philadelphia. I'm almost proud to say that our company's logo was the second one they recognized behind the Golden Arches, and even though we don't give away free toys with each of the kid's meals at our restaurants, our fries are preferred two-to-zero by our own children.

With the way technology is moving, videoconferencing is becoming a bigger part of the business world. Mariah and I may be able to retain majority ownership of our company and work with our executive managers to run it from afar. I could teach in the winters and return to Delaware in the summers to help a whole team of thinkers run the company. While in Massachusetts I could have weekly videoconference meetings and keep up with everything by e-mail. I envision us having a yurt in the backyard with a small brewing system and lab where I could experiment with new ideas to my heart's content. I could invite my managers and brewers up to New England to try the latest beers and discuss the marketing and growth opportunities that are facing us. This might be how things work out, or it might not.

I just hope that whatever decision we make, it is reached because it represents the best opportunity for the company. This company has been so good to Mariah and me that I feel like we owe it the same consideration in return. If and when some level of separation comes between me and Dogfish Head I know it won't be easy. You hear about amputees who swear that they still can feel their missing limb. I imagine it would be something like that for me. I grew a company from nothing to something, and during that period I became a part of that company and it became part of me. It doesn't matter to me that we are still a small company or that most of the people that buy beer have probably never heard of Dogfish Head. What matters is that I was given the opportunity to express myself and create something and the thing that I created has brought a lot of enjoyment and value to a growing number of off-centered consumers and coworkers. Listen to me, I sound like I'm writing my own eulogy. I'll stop now.

I think of these exit strategy options occasionally, but I don't even have my blinker on yet to get over to the exit lane. I'm only 35 so even if I hit my target age of 45 to start teaching, I have 10 years to wear flip-flops to work and the occasional wig. Dogfish Head is still as fun as it was when I started. We are at least as innovative as we were 10 years ago. Most important, I still work in an environment rich with respect. I am respected by the people I work with and the customers that I sell my beer to, and I give them that respect right back. I know that they could work for another brewery or buy beer from another brewery in a heartbeat. I know that the reason they choose to believe in Dogfish Head is that we deliver an experience unlike any other company out there. Our passion, dedication, and distinction is palpable in every case of beer that comes off our bottling line, every pizza that comes off our wood grill, and every bottle that comes out of our distillery. A respect for people comes from a respect in yourself. The decision to start your own company comes from a position of self-respect. You must believe in yourself so strongly that you are willing to see your idea through regardless of the obstacles you will surely face. You must believe that your vision is worth sharing with the world and is noble enough to be taken up by your coworkers as their own. I commend you on your efforts to make your dream a reality. With this in mind I would like to share a Theodore Roosevelt quotation that I hope to someday read to my class on my first day of teaching high school English.

> It is not the critic who counts, not the man who points out how the strong man stumbled, or where the doer of deeds could have done them better. The credit belongs to the man who is actually in the arena: whose face is marred by the dust and sweat and blood; who strives valiantly; who errs and comes short again and again. . . . who knows the great enthusiasms, the great devotions and spends himself in a worthy cause; who, at the best, knows in the end the triumph of high achievement; and who, at the worst if he fails, at least fails while daring greatly, so that his place shall never be with those cold and timid souls who know neither victory or defeat.

chapter 14
TO SMALL-BUSINESS SUCCESS

The *art* of brewing is not something that you hear or read about often. But we really do treat what we do as an art form. Like Black Mountain College, Jackson Pollock, and bands like Radiohead and Wilco, Dogfish Head tries to make challenging but beautiful art. The difference is that our art is in liquid form and we don't get royalties if some hot chick drinks one of our beers on *The O.C.* Small is relative. Dogfish Head is still a small brewery in the eyes of most consumers and the government as well. This reality will never stop us from thinking big.

In 2003 Dogfish Head was the fastest-growing brewery in the country, and as I finished writing this book at the end of 2004 we were maintaining our breakneck growth. I'm not worried that we'll grow too big or forget what we are all about because our neck muscles are getting acclimated to this jolting growth. Just because something is popular doesn't mean it has to be bland and disposable (try to say that Ben & Jerry's ice cream sucks). We will be considered a small brewery in the eyes of the average beer consumer for many years to come. But we are getting bigger. Becoming popular and selling out aren't necessarily synonymous, but as you become a bigger company with more responsibilities to more coworkers, it becomes more difficult to walk the line unless you indoctrinate everyone that surrounds you with an understanding of what you stand for as a company, as a brand. Dogfish Head will never let the tail of money wave the dog of inspiration.

The decision to go into business for yourself involves the ultimate leap of faith; the faith necessary to fully believe in your big idea. But I think you can increase your chances for success by expanding the realm of what you put your faith in. The obvious answer is that you are basing the decision to make this leap in the faith you have in yourself. Fair enough; it's true that everything must start from your own conviction and passion. But I have found it to also be true that the more I put faith in other people, the better Dogfish Head does. The next step after having faith in yourself is having faith in your coworkers. After that you need to have faith in your customers. Unfortunately, for many small companies it seems that this is where the outer boundaries of faith exist. I believe in a business-karma equation: the more time and effort you spend as a company helping groups of people who do not directly influence your monetary success, the more monetary success you will have. The entities I would include in this category would be fellow small businesspeople who don't compete directly with your business, businesspeople from outside your immediate area but within the same industry, and your local community in general. To survive and thrive in the world of commerce you need to embrace risk, creativity, passion, and an ethical business philosophy centered around a compassion for everyone your business comes in contact with. You will need to be savvy enough to convert limited resources into a significant impact on the business world. But if you can gather the right people around your righteous idea, customers and coworkers alike, you will succeed.

If you are in business you are bound to make mistakes. If you aren't making mistakes then you aren't taking enough risks. Roam. Learn about your business outside of the world of your business. As much as you learn, you will always be exposed to risk. This is good. Expose your bad self. Your opportunity to do so is your greatest advantage over larger, risk-adverse companies. You stand to learn as much from your mistakes as you do from your successes. How you respond to your mistakes will tell your customer a lot about what kind of company you are trying to create. Mistakes are experiences that you live through and your customer lives through. I honestly believe that Dogfish Head has provided a richer experience for our customers because of, not in spite of, the mistakes that we've lived through, owned up to, and made good on.

In Buddhism there is an ideal of nonattachment: a nobility in letting go of the desire for material success that, at face value, seems to represent the absolute opposite ideal of capitalism. But the idea is based on de-emphasizing the self; the *doer* is less important than the *doing*. I think this is a worthy ideal in small business. As small businesspeople, we are doers—we make something that we offer up for sale. This activity is useless without the doing—the actual selling of what we make. If the market doesn't exist for your product, then it doesn't matter how good the product is.

The difficulty we have in accessing the market is something that we share with the other small businesspeople in our industry and in our neck of the woods. It doesn't matter what we make if there is no one there to buy it. That's why it makes more sense to work together, as small business-people, to gain access to the marketplace than it does to work apart. Small is beautiful. Small and growing is even more beautiful. Support your local breweries, support your local restaurants, your local bakeries, coffee mills, blacksmiths, and independent local businesses of all shapes and sizes, and that support will come back to you. You will receive support from the community that you build and the greater one that you work within.

I wish you luck on your journey into business. It may not be easy, but it will be rewarding.

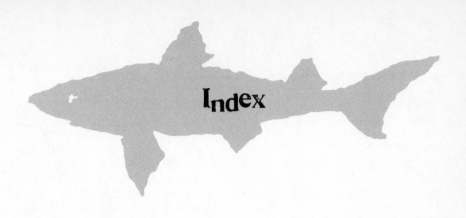

Index